Taxation is Slavery
The Biblical Case for Libertarian Politics

Nick Watts

Copyright © 2020 Nicholas Watts

All rights reserved.

No part of this book may be reproduced or transmitted in any form or by any means, electronic, mechanical, photocopying, recording, or otherwise, without express written permission of the author or publisher.

However...

The express written permission of the author is hereby given for the purchaser to retain unlimited copies of this work for personal use in any format so long as they are not distributed.

ISBN: 978-0-6489087-1-5

Detailed referencing information is available at beingbiblical.com/referencing

To see more of Nick's work, go to beingbiblical.com/books

Acknowledgements

I would like to thank the many people who provided feedback and helped me to develop the ideas in my original theological-college project, and ultimately in this book. Thank you to Kate, who reviewed the college project and raised some tough questions that I had left unanswered. Thank you to Mark, who supervised my project, provided lots of great input, and graciously took me seriously even after realising that I was going to argue a fairly radical point of view.

A huge thank you to my dad, who read diligently over my first shaky draft of this book, provided lots of great feedback and a ton of personal encouragement.

Thank you to Rick, who first challenged me to think outside the box on Christian approaches to politics and to investigate Austrian economics via the Mises Institute.

A corresponding thank you to the Mises Institute itself, which has made available many of the works cited in this book free of charge. If they had not done this, I would probably not know anything substantial about Austrian economics today and this book would look very different. Many thanks also to Tom Woods and Bob Murphy for their podcast content, which has been a great help to me, sharpening my thinking in many areas along the way.

Thanks also to Matt, Dave, Laurence and Dan who all provided feedback on my early drafts. A big thanks to Elizabeth, who proofread the manuscript.

My warmest thanks to my beloved wife, Katelyn. Without her support, this book would not have been completed. She loved me, encouraged me and supported me, while I spent over a year pouring my free time into researching and writing. She has put up with my ramblings about economics and politics, just to help me gather my thoughts. She is my light, my love and my treasure.

Finally, may any glory for this work be directed to the Lord Jesus. He alone is fit to be our King. He alone is worthy of all honour and praise. He alone is our hope for a final end to State tyranny, for salvation from sin and death, and for everlasting life. The many shortcomings that exist within this work are my own, whatever is helpful within it belongs to Christ.

Soli Deo Gloria

Table of Contents

Introduction: Taxes – The Question That Started It All...........11
Limited Government – The Typical Protestant View...........15
   The Usual Reading of Romans 13...........15
   Civil Government in Historic Reformed Theology...........19
      The Magdeburg Confession...........19
      The Westminster Confession of Faith...........20
      Calvin's *Institutes of the Christian Religion*....21
   Abraham Kuyper: Reformed Theology in the Age of Democracy...........24
      Kuyper's Concept of Sphere Sovereignty.......25
      Kuyper's Tax Policies in Practice...........28
      Kuyper's View of the Origin of the State........32
   Serious Problems with the Reformed View of Civil Government...........33
      This Typical Protestant View Cannot Explain the Biblical Data...........34
      The Typical Protestant View is Internally Inconsistent...........41
   Conclusion: I Needed a New Paradigm for Taxation...........44
Understanding Slavery in the Bible...........45
   Biblical Slavery: Conquerors and Contracts......47
      Examples of Slavery by Contract...........49
      Examples of Slavery by Conquest...........53
      Slavery as Retribution...........58
   Should a Debt-Repayment Contract Really be Called "Slavery"?...........61
      The Case of Paul, Onesimus and Philemon...62

Key Biblical Terminology on Slavery...................67
  δουλος (doulos) – Greek for "Slave"..............67
  διακονος (diakonos) – Greek for "Servant" or "Minister"..68
  עבד (ebed) – Hebrew for "Slave"...................69
The Biblical Answer: Taxation is Slavery..............70
  1 Samuel 8 – Israel Demands a King................70
    The LORD Responds through Samuel............74
  Nations Pay Tribute When They Become "Slaves"..77
  The Man Who Slays Goliath will be "Free" in Israel...79
  Sons Do Not Pay Tax Because the Sons are "Free" 81
  Bonus – The Early Church Fathers and The State 83
    Ireneaus (*Against Heresies*) – The Impossibility of a "Christian King"..................83
    Tertullian (*The Apology*) – Tribute is the "Mark of Servitude"..88
    Augustine (*City of God*) – Kingdoms as "Great Robberies"...94
Taxation in the New Testament Epistles.............102
  1 Peter 2 – Free People, Yet Slaves of God........103
  Titus – Testifying to the Gospel by Godly Living 105
  Romans 13 – Love Your Enemies, Even the Emperor..110
  Romans 13 cont. – How Does the Authority of Rulers Come from God?...................................114
  Romans 13 cont. – Why Then Do We Pay Taxes? 118
  Conclusion: Tactical Pacifism...........................121

Taxation in the Gospels...125
  Matthew 22:15-22 – Give to Caesar What is Caesar's...125
    Reframing the Question: Is It *Lawful* to Pay Taxes?..129
    Bitcoin – The Separation of Money and State 131
  Luke 3:10-14 – Bureaucrats and Police.............136
    To The Crowds: Voluntary Charity................138
    To The Tax Collectors: Do Not Be a Part of The Problem..140
    To The Soldiers: Do Not Engage in Extortion 145
  Matthew 17:24-27 – Not Giving Offence...........147
A Systematic Theology of Property Rights...........150
  Where Does "Property" Come From?.................150
    Ownership as a Feature of Human Law.......152
    Divine Ownership and Human Ownership 154
  Two Schools of Thought on Delegated Human Ownership (Locke versus Aquinas)....................159
    Natural Law and Positive Law.......................161
    Thomas Aquinas: Property Rights are a Feature of *Positive* Law.......................................168
    Implications of this Positive-Law View........171
    John Locke: Property Rights are a Feature of *Natural* Law...175
    Implications of this Natural-Law View........179
  Biblical Examples of Acquired Ownership......181
    Abraham...182
    Isaac...185
    Homesteading by Animals.............................188
The Doctrine of Creation and Economics............192
  Bastiat's Doctrine of Economic Harmony.........193

- How Free Markets Work..................................198
  - Market Prices.......................................200
  - Division of Labour..................................208
  - Capital Interest....................................213
- Society without the State.............................217
  - The Nature of the State............................218
  - All Taxes Cause Disharmony and Class Warfare..220
  - What About Infrastructure (Schools, Hospitals, Roads)?...............................224
  - What About Public Safety (Fire Departments, Certifying Doctors)?..........................227
  - What About Handling a Virus Epidemic?....230
  - What About Law and Order?......................233
  - What About Negative Externalities (Pollution)?......................................241
  - Tort Law...244
  - Property Titles to Easements....................246
  - What About the Poor?.............................249
- Free Markets are an Expression of Faith in God 254
- Intelligent Design Theory and Economics............258
  - Intelligent Design Explains Why Economic Harmony Exists....................................260
  - Intelligent Design Explains Why Landowners Don't Control Everything.......................264
  - Intelligent Design Clarifies Private Property Boundaries..271
- Property and Politics in Old Testament Israel......276
  - Israelite Slaves versus Foreign Slaves..............280
  - Capital, Labour and Interest in Mosaic Law....285
    - Wages and Time Preference.......................285
    - Returns on Capital Investment..................288

Lending Money at Interest..................291
Land Boundaries in Ancient Israel..............296
Rejection of Class Warfare Between Rich and Poor..................................299
A Justice System Without a King................302
Open Right to Enact Retribution................302
Multiple Independent Judges..................308
Was Pre-Monarchical Israel "Minarchist" or "Anarchist"?..................315
Common Law as a Pragmatic Approximation of Natural Law..................316
The Transition to Monarchy..................320
Why Did the Monarchy Arise?..................321
The Legal Basis for Israel's Monarchy..........328
First Argument: The Human Monarchy is Derived from God's Kingship.......................330
Second Argument: Precedent from Israel's History in Egypt..................336
Third Argument: Resolving the Multi-Generational Nature of the Contract............338
Are Modern Taxes Justified by Ancient Contracts?..................340
The Gospel Implications of Israel's Monarchy 346
Is Monarchy Preferable to Anarchy?............346
The Divine Monarchy Fulfilled in Christ.....352
Appendix 1: What About Democracy?..................365
Australian Childcare Subsidy – A Case Study in the Failure of Democracy..................366
Flaw Number One: Power Corrupts............369
Flaw Number Two: Weaponised Boredom. 370
Lesser Magistrates: Kuyper's Justification for Democracy..................371

Lysander Spooner's Critique of Democratic "Consent"..377
The Silence of Scripture on Democracy............381
Can a Christian Vote or Hold Political Office?. 382
Appendix 2: Assorted Q&A..384
1. Cut to the chase! As a Christian, do I have to pay my taxes or not?..384
2. If we *don't* get involved in politics, how else can we apply this way of thinking in our everyday lives?..386
3. Does Acts 4 show that early Christians embraced socialism?..389

Introduction: Taxes – The Question That Started It All

Towards the middle of my time at theological college, I actually considered becoming a politician. I did not think that being a pastor of a church was for me. I saw that there was an increasingly powerful wing of the political left that was openly hostile to the Christian worldview. Inspired by stories of Christian parliamentarians like William Wilberforce, I wondered if I should enter into politics to defend Christianity in the public square.

That thought led me to wonder about how I would make certain policy decisions as a Christian. In particular, I felt unsure about how I would handle tax policy. What if someone asked me whether we should tweak the tax-bracket thresholds, so that costs would be shifted from the bottom 20% of taxpayers up to the middle income brackets? I realised that I didn't have a clear biblical framework for answering such a question. As a Christian, when I asked myself, "What does the Bible say about taxes?" my mind basically went to two passages. If you've grown up in church, you might even be able to guess what they are.

One is Matthew 22:15-22. In that passage, Pharisees come to Jesus and ask him about paying taxes to Caesar. Jesus replies with that well-known quote "Give to Caesar what is Caesar's, and to God what is God's." The other is Romans 13:1-7. In that passage Paul tells the church in Rome that rulers are "God's servant for good... an avenger who carries out God's wrath on the wrongdoer." Paul then tells them "for the same reason you also pay taxes, for the authorities are ministers of God, attending to this very thing."

In the minds of all the Christians I knew, these two passages contained everything that they needed to know about the matter of taxes. The question they were asking was, "Do I have to pay all of my taxes?" Their answer, of course, was, "Yes, we give to Caesar what is Caesar's, just as Jesus said." In their understanding, the government is a good thing, given to us by God to produce an orderly society. Taxes are simply the wages that government employees deserve to be paid for facilitating that order.

But I needed to go deeper. I needed to ask more subtle questions than that. If I actually did become a parliamentarian, then effectively, I would be Caesar. I would have completely different questions about taxes than other Christians. They were asking, "Do I have to pay?" I was asking, "How much am I supposed to charge?" That became my fundamental question. If we are to "render to Caesar what is Caesar's" – well then, what exactly *is* Caesar's?

This question bothered me a lot. I realised that I simply didn't have a consistent, principled answer.

One possibility is that Caesar himself would get to decide what is his. Whatever tax rate the government comes up with, it is their right to do it, and we as Christians ought to be obedient and pay it. But that view, taken to its logical conclusion, seems to border on absurdity. There have been some incredibly oppressive governments in history. Are we really supposed to believe that a government imposing a 99% tax rate, and thereby forcing its people into starvation, is acting completely within its God-given rights? If that is our conclusion, then surely we've made a mistake somewhere.

On the other hand, I knew that there was this group calling themselves "libertarians", who continually proclaimed the slogan that "taxation is theft". I was persuaded that the teaching of the Bible, and of Romans 13 in particular, required Christians to be obedient taxpayers. For that reason, I imagined that there must be some fundamental flaw in identifying taxation with "theft". But I was not certain that I could properly articulate what that problem was.

I decided to make this question the focus of my capstone project for completing my Master of Divinity degree. That gave me a lot of time to read, study and reflect on different approaches that Christians have taken to the subject of politics. I learned a lot over this period. But one point stood out above the rest: the libertarians were *not* crazy. In fact, by the time that I was done, I had become persuaded that the libertarian view of taxes was the only one that truly made sense of the biblical data.

This was not an easy journey for me. I had always been taught that the Bible said government was a good thing ordained by God. I went through several intermediate stages, trying to redeem some vestige of that mainstream view. But eventually, the weight of evidence simply compelled me to change my mind.

In this book, my goal is to present that evidence to you, step by step, in the hopes that it helps you to wrestle with God's word and to understand the world of politics in a way that is thoroughly and vigorously biblical.

Limited Government – The Typical Protestant View

We must begin our journey from some kind of starting point. I myself am a settled Protestant, of a Reformed and Calvinistic variety. That is where I began, and so that is where this book will begin. We will start with the view of taxes and government that is held by a majority of Protestants in the Reformed tradition.

The Usual Reading of Romans 13

To understand the typical Protestant view of the State and taxation, you must understand how Protestants interpret Romans 13:1-7. For most Protestants, Romans 13 is *the* critical passage on the issue of taxation. They will often quote "give to Caesar what is Caesar's", but that statement is comparatively vague and open to many interpretations. It is Paul's practical instructions in Romans 13 that really drive their convictions. Let us review that passage for good measure, just so that we know what we are talking about.

> Let every person be subject to the governing authorities. For there is no

> authority except from God, and those that exist have been instituted by God. Therefore whoever resists the authorities resists what God has appointed, and those who resist will incur judgement. For rulers are not a terror to good conduct, but to bad. Would you have no fear of the one who is in authority? Then do what is good, and you will receive his approval, for he is God's servant for your good. But if you do wrong, be afraid, for he does not bear the sword in vain. For he is the servant of God, an avenger who carries out God's wrath on the wrongdoer. Therefore one must be in subjection, not only to avoid God's wrath but also for the sake of conscience. For the same reason you also pay taxes, for the authorities are ministers of God, attending to this very thing. Pay to all what is owed to them: taxes to whom taxes are owed, revenue to whom revenue is owed, respect to whom respect is owed, honour to whom honour is owed.
>
> Romans 13:1-7

If you were wondering about the Christian view of taxes, this might seem like an open-and-shut case. It appears to be right there in verse seven: "pay to all what is owed to them: taxes to whom taxes are owed..."

If you pick up a Protestant commentary on Romans, the explanation that you will find there is fairly predictable. We are to pay taxes because the State is a good thing, which is instituted by God to wield the sword for punishing evil (meaning that the State holds the authority to execute capital punishment). These excerpts from Stott's commentary[1] are fairly typical. Stott writes:

> Paul begins with a clear command of universal application: Everyone must submit himself to the governing authorities (1a). He then goes on to give the reason for this requirement. It is that the state's authority is derived from God, and this he affirms three times.
>
> 1. There is no authority except that which God has established (1b).
>
> 2. The authorities that exist have been established by God (1c).

---

[1] John R. W. Stott, *The Message of Romans*, 340-347.

> 3. Consequently, he who rebels against the authority is rebelling against what God has instituted (2a).
>
> Thus the state is a divine institution with divine authority. Christians are not anarchists or subversives.
>
> ...
>
> Paul gives us in these verses a very positive concept of the state. In consequence Christians, who recognize that the state's authority and ministry come from God, will do more than tolerate it as if it were a necessary evil. Conscientious Christian citizens will submit to its authority, honour its representatives, pay its taxes and pray for its welfare. They will also encourage the state to fulfil its God-appointed role and, in so far as they have opportunity, actively participate in its work.

In most Protestant and Reformed circles, this reading of Romans 13 is uncontroversial. It is the accepted wisdom of our day.

Civil Government in Historic Reformed Theology

Let us take a step back in history and consider the roots of Protestant Christianity. In particular, let us consider the view of civil government that was held by key figures during the era of the Protestant Reformation.

The Magdeburg Confession

In 1548, Charles V issued the Augsburg Interim to curb the spread of Protestantism. While certain concessions were made, such as allowing Protestant clergy to marry, they were commanded to re-institute all seven Roman Catholic sacraments (these having been reduced by Luther to two, Baptism and the Lord's Supper). They were also ordered to affirm transubstantiation and to reject the doctrine of *sola fide* (justification by "faith alone")[2]. Needless to say, many Protestant pastors resisted these orders. One such group of resistors was the German Protestant city of Magdeburg. The pastors of Magdeburg wrote a lengthy confession detailing their Protestant convictions and appealing to Charles V to allow them to exercise their Christianity in the manner prescribed by their own conscience. Ultimately, the city of Magdeburg was besieged by imperial forces

---

2 Grant and Trewhella, *The Magdeburg Confession*, 52.

because of their refusal to re-adopt these Roman Catholic dogmas.

The events surrounding the siege of Magdeburg are fascinating, but one point that stands out is how desperate those pastors were, who wrote the Magdeburg Confession, to affirm their love for the emperor (Charles V). They pledged their loyalty to the emperor; they promised to pay all tributes and duties; they even claimed that they would be the most obedient and loyal citizens in the emperor's whole dominion – if he will only grant them this one favour, that he would allow them to freely practice their Protestant Christianity.

The Westminster Confession of Faith

The Westminster Confession is an iconic document of the Protestant Reformation. It is a foundational document for the Presbyterian tradition, but its theology also stands in large measure behind both the Reformed Baptist tradition (since the Westminster Confession was the primary precursor to the London Baptist Confession of 1689) and the Anglican tradition (since the Westminster Confession was originally written to serve as the official confession for the Church of England, though it was later displaced by the so-called "39 Articles").

The Westminster Confession's stance on civil government is outlined in its 23rd chapter. Right out of the gate, this chapter references Romans 13 and claims that God has ordained and endowed "civil magistrates" (a generic term for secular rulers, whether kings, presidents, or whatever) with the power of the sword to serve God's glory and the "public good". The Westminster Confession also states that it is entirely lawful for Christians to accept the office of a civil magistrate and to wage war upon "just and necessary occasion" (though the nature of such occasions is not defined).

The Westminster Confession states, matter-of-factly, that it is the duty of the people to honour the civil magistrates and to pay them "tribute or other dues".

Calvin's *Institutes of the Christian Religion*

In the period of the Reformation, John Calvin stands as the leading theological thinker. Calvin's *Institutes of the Christian Religion* is one of the most influential books written in the history of the world, and Calvin stands indelibly as one of the "greats" of theology. Calvin leaves a grand legacy on two big issues of theology, namely, soteriology (how we are saved) and the sovereignty of God in all things.

Calvin is also among the strongest defenders in church history, of the legitimacy and goodness of the State. His final chapter in the *Institutes* is dedicated to the issue of civil government. In that chapter, Calvin makes some breathtaking claims about God's support of kings and rulers. The extent to which Calvin regards the office of a ruler as "given by God" is so great that it even eclipses extremely wicked conduct by the ruler. No matter how terrible your ruler is, Calvin argues that you are honour bound to give them all of the esteem and reverence which you would give to a wise and benevolent ruler. Calvin writes[3]:

> But if we have respect to the word of God, it will lead us farther, and make us subject not only to the authority of those princes who honestly and faithfully perform their duty toward us, but all princes, *by whatever means they have so become,* although there is nothing they less perform than the duty of princes.
>
> ...even an individual of the worst character, one most unworthy of all honour, if invested with public authority, receives that illustrious divine power

---

[3] John Calvin, *Institutes of the Christian Religion*, IV.20.25.

> which the Lord has by his word devolved on the ministers of his justice and judgement, and that, accordingly, in so far as public obedience is concerned, he is to be held in the same honour and reverence as the best of kings.
>
> [Emphasis Added]

Even more shocking than Calvin's insistence that bad kings should receive equal reverence to good kings, Calvin even insists that it does not matter how someone came to be the ruler over a territory in the first place. For Calvin, it does not matter whether the ruler was put into power by a democratic election or whether they simply marched their army into town and began slaughtering all those who opposed their rule. Once they have become established as the ruler of an area, they are to be regarded as having a divine authority and mandate to rule over the people, to receive taxes and to decree whatever laws they see fit.

There is no escaping the fact that Reformed theology has historically been very "Statist" in its outlook (that is to say, it has generally had a very positive view of the State). I believe that the reasons for this are primarily contextual. As with all of us, these Reformation theologians were, to some degree, products of their time. How could they be expected to be otherwise? After over 1,000 years of living within "Christendom", being reigned over by ostensibly "Christian" kings and popes, the assumption that Christianity was compatible with such a system of rulers must have been as pervasive as the air that they breathed. To even contemplate a society with *no king* would probably have struck them as absurd and even perverse. As Protestants in the tradition of Reformed theology, this is the heritage that we have had passed down to us. We must understand where we have come from before we strike out to form opinions of our own.

Abraham Kuyper: Reformed Theology in the Age of Democracy

This all brings us to the work of Abraham Kuyper. From 1901-1905, Kuyper was the Prime Minister of the Netherlands, heading the "Anti-Revolutionary" party. Crucially, Kuyper was *also* a Calvinist theologian. If anyone ought to have well thought-out opinions on how a Protestant should engage with the political realm, it would be Kuyper.

At this point, I should stress that not everyone who favours Reformed theology is necessarily a Kuyperian political thinker. However, Kuyper's thought has unquestionably been influential in the Reformed camp, and Kuyper is one of the few people who have tried to build a rigorous, theological foundation for political thought. Therefore, Kuyper will serve as a helpful case study in Protestant political theology.

Kuyper's Concept of Sphere Sovereignty

The idea that overwhelmingly framed and shaped Kuyper's political thought was something called "sphere sovereignty". For Kuyper, human life could be thought of as working itself out in different "spheres". Examples of such spheres include the sphere of family, the sphere of art, the sphere of science, and importantly, the sphere of the State.

These spheres are not sealed off from one another. A father doing a science experiment with his child is operating simultaneously in the sphere of family and the sphere of science. Nevertheless, these spheres can be distinguished from one another and we can think about them separately.

Kuyper understood the spheres as being a part of God's created order for the world. In each sphere, Kuyper believed that there was a separate structure of authority and that the authority that exists in each sphere is ultimately an authority given by God. So then, in the sphere of family, it is part of God's good design that parents should have authority over their children. In the sphere of art, there are natural geniuses in each artistic field, around whom "schools" of followers naturally form. This too is a part of God's good design for the governance of the sphere of art.

In Kuyper's thinking, each of these authority structures occurs naturally, simply by the righteous outworking of potencies which God has put within the nature of mankind. No sin needs to be committed in order for parents to have authority over their children. No one needed to sin for Albert Einstein to become an authority in the field of theoretical physics or for Plato to exercise such strong influence over the field of philosophy. These people are the natural authorities within those spheres of human endeavour.

However, Kuyper saw a distinction regarding the sphere of the State. Family, art and science are what we might call "organic" spheres, that is, spheres which occur naturally through the God-intended design of the created order. But the sphere of the State is a "mechanical" sphere. It is not organic, it does not occur naturally, and in a perfect world it would not even be necessary. For Kuyper, the sphere of the State, and the authorities which govern it, are alien to the original design of the created order. It is only as a merciful response to the Fall of man that God has seen fit to impose the authority of the State upon society.

As a result, in our fallen world, the State has a rightful authority given to it by God to rule over society in order to reward good and to restrain evil. Precisely because this authority comes from God, it is no less legitimate than the authorities in the organic spheres. The authority of the State and the authorities over the organic spheres are equally delegated by God, who is the ultimate authority over all things.

What this view meant for Kuyper is that the State has a *legitimate* authority, but that authority is *limited*. The State has authority within the sphere which God has assigned to it, but it must not usurp the legitimate authorities within the other spheres. For example, the State should *not* seek to dictate which avenues of inquiry will be pursued by scientists. This area is the purview of those naturally occurring authorities which rise to the top within the scientific academy. The State should also *not* seek to intervene and to decide that children should be raised in State-run group homes, rather than being raised by their own parents. To do so would be to usurp the legitimate authority of parents within the organic sphere of "family".

In this way, Kuyper's "sphere sovereignty" concept provides a theological foundation for what has become the standard view among most Western Christians, and especially Protestants: the view that we should have some kind of "limited government".

Kuyper's Tax Policies in Practice

How then was this limited-government idea applied by Kuyper himself? Since Kuyper was a politician, it is natural to ask what kinds of tax policies Kuyper himself proposed.

To answer that question, we turn to the policy manifesto that Kuyper wrote for the Anti-Revolutionary party. That manifesto is simply called "Ons Program"[4]. In Ons Program, we find several proposals for tax policies to be implemented by the party, as well as rationales for those proposals.

First, we may note that Kuyper does not see taxes as something taken by the State from particular individuals. Rather, Kuyper sees taxes as something to be taken from "the organic property

---

4   Dutch for "Our Program".

of the nation"[5]. In Kuyper's thinking, a nation is not merely a conceptual grouping of individuals. The "nation" is a real, tangible entity with its own existence. The nation is something greater than the sum of the individuals who are a part of it. The nation has a particular cultural heritage, the nation is naturally associated with a particular area of land, and so on. The State, by providing a system of law and order to "the nation", is doing the job that God gave it. Therefore, in Kuyper's mind, taxes are to be seen as a "a nation's sacred offering, rendered to God in order that God should rule the nation by means of the authorities he has ordained."[6]

Second, however, Kuyper *does* recognise the need for individuals to be "sovereign over their own purses"[7]. In this way, Kuyper does appear to believe strongly in the notion of private property. He considers the money possessed by individuals to be their own, and believes that they should have the authority and the dignity to spend it as they wish[8]. To this end, Kuyper sees the strong need to balance the financial interests of individuals against those of the government. Kuyper proposes a series of checks and balances to achieve this goal[9]. While this desire to preserve private

---

5 Ons Program, section 209.
6 Ibid.
7 Kuyper, *Lectures on Calvinism*, 83.
8 Ons Program, section 126.
9 Ons Program, section 105.

property is admirable, Kuyper seems to sleepwalk into a contradiction here. On the one hand, he wishes for taxes not to be levied on the nation unless the nation "has lawfully given its consent" (presumably, "consent" here refers to the consensus reached by its representative democracy)[10]. Yet on the other hand, Kuyper himself recognises, elsewhere in the manifesto, that majority vote cannot truly tell you whether something is just or unjust, only whether it is popular[11].

How does Kuyper manage to believe that representative democracy legitimises taxation, while also believing that majority vote does not determine what is just? These two ideas can be held together for Kuyper because he does not see the democratic consensus as giving the government the right to tax particular individuals (potentially unjustly). Rather, in Kuyper's view, the democratic consensus only justifies the government in taxing "the nation" as some sort of abstract entity in its own right. Since taxation is not carried out against particular individuals, it is not dealing with them unjustly. However, this is a distinction which occurs entirely within Kuyper's own mind. Those individuals who voted against the present government will certainly notice that their

---

10 Ibid.
11 Ons Program, section 175.

property is being taken away whenever "the nation" is taxed.

Third, Kuyper appears to be quite comfortable with the idea of his government levying taxes upon people who live in places which, at that time, were Dutch colonies. Kuyper specifically mentions "land rent" collected by the Dutch government from the chiefs of various villages in Java as an example[12]. This is a particularly striking point because it seems impossible to square with Kuyper's notion that taxes are taken from the nation "as a nation". How can Kuyper possibly consider the Javanese under Dutch-colonial rule to be a part of the Dutch "nation"? The Javanese people live on a separate (and distant) area of land, previously disconnected entirely from the Dutch civilisation. The Javanese have a different culture, a different language, a different history and even their own existing system of rule (the aforementioned chiefs). If the Dutch government has any "God-given" right to receive taxes from these Javanese villages, it must mean that conquering and occupation are then sufficient grounds to declare one's *ongoing* rule of an area to be God's will. This may well have been Kuyper's view. After all, Kuyper was a devout student of John Calvin, and it was Calvin who argued that the process by which a ruler comes to power has no bearing upon that ruler's legitimacy.

---

[12] Ons Program, section 268.

Kuyper's View of the Origin of the State

Before we dismiss Kuyper as a chest-thumping conqueror of neighbouring peasants, we should understand that he fully expects the governing State to *typically* be formed by peaceful means.

Kuyper proposes a "creation myth" of sorts for the initial formation of a functioning State. In this myth, the hypothetical colonial group "makes landfall" in a new area and begins to settle there[13]. At first, Kuyper envisions all of their efforts being directed to the common good simply in order to survive. This would include all property being held in common. However, as things progress and the colony becomes better established, Kuyper expects that the people would gradually delegate more and more of these communal holdings into the hands of specific people. This would allow those resources to be organised into more manageable-sized allotments. Since these holdings were initially communal, the right of the whole community to reap a benefit from them would remain intact, and this provides the foundation for the delegated owners to pay taxes. The taxes would represent the ownership stake that the whole community still retained in the delegated resource.

---

13 Ons Program, section 212.

This is a nice story in theory, but as people acquainted with history will be painfully aware, it is anything but typical of reality. Far from being the general rule, this sort of peaceful origin for a State is a vanishingly rare exception. In the vast majority of cases, nations live under the rule of whomever has conquered them the most recently. Nevertheless, if we assumed that a nation had been formed in the manner that Kuyper describes, then we can see how taxes might be a way of expressing the historic, communal ownership of the national wealth.

Serious Problems with the Reformed View of Civil Government

While this theory of Kuyper's may seem plausible on the surface, I have gradually, even begrudgingly, come to the conclusion that the whole Reformed tradition has been woefully misguided on this issue of civil government. It was extremely unsettling for me to find myself in strong disagreement with theological heavyweights like John Calvin. But as the evidence has accumulated from history, from theology, and most importantly from Scripture itself, I have been forced to abandon the mainstream view described above.

Before I propose an alternate theory of civil government (one which I believe to be much more biblical), I first want to show you the serious, gaping inconsistencies which appeared as I thought through this typical Reformed view.

This Typical Protestant View Cannot Explain the Biblical Data

To recap, let me share once more this summary line from John Stott, which is fairly typical of Reformed thought on the nature of the State. Stott writes:

> In consequence Christians, who recognize that the state's authority and ministry come from God, will do more than tolerate it as if it were a necessary evil. Conscientious Christian citizens will submit to its authority, honour its representatives, pay its taxes and pray for its welfare.

Submit to the State's authority, honour its representatives, pay its taxes and pray for its welfare. That is what I believed was necessary. From this starting point, I began reading through the Bible. I had decided that if I wanted to arrive at a thoroughly biblical view of taxes, I could not simply read Romans 13:1-7 and leave it at that. I needed to pool together *everything* that the Bible said about taxes, from Genesis to Revelation. What I discovered was a completely different picture of the State and taxation from the one that I was expecting. I asked myself, "Are there any examples in the Bible of someone *refusing* to pay their taxes?" As it turns out, there are several.

The first big example I came across was Ehud in Judges. Notice how the scene is set for us in Judges 3:12-14.

> And the people of Israel again did what was evil in the sight of the LORD, and the LORD strengthened Eglon the king of Moab against Israel, because they had done what was evil in the sight of the LORD. He gathered to himself the Ammonites and the Amalekites, and went and defeated Israel. And they took possession of the city of palms. And the people of Israel served Eglon the king of Moab eighteen years.
>
> Judges 3:12-14

So Israel had been conquered by Eglon, the king of the Moabites. How does Eglon express his dominion over Israel? He expresses it by requiring that Israel pay him "tribute" (i.e., taxes). The book of Judges unblushingly views this as Moab oppressing Israel. The people of Israel cry out to the Lord for deliverance, and God faithfully raises up a deliverer for them, a man named Ehud. As we read on, we see what Ehud does to rescue Israel.

> Then the people of Israel cried out to the LORD, and the LORD raised up for them a deliverer, Ehud, the son of Gera, the Benjaminite, a left-handed man. The people of Israel sent tribute by him to Eglon the king of Moab. And Ehud made for himself a sword with two edges, a cubit in length, and he bound it on his right thigh under his clothes. And he presented the tribute to Eglon king of Moab. Now Eglon was a very fat man. And when Ehud had finished presenting the tribute, he sent away the people who carried the tribute. But he himself turned back at the idols near Gilgal and said, "I have a secret message for you, O king." And he commanded, "Silence." And all his attendants went out from his presence. And Ehud came to him as he was sitting alone in his cool roof chamber. And Ehud said, "I have a message from God for you."

> And he arose from his seat. And Ehud reached with his left hand, took the sword from his right thigh, and thrust it into his belly. And the hilt also went in after the blade, and the fat closed over the blade, for he did not pull the sword out of his belly; and the dung came out.
>
> Judges 3:15-22

Here we have an Israelite tasked with carrying Israel's taxes to their ruler. Instead, he deceives the ruler, kills him, and liberates Israel so that they never have to pay those taxes again. In fact, the story of Ehud is a story of a taxpayers' revolt.

When I first came across this example, I thought that perhaps this was a special case, because Ehud is actively leading a campaign to free Israel from Moabite rule. Perhaps Ehud and the other Israelites would be obliged to pay their taxes to Eglon if they were not in the process of actively opposing him. Perhaps tax evasion is only truly sinful when it is covert and deceptive, rather than open and public. But as I read on, I found another example that forced me to abandon that solution. I came across Gideon. When we are first introduced to the character of Gideon, you might suppose that we would find him out in the field, harvesting crops or tending a flock, waiting for God to call him into service. Instead, when we first meet Gideon, he is committing an act of secretive tax evasion.

> Now the angel of the LORD came and sat under the terebinth at Ophrah, which belonged to Joash the Abiezrite, while his son Gideon was beating out wheat in the winepress to hide it from the Midianites.
>
> Judges 6:11

At this later stage, it is the Midianites who are ruling over Israel, rather than the Moabites. Gideon is not a captain leading soldiers into battle. He is just a random Israelite peasant. But here he is, actively hiding crops from the Midianites so that they will not be able to take their cut.

Seeing these two examples left me with a very difficult question. What would the apostle Paul say to Ehud and Gideon? Would Paul, the inspired author of Romans 13, condemn Ehud and Gideon as wicked sinners? Would he have told them that they ought to have submitted to Moabite and Midianite rule and dutifully paid the tribute? That seemed absurd, for it was God who raised up Ehud and God who directly instructed Gideon to go and fight the Midianites.

> Then the people of Israel cried out to the Lord, and the Lord raised up for them a deliverer, Ehud, the son of Gera, the Benjaminite, a left-handed man.
>
> Judges 3:15

> And the Lord turned to [Gideon] and said, "Go in this might of yours and save Israel from the hand of Midian; do not I send you?"
>
> Judges 6:14

Nevertheless, I could not simply dismiss the instructions of Paul in Romans 13. How could the same God who raised up Ehud and Gideon to throw off the tax shackles of their pagan conquerors also inspire the apostle Paul to write:

> Therefore one must be in subjection, not only to avoid God's wrath but also for the

> sake of conscience. For the same reason you also pay taxes, for the authorities are ministers of God, attending to this very thing.
>
> Romans 13:5-6

Perhaps we might assume that Ehud and Gideon were justified because they were not resisting the taxes imposed by their own king, but rather, they were resisting taxes imposed by a foreign ruler. But of course, when Paul tells the believers to pay taxes in Romans 13, he is speaking of paying taxes to Rome. For Paul, a Jew, Rome *is* a foreign power. Rome is no less of a foreign conqueror to Paul than Midian was to Gideon.

Something here was just not adding up. I needed an explanation that was sufficiently robust to make sense of the whole Bible, not just one part or the other. All Scripture is breathed out by God, and God does not speak to us with a forked tongue (that is to say, God does not speak in contradictions). There had to be some way of understanding taxation that could make sense of all of this data.

The Typical Protestant View is Internally Inconsistent

While answering these questions about the biblical data is critical, there is a further problem with the usual Reformed view. The additional problem is that this view is incapable of consistency, even on its own terms.

If the Reformed position is that Christians have a moral and ethical obligation to pay taxes, how are we to deal with the atypical situations that can and do arise? The majority of people who have ever lived have lived in situations where they are among the great masses of people being ruled over by a tiny group of political elites. But not everyone is in that position.

Eventually, a person will find themselves in the position where they are a Christian who is in political power. This may happen either because they rose to power as a Christian or because they became a believer after they were already in power. If paying taxes is part of being a faithful Christian, to whom – if anyone – should a Christian *king* pay taxes?

Some people are not necessarily in a position of political authority but are nonetheless living in a situation where no one is imposing taxes upon them. They are effectively "stateless". The vast majority of the world's land area today has at least one State claiming the right to rule that area (and in some cases, multiple States proclaiming their authority to rule in opposition to one another). But there are places where that is not the case. A narrow tract of land known as "Liberland" was, until very recently, an area not claimed by any existing State[14]. Liberland sits between Croatia and Serbia, but neither of those countries' governments considered it to be a part of their own territory. If a Christian wandered onto Liberland's area, pitched a tent, and declared it to be their home, to whom would they be obliged to pay taxes? Could a person be a faithful Christian and live in Liberland without paying taxes to anyone? Or would this mean that they were being disobedient to God's injunction in Romans 13 to pay their taxes?

Turning from the modern day back to Biblical examples, we find Abraham. Abraham lived under no king. He sojourned for various periods in territory ruled by kings, but he himself never pledged long-term allegiance to any of them, and for significant periods he was simply a roaming nomad. His family and his servants dwelt in tents, raising their own herds, not living as subjects of

---

14 An attempt to claim this area and turn it into a separate micronation has been underway since April 13, 2015. More information about this fascinating project can be found at http://liberland.org

any kingdom at all. Was Abraham in sin because he did not live under a ruler to whom he could pay taxes?

A more hypothetical (though still important) question is, What about Caesar in the time shortly after Christ's resurrection? Paul requires that taxes be paid "to whom they are owed", and Jesus instructs the people to "render to Caesar what is Caesar's". But what if Caesar were to *renounce* his claim over Israel? Suppose Caesar had a change of heart. Suppose that Caesar repented of his desire to conquer the world and issued a decree. The decree states that all the Roman people and soldiers occupying Israel must immediately pack up their families and return to Rome, stopping at every village that they passed by to beg forgiveness for invading that territory. Suppose that Caesar proclaimed that Israel was not his to rule, that the land of Israel belonged to the Lord God, and that Rome would no longer be accepting any tribute from Israel. What would a faithful Christian in the late first century need to do in this scenario?

Would a faithful Christian be obliged to demand that Caesar continue extracting tribute, lest the people fall into sin by not paying taxes? Or would they be forced to seek out another conqueror who would take Caesar's place so that taxes would continue to be levied?

These are all questions for which the Reformed tradition does not appear to have a robust answer. The tradition is one steeped in the assumption that there will always be a king and the people will always be taxed. But given a situation where this is not the case, the Reformed tradition has no deeper ethic upon which to establish a system of taxation.

Conclusion: I Needed a New Paradigm for Taxation

After many late nights, tossing and turning in my bed, reeling from the cognitive dissonance, I was forced to admit that the Reformed Protestant tradition could not answer my most fundamental questions about the ethics of taxation.

If I was going to understand how a Christian politician should view the issue of taxes, I was going to have to reach beyond the framework of standard Reformed answers and find something with a lot more substance.

I prayed for God's help and trusted that there was one place to go to find the answer. It was time to set the teachings of my tradition to one side and begin with the Bible.

Understanding Slavery in the Bible

I wanted to understand how taxes fit into the broad, overarching storyline of the Bible. In many ways, the Bible is a history book, beginning with the creation of the world and finishing with mankind redeemed by God, living in the New Heavens and Earth.

I wondered how the first taxes originated in history. At one point, the only people on earth were Adam and Eve. There is no reason to think that either one of them was levying taxes upon the other. Then their children were born. I was not sure what would prompt them to require taxes from one another either. At what point then did one human first say to another, "You must pay taxes to me"?

After searching the early books of the Bible, I did not find a definite answer to the question of how the first taxes originated. I did stumble across a passage from Augustine which may give us some indication – but more on that later when we discuss the church fathers. What I did find in the Bible was a clear, consistent, universal understanding of where taxes come from in general. That biblical understanding of taxes can be summed up in three words, which form the title of this book: *taxation is slavery.*

If we understand that one point, then we will understand everything else that the Bible says about taxes. We can make sense of the tales of Gideon and Ehud, and also make sense of Romans 13, all at the same time.

I am aware that equating taxation with slavery is a very controversial position to take. Some of you reading this may already consider yourselves libertarians and may already be sympathetic to the more common formulation that "taxation is theft". I understand what is meant by this statement, and ultimately I do agree with it[15]. However, I believe that for the Christian trying to understand taxes biblically, the relatively plain idea of "theft" does not fully capture all that needs to be said. What the libertarian usually means by calling taxation "theft" is that it is a violation of property rights, achieved by the threat of violence. This is certainly true, but we can be more nuanced than that. Taxation is a particular subset of regularised, coercive arrangements between people. By saying that taxation is "slavery", we are articulating much more accurately how that subset of coercive acts is defined.

---

15 That is, I agree with the fundamental Rothbardian assertion that all acts of aggression, including taxation, are unethical.

Some of you reading this may not be libertarians at all. I hope and trust that many people who read this will be from my own Reformed Protestant tradition and will come to this book holding to some of the same limited-government type views that I have described in the first chapter. For those readers, I fully appreciate that the statement "taxation is slavery" may initially seem quite harsh and incendiary. My goal in this chapter is to take you on a tour through Scripture and to show you that if we are to properly understand what the Bible says about politics, then the language of "slavery" is simply inescapable. For the biblical writers, the concept of slavery permeates the entire discussion.

Before we begin that process, however, there is an important piece of groundwork that must be laid. We need to define our terms. We need to understand what the word "slavery" meant in the minds of the biblical writers.

Biblical Slavery: Conquerors and Contracts

Slavery in the Bible can be divided into two broad categories. The first category is slavery by *conquest*. In the modern world, this is what we typically think of when we use the term "slavery". This type of slavery is what was done to African slaves by European slave owners in earlier years in America.

Let us be clear: this type of slavery, slavery by conquest, is consistently and viciously condemned throughout the whole Bible.

This fact may be a surprise to some of my readers. Some of you may have read works from the so-called "New Atheists" and others, claiming that the Bible is "okay" with slavery. They see passing mentions of slavery throughout the Bible where it does not appear to be condemned and conclude from this that the biblical writers were comfortable with *all* forms of slavery. This is a mistake. Most often, this misunderstanding is caused by confusing slavery by *conquest* with our second category, that is, slavery by *contract*.

The distinction is a very simple one. Slavery by conquest is what occurs when a person is captured, kidnapped, threatened with violence, or otherwise forced into the position of a slave. Slavery by contract is what occurs when a person *voluntarily* chooses to enter into the position of a slave.

Slavery by conquest is condemned by Scripture, everywhere and without exception. Slavery by contract is typically regarded as a normal feature of society, and one which does not especially demand to be overturned or outlawed.

Examples of Slavery by Contract

This distinction between contract and conquest may initially seem absurd. Why would a person voluntarily enter into the position of being a slave? In the ancient world, there were a number of reasons why someone may have wanted to do this, and many of them are surprisingly reasonable.

A common scenario was that a person may enter into a slavery contract in order to pay off a debt that they owed. If they could not pay, they would offer their services as a slave to their creditor. This may have been for a fixed period of time, which was considered equivalent to the money that they owed. An example of this occurs in Genesis 29:18, where Jacob makes an arrangement with Laban that he will work for Laban for seven years, in lieu of a dowry, so that he may marry Laban's daughter Rachel.

Another common arrangement, crucial for our discussion, is that a person may resolve a debt by entering into a slavery contract, not for a limited time, but until they had paid off a certain amount of money. In this scenario, the slave contract functioned more like a payment plan on the debt. The slave would continue working and would give a portion of their income to their master until the debt was paid off, at which point they would go free. In such an arrangement, a slave master may be relatively "hands off", leaving the slave a large degree of independence. While many slaves did live in their master's household, slaves operating under a payment contract could also sometimes live in their own dwelling, conduct their own business, etc. Their only obligation was to pay the required instalments to their master.

An example of this type of arrangement can be seen in a parable that Jesus tells in Matthew 18:23-35 (the parable of the unforgiving slave).

> Therefore the kingdom of heaven may be compared to a king who wished to settle accounts with his slaves. When he began to settle, one was brought to him who owed him ten thousand talents. And since he could not pay, his master ordered him to be sold, with his wife and children and all that he had, and payment to be made. So the slave fell on his knees, imploring him, "Have patience with me, and I will pay you everything." And out of pity for him, the master of that slave released him and forgave him the debt. But when that same slave went out, he found one of his fellow slaves who owed him a hundred denarii, and seizing him, he began to choke him, saying, "Pay what you owe." So

> his fellow slave fell down and pleaded with him, "Have patience with me, and I will pay you." He refused and went and put him in prison until he should pay the debt. When his fellow slaves saw what had taken place, they were greatly distressed, and they went and reported to their master all that had taken place. Then his master summoned him and said to him, "You wicked slave! I forgave you all that debt because you pleaded with me. And should not you have had mercy on your fellow slave, as I had mercy on you?" And in anger his master delivered him to the jailers, until he should pay all his debt. So also my heavenly Father will do to every one of you, if you do not forgive your brother from your heart.
>
> Matthew 18:23-35

Notice here that, in the scenario Jesus describes, the master has "accounts" with his slaves for particular amounts of money that they owe him. This only makes sense if *that debt itself* is the basis for their position as slaves.

If they had entered into a slave contract for a fixed period of time (like Jacob), then there would not be a financial amount owing. They would simply have been waiting out their time. If they had become slaves because they were captured and kidnapped, then there would also have been no fixed amount owing, but rather, they would simply be trapped permanently in their position as slaves. Therefore, this slavery to the king must have been grounded in the specific amount of debt that stood between the king and the slave.

A final clear indication of the existence of contract slavery is found in 1 Corinthians 7:23. Paul is writing practical instructions to the Corinthians, including advice on how they should think about the institution of slavery in their context. What is striking is that he finishes these instructions with a simple imperative statement:

> You were bought with a price; do not become slaves of men.

How can Paul tell them not to become slaves of men if they have no choice in the matter? It seems silly to command someone not to be conquered or kidnapped. Nobody would choose that fate for themselves anyway. Clearly what Paul is telling them is that God has set them free from slavery to sin by ransoming them through the cross ("you were bought with a price"). Therefore, they are to avoid subjecting themselves to slavery contracts, because a slavery contract is a poor way to live out the reality of their new-found spiritual freedom.

So there are clear examples of slavery by contract in biblical times. Contracts were not identical. They differed both in terms of what was expected of the slave and in the form of repayment. But it is clear that such slavery contracts did exist in both Old Testament and New Testament societies. These arrangements were not viewed as sinful and were basically a normal part of human affairs.

Examples of Slavery by Conquest

Sadly, slavery by conquest also existed in biblical times. Once again, slavery by conquest is roundly condemned by Scripture in both the Old and New Testaments. Slavery by conquest is what would happen when either (a) a group of bandits kidnapped an individual and put them into slavery or (b) an army invaded a territory and put the entire population into slavery. Both of these things happen in Scripture. A classic example of an individual being abducted into slavery is the story of Joseph in Genesis. You may recall that Joseph was a favourite of his father and was hated by his brothers. The brothers conspire to kill Joseph, but ultimately end up selling him into slavery to some passing traders.

> They saw him from afar, and before he came near to them they conspired against him to kill him. They said to one another, "Here comes this dreamer. Come now, let us kill him and throw him into one of the pits. Then we will say that a fierce animal has devoured him, and we will see what will become of his dreams." But when Reuben heard it, he rescued him out of their hands, saying, "Let us not take his life." And Reuben said to them, "Shed no blood; cast him into this pit here in the wilderness, but do not lay a hand on him"—that he might rescue him out of their hand to restore him to his father. So when Joseph came to his brothers, they stripped him of his robe, the robe of many colors that he wore. And they took him and cast him into a pit. The pit was empty; there was no water in it. Then they sat down to eat. And looking up they saw a caravan of Ishmaelites coming from Gilead, with their camels bearing gum, balm, and myrrh, on their way to carry it

> down to Egypt. Then Judah said to his brothers, "What profit is it if we kill our brother and conceal his blood? Come, let us sell him to the Ishmaelites, and let not our hand be upon him, for he is our brother, our own flesh." And his brothers listened to him. Then Midianite traders passed by. And they drew Joseph up and lifted him out of the pit, and sold him to the Ishmaelites for twenty shekels of silver. They took Joseph to Egypt.
>
> Genesis 37:18-28

There are also examples of this happening on a national scale, rather than an individual scale. This is what happens to the prophet Daniel. He is among those who are carried off to Babylon after the Babylonians invade and conquer Israel.

> In the third year of the reign of Jehoiakim king of Judah, Nebuchadnezzar king of Babylon came to Jerusalem and besieged it. And the Lord gave Jehoiakim king of Judah into his hand, with some of the vessels of the house of God. And he brought them to the land of Shinar, to the

> house of his god, and placed the vessels in the treasury of his god. Then the king commanded Ashpenaz, his chief eunuch, to bring some of the people of Israel, both of the royal family and of the nobility, youths without blemish, of good appearance and skillful in all wisdom, endowed with knowledge, understanding learning, and competent to stand in the king's palace, and to teach them the literature and language of the Chaldeans.
>
> Daniel 1:1-4

Sadly, ancient societies were no more immune to violence and war than are modern societies. Slavery resulting from the conquest of nations or the kidnapping of individuals was a known reality. The Bible roundly condemns this practice. To underscore that point, here are relevant quotations from both the Old and New Testaments. The first is from Deuteronomy, where Moses is recounting the laws by which the newly formed Israelite society is to live. He gives them this command concerning escaped slaves who turn up on their doorstep as refugees:

> You shall not give up to his master a slave who has escaped from his master to you. He shall dwell with you, in your midst, in the place that he shall choose within one of your towns, wherever it suits him. You shall not wrong him.
>
> Deuteronomy 23:15-16

When a victim of conquest slavery escapes from their conquerors, Israel is to be a place of shelter and refuge. The slave must not be given up and handed back over to their former oppressor. God's people are supposed to be a safe haven for escaped slaves.

Turning forward to the New Testament, we find Paul condemning conquest slavery in his first letter to Timothy, among a long list of other sins:

> Now we know that the law is good, if one uses it lawfully, understanding this, that the law is not laid down for the just but for the lawless and disobedient, for the ungodly and sinners, for the unholy and profane... *enslavers*... and whatever else is contrary to sound doctrine, in accordance

> with the glorious gospel of the blessed God with which I have been entrusted.
>
> 1 Timothy 1:8-11

It is necessary to be very clear on this point: conquest slavery is a terrible sin and runs contrary to the gospel of Jesus Christ. That is a necessary point to make because a much more subtle discussion of the rules surrounding slavery in ancient Israel will be coming up later (and particularly when we develop our systematic theology of property rights). What must be remembered at every point is that *conquest* slavery is condemned at all times, while *contract* slavery may be permissible.

Slavery as Retribution

There is one final category of slavery in biblical times that warrants discussion, even though it is less prominent. There is the edge case of slavery as retribution. This is a slavery arrangement that is not voluntary on the part of the slave, so it is by no means contractual, but it is also not precisely an act of aggression by the slave master. This is the situation that arises when the aggressor party in a war is vanquished by the defending party. The defending party must now consider what to do with their vanquished foes.

As a matter of practicality, the surviving soldiers of the vanquished army cannot simply be allowed to go free. They have every incentive to do harm and violence out of bitterness over their defeat. Additionally, the vanquished aggressor has committed a crime against the defending community, and it is just for the defending community to impose a retributive punishment upon the aggressor army for that crime.

For this reason, retributive slavery arises as a solution to a practical issue. The aggressor army is put into slave labour in order to make restitution for the damage that they have done to their victims. This may be done by forcing members of the aggressor army into direct service of the victims. This may be advisable if letting them roam free would likely lead to them mounting a new attack. But retribution may also be achieved by imposing a regular payment to the victims from the aggressors. Instead of bringing the aggressors into direct service, the defending army could periodically demand a payment. The aggressors, who by that time would have already returned to their homeland, would be forced to pay the reparations demanded by the defenders, under threat of a counter-invasion.

Again, this is not an act of aggression on the part of the defending army (unless it eventually grows out of proportion to the initial crime). Rather, it is merely an act of retribution.

We can see the acknowledgement of this practicality in the lead-up to the battle between the Israelites and the Philistines in 1 Samuel 17, prior to the iconic showdown between David and Goliath. Goliath, the Philistine champion, approaches the Israelite battle line and proclaims:

> Am I not a Philistine, and are you not servants of Saul? Choose a man for yourselves, and let him come down to me. If he is able to fight with me and kill me, then we will be your slaves. But if I prevail against him and kill him, then you shall be our slaves and serve us.
>
> 1 Samuel 17:8-9

The story doesn't play out this way. Neither nation ends up respecting the results of the battle and becoming slaves to the other. But the recognition of the principle is clear. After a battle like this, the expectation is that the vanquished army would be put into slavery. Whether this was a form of conquest slavery or a form of retribution slavery depends upon whether the aggressor wins the battle (conquest) or whether the defending victim is the winner (retribution).

Should a Debt-Repayment Contract Really be Called "Slavery"?

Making these subtle distinctions raises an important question about terminology. Is it right to lump in people who have been abducted from their homeland and sold into slavery along with people who have arranged a payment plan for a debt? Are we confusing many of the issues by referring to both of these things using the word "slavery"?

While this is a valid concern, it is important that we do not discard the term "slavery" when discussing contractual slavery arrangements. While it may seem more clear and convenient to reserve the word "slavery" only for conquest circumstances, the Bible itself does not do that. The Bible uses the language of slavery to refer to both contract *and* conquest scenarios. Therefore, if we are to understand the Bible on its own terms, we must understand the language of slavery in the sense that the biblical authors use it.

Let us now consider a key example which demonstrates that the biblical authors *do* make a distinction between conquest and contract slavery, even though they refer to both with the same terminology.

The Case of Paul, Onesimus and Philemon

Onesimus is a slave with a master named Philemon who is a Christian. Onesimus flees from Philemon, and on his travels he encounters the apostle Paul. After meeting Paul, Onesimus himself becomes a Christian. As it turns out, Paul also knows Philemon and writes a letter to Philemon on behalf of Onesimus. Paul writes to Philemon that, even though Paul loves Onesimus like a son, he is sending Onesimus back to Philemon. Paul asks Philemon to release Onesimus from his service.

This episode is fascinating and enlightening on several points.

First, Paul clearly uses the language of "slave" to refer to Onesimus' relationship to Philemon:

> For this perhaps is why [Onesimus] was parted from you for a while, that you might have him back forever, no longer as a slave [δουλον] but more than a slave, as a beloved brother—especially to me, but how much more to you, both in the flesh and in the Lord.

Philemon 1:15-16

Whatever else we might infer about the arrangement between Philemon and Onesimus, we must infer that in the cultural context of the New Testament, it was legitimate to use the language of "slavery" to describe what was happening.

Paul does not condemn Philemon as a wicked sinner for holding Onesimus as a slave in the first place. Yes, Paul does request quite strongly that Philemon should release Onesimus. But it is still a *request*. Paul does not *command* Philemon to do this (verse 8-9). This does not make sense if Philemon is committing a grave sin by holding Onesimus as a slave. If that were the case, why should Paul have given Philemon any say in the matter at all? If that were the case, Paul would be commanding him to immediate repentance. This is the same Paul who wrote to the Corinthians that:

> [You are] not to associate with anyone who bears the name of brother if he is guilty of sexual immorality or greed, or is an idolater, reviler, drunkard, or swindler—not even to eat with such a one.

1 Corinthians 5:11

Paul commanded the Corinthians to have a zero-tolerance policy toward unrepentant sin in their church. Do not even share a meal with someone, he says, if they claim to be a Christian but they make a consistent practice of gross sin. It is clear then that, for Paul, he is imploring Philemon to an act of *mercy and grace*, rather than to an act of *repentance and justice*. Paul is very adamant that this mercy and grace ought to be forthcoming, but he refrains from absolutely demanding it. Whatever else we may say, we must admit that Paul is *not* treating this arrangement between Philemon and Onesimus as one of aggressor versus victim.

Third, this view is further confirmed by Paul's failure to apply the command of Deuteronomy 23:15 (which we saw above) that a Jew must give shelter to an escaped slave. Onesimus meets Paul and clearly describes his situation (how else could Paul write to Philemon about it?). Does Paul, this Pharisee of Pharisees who knows the Mosaic law back-to-front, not remember that he is supposed to shelter escaped slaves? The same Paul who himself condemned enslavers in 1 Timothy 1:10? This seems extremely unlikely. Again, we see that Paul is using the terminology of "slavery", but obviously he regards Philemon's relationship to Onesimus as something different than what is being referred to in both Deuteronomy and in 1 Timothy.

How then does Paul actually conceive of this arrangement? Paul is writing as though Philemon and Onesimus have a contractual agreement for Onesimus to render service to Philemon as a slave. Most likely this arrangement was in repayment of a debt that Onesimus owed to Philemon.

And so Paul appeals to Philemon to release Onesimus with these words:

> So if you consider me your partner, receive him as you would receive me. If he has wronged you at all, or owes you anything, charge that to my account. I, Paul, write this with my own hand: I will repay it—to say nothing of your owing me even your own self.
>
> Philemon 1:17-19

Paul is sending Onesimus back to Philemon because, as a matter of justice, Onesimus still has an outstanding debt which must be repaid. Yet at the same time, Paul is requesting that Philemon give grace to Onesimus and release him from that debt. Further, Paul is asking that Philemon should consider this a personal favour to Paul, to whom Philemon owes a great debt of gratitude. Paul is saying that Philemon should treat his account with Onesimus as settled, on the basis of what Onesimus has done for Paul and what Paul in turn has done for Philemon. Therefore, he beseeches Philemon to let the whole incident be swallowed up in gospel-driven grace, to allow the slate to be wiped clean, debts to be forgotten, and Onesimus to be received as a brother in the Lord rather than as a slave.

This is clear, exegetical evidence that the biblical authors make a firm distinction between contract slavery, where they require the honouring of the contract, versus conquest slavery, where they require bystanders to offer aid and comfort to escaped slaves who are fleeing from their masters. In spite of making this clear distinction, the biblical writers habitually use the word "slave" to refer to both scenarios.

This is why it is important, when reading biblical passages on slavery, to keep this distinction at the forefront of our minds, lest we be muddled by mistaking a contract for a conquest or vice versa.

Key Biblical Terminology on Slavery

In the next chapter, we will move on see how the Bible consistently connects the practice of levying taxes with the institution of slavery. Before we do that, let's take a moment to review the original-language terms that are used in scripture. This is necessary because English translations do not always handle the same Greek or Hebrew word consistently.

δουλος (doulos) – Greek for "Slave"

In the Greek, the most important term we must be familiar with is the word δουλος ("doulos"). This word is variously rendered as "slave", "servant" or "bondservant" in English translations of the Bible. Part of the reason for this is precisely because of the distinction we have outlined above. The translators are trying to recognise that the term δουλος covers a broad set of arrangements, not just conquest slavery. So they try to use the term "servant" or "bondservant" when they think that a more contractual relationship is being described. For example, I have a quotation above from Matthew 18:23-35, Jesus' parable of the wicked slave. The translation is taken from the ESV, but the ESV renders δουλος as "servant" throughout that passage. I have rendered it as "slave" in that quotation to emphasise the point that Matthew is using the term δουλος. In many other cases, including when referring to Onesimus in Philemon, the ESV renders δουλος as "slave".

The point is, the patterns of when an English translation will render δουλος as "servant" versus "slave" are not overly consistent. So, in what follows, I will be careful to point out when passages often translated as "servant" are actually rendering the term δουλος in the original text.

διακονος (diakonos) – Greek for "Servant" or "Minister"

Another Greek term which we should not confuse with δουλος is διακονος. This is the term from which we get the English word "deacon". It means one who serves or ministers to others. It can be used (and is used in the New Testament) of people who serve in the king's court, but it is also used of people who carry out various volunteer roles in the church. In the introduction of Paul's letter to the Philippians, we see these terms used side-by-side, which give us a helpful contrast:

> Paul and Timothy, servants [δουλοι, plural of doulos, i.e., "slaves"] of Christ Jesus, To all the saints in Christ Jesus who are at

> Philippi, with the overseers and deacons [διακονοις, plural of diakonos, i.e., "servants"].
>
> Philippians 1:1

The other classic example, which gives us our paradigm for how deacons are to function in the church, is Acts 6:2. In that passage, a group of men are appointed to the logistical task of ensuring that all the widows in the church are being provided with food. This is done to free up the apostles for the work of teaching and preaching the gospel. The men appointed to this logistical task are said to be "deacon-ing".

עֶבֶד (ebed) – Hebrew for "Slave"

In Hebrew, the most common term for a slave is עֶבֶד (ebed), or the plural form עֲבָדִים (ebedim), along with the verb "to serve" or "to act as a slave", which is "abad" coming from the same three-letter root.

This term is used very often throughout the Old Testament and again can be translated in English as either "servant" or "slave", depending on context.

The Biblical Answer: Taxation is Slavery

Now that we have some understanding of how the Bible uses the term "slavery", we are ready to survey the biblical text. As we go, we will see that the Bible consistently uses the language of slavery to describe relationships between those who pay a tax and those who impose it. The Bible consistently assumes that "taxes" and "slavery" are inseparable ideas. Once we understand that these two concepts go hand in hand, all of the Bible's instruction about slavery then becomes a part of our source material for understanding taxation.

With that goal established, let us consider the text.

1 Samuel 8 – Israel Demands a King

We begin with this passage in 1 Samuel 8. Firstly, because it is clear and direct. Secondly, because it gives us a good central point from which to discuss a variety of related passages.

Before diving into the passage, some historical background will be helpful. Israel lived as slaves in Egypt for about 400 years. God freed them from Egyptian slavery by spectacular and miraculous judgements against Pharaoh, the king of Egypt. Ultimately, God has Moses lead them out towards the promised land of Canaan, which we now know as the land of Israel. When they arrive in Canaan, the period of the judges begins. In this period, Israel has no king. Most of the other nations around Israel have kings, but Israel does not. Israel is supposed to have God as their king, following God's law as given to them by Moses. Disputes that arose between people on a day-to-day basis were to be settled by the various "judges" who arose during that time. 1 Samuel 8 marks the transition from Israel's period of being led by the judges into its period of being ruled by a king. It begins with Samuel, a prophet of God, who is also operating as a judge in the land.

> When Samuel became old, he made his sons judges over Israel. The name of his firstborn son was Joel, and the name of his second, Abijah; they were judges in Beersheba. Yet his sons did not walk in his ways but turned aside after gain. They took bribes and perverted justice. Then all the elders of Israel gathered together and came to Samuel at Ramah and said to him, "Behold, you are old and your sons do not walk in your ways. Now appoint for

us a king to judge us like all the nations." But the thing displeased Samuel when they said, "Give us a king to judge us." And Samuel prayed to the LORD. And the LORD said to Samuel, "Obey the voice of the people in all that they say to you, for they have not rejected you, but they have rejected me from being king over them. According to all the deeds that they have done, from the day I brought them up out of Egypt even to this day, forsaking me and serving other gods, so they are also doing to you. Now then, obey their voice; only you shall solemnly warn them and show them the ways of the king who shall reign over them." So Samuel told all the words of the LORD to the people who were asking for a king from him. He said, "These will be the ways of the king who will reign over you: he will take your sons and appoint them to his chariots and to be his horsemen and to run before his chariots. And he will appoint for himself commanders of thousands and commanders of fifties, and some to plough his ground and to reap his harvest, and to make his implements of war and the equipment of his chariots. He will take your daughters to be perfumers and cooks and bakers. He will take the best of your fields and vineyards and olive orchards and give them to his servants. He will take the tenth of your grain and of your vineyards and give it to his officers and to his servants. He will take your male servants and female servants and the best of your young men and your donkeys, and put them to his work. He will take the tenth of your flocks, and you shall be his slaves. And in that day you will cry out because of your king, whom you have chosen for yourselves, but the LORD will not answer you in that day." But the people refused to obey the voice of Samuel. And they said, "No! But there shall be a king over us, that we also may be like all the nations, and that our king may judge us and go out before us and fight our battles." And when Samuel had heard all the words of the people, he repeated them in the ears of the LORD. And the LORD said to Samuel, "Obey their voice and make them a king." Samuel then said to

> the men of Israel, "Go every man to his city."
>
> 1 Samuel 8:1-22, ESV

You may immediately have noticed verse 17, which simply states: "He will take a tenth of your flocks, and you shall be his *slaves* [עבדים, ebedim]." Here we see a clear example of Scripture connecting the tax income of a king with the enslavement of his subjects.

This sets the king apart from the "judges" who had been leaders in Israel up until this point. The judges took voluntary contributions, but they did not have the power to tax. By contrast, a king does have the power to tax. We will examine this distinction in more detail in a later chapter.

The LORD Responds through Samuel

The LORD God hears this request from Israel and is gravely offended. He takes this request for a human king as a rejection of His own reign over them. What is interesting, however, is that God does not come down upon them in wrath. God instead warns them that fulfilling this request will have dire consequences. Yet God ultimately allows

Israel to have the human king for whom they have asked. In fact, provision was made in the Mosaic law for the day (should it ever come) when Israel would choose to place a human king into power over them.

> When you come to the land that the LORD your God is giving you, and you possess it and dwell in it and then say, "I will set a king over me, like all the nations that are around me", you may indeed set a king over you whom the LORD your God will choose.
>
> Deuteronomy 17:14-15

Among many interesting things about this, we should note that a human king was *not a requirement* for Israel. When God first brought them out of Egypt and established their nation, He gave them no human king, and so there was no one to whom they could pay taxes. The setting up of a king who would levy taxes was an entirely optional event.

Nevertheless, in 1 Samuel 8, Israel has requested to exercise that option. The LORD's answer is simple: having a king is *not* going to solve their problems.

God tells Samuel to spell out for Israel the heavy consequences of the request that they are making. And these consequences culminate with the key verse of this passage, verse 17: "he will take the tenth of your flocks, and you shall be his *slaves*."

All scripture is breathed out by God, and the scriptures here are clear. If you are forced to continually give a tenth of your produce to the State, then you are effectively a slave.

That statement may initially seem absurd. Ten percent sounds like a very small tax burden to the modern ear. The income tax brackets in most of the English-speaking world today go up to 40% or even 50%. Once we factor in sales taxes, tariffs, excises, duties and so on, many of us are paying substantially more than half of our income to the State. We wish that we could be so lucky as to be burdened with a mere ten percent. But there it is, plain as day, right there in the word of God.

Now, at this point we must be careful with our terms. We should not make the mistake of thinking that the slavery Israel experiences under their king is equivalent to the enslavement of Africans by European slave traders.

What is happening here is not a situation of brutal slavery by conquest. Rather, Israel is asking to enter into an extensive, long-term, multi-generational arrangement of slavery by contract. As with the distinction between judges and kings, the details of this contract are something we will discuss more in a later chapter. For now, let us move on to further examples where the Bible connects taxation with slavery.

Nations Pay Tribute When They Become "Slaves"

In the books of the Old Testament which detail the history of Israel's kings, we see a repeated refrain that, as nations are defeated by Israel, they become "slaves" of the king. They express this slavery by paying "tribute". A selection of examples is below:

> And he defeated Moab, and the Moabites became servants (עבדים, ebedim) to David and brought tribute.
>
> 1 Chronicles 18:2
>
> Then David put garrisons in Aram of Damascus, and the Syrians became servants (עבדים, ebedim) to David and brought tribute. And the LORD gave victory to David wherever he went.

> 2 Samuel 8:6
>
> Against him came up Shalmaneser king of Assyria. And Hoshea became his vassal (עֶבֶד, ebed) and paid him tribute.
>
> 2 Kings 17:3

The term "vassal" here is used by the English Standard Version based upon the context of the passage. The word translated "vassal" is the same word usually translated as "slave". The term "vassal" refers to a country which has its own distinct government, identity, etc. but which is ruled over by another country. A "vassal" king is effectively enslaved to the "suzerain" king who has conquered the area. In practice, a vassal king operates as a local governor and collects taxes on behalf of the suzerain.

Throughout these examples, we see that it is precisely because the people have become "slaves" (עֲבָדִים) of the king that they are forced to bring him tribute.

The Man Who Slays Goliath will be "Free" in Israel

In 1 Samuel 17 we see Israelite soldiers preparing to face off against the Philistines. The Philistines' champion, Goliath, comes and poses his challenge to the Israelite army. In verse 25, we read that the soldiers were discussing among themselves what great things the king would do for the man who would kill Goliath:

> And the men of Israel said, "Have you seen this man who has come up? Surely he has come up to defy Israel. And the king will enrich the man who kills him with great riches and will give him his daughter and make his father's house *free in Israel*."
>
> 1 Samuel 17:25 (emphasis added)

What does it mean for the man's father's house to become "free in Israel"? Isn't Israel already a free nation? The Philistines have not conquered them. From what were they to be freed? Virtually everywhere this word "free" is used in the Old Testament, it explicitly refers to the freeing of a slave. There are only two counterexamples. In one case, it is used poetically and ambiguously in a psalm (Psalm 88:5). In the other example it refers to releasing a donkey (Job 39:5). But everywhere else, throughout Exodus, Deuteronomy and the prophets, it consistently refers to releasing a slave. So what about this case?

The answer is simple: the soldiers expect that what the king (Saul) will do for the man who kills Goliath is to make his father's house *exempt from taxes*. The New King James Version even translates the phrase this way for clarity:

> So the men of Israel said, "Have you seen this man who has come up? Surely he has come up to defy Israel; and it shall be that the man who kills him the king will enrich with great riches, will give him his daughter, and *give his father's house exemption from taxes* in Israel."
>
> 1 Samuel 17:25 (NKJV, emphasis added)

From context, this is what the term must plainly mean. To be "free", to be a "non-slave" with regard to one's own king, is to be exempt from the king's taxes.

Sons Do Not Pay Tax Because the Sons are "Free"

We also see a key example on the lips of the Lord Jesus himself. There is an incident where Jesus and Peter pull a coin out of the mouth of a fish in order to pay the temple tax. Let us re-read that incident and see exactly what Jesus says to Peter about it.

> When they came to Capernaum, the collectors of the half-shekel tax went up to Peter and said, "Does your teacher not pay the tax?" He said, "Yes." And when he came into the house, Jesus spoke to him first, saying, "What do you think, Simon? From whom do kings of the earth take toll or tax? From their sons or from others?" And when he said, "From others", Jesus said to him, *"Then the sons are free.* However, not to give offense to them, go to the sea and cast a hook and take the first fish that comes up, and when you open its mouth you will find a shekel. Take that and give it to them for me and for yourself."
>
> Matthew 17:24-27 (ESV, emphasis added)

Notice that phrase "then the sons are free". What does that mean? The Greek term here translated as "free" is ελευθεροι (eleutheroi). This term is consistently used as the opposite of δουλος (slave) in the New Testament. This is the term employed when Paul utters those beautiful words about the unity of the church in Galatians 3:28: "there is neither Jew nor Greek, there is neither slave (δουλος) nor free (ελευθερος).

What then is Jesus saying? He is saying that taxes are not paid by sons, taxes are paid by *slaves* (i.e. those who, unlike the sons, are not "free"). It is precisely because Jesus is a *son* (and therefore free in his Father's house) that he has no need to pay the temple tax.

There are many more examples that could be given where context makes clear that it is because of conquering aggression that tributes and offerings must be given over to kings. However, these examples have been presented because they so clearly link the very *language* of slavery to the practice of taxation.

It should be clear now that, from the perspective of biblical history, the statement that "taxation is slavery" hardly needs proving. For ancient peoples and societies (including first-century Israel), the connection between slavery and taxes was as plain as the colour of the sky. They lived it every day. Tax collectors did not show up at their door claiming to be gathering funds that were owed as part of a "social contract", nor with assurances that the money would go towards some "public good". The tax collectors were there to extract the tribute that Eglon of Moab or Nebuchadnezzar of Babylon or Caesar of Rome demanded from Israel in order to keep their armies from crushing Israel into the dust.

Bonus – The Early Church Fathers and The State

Before we conclude this chapter, I want to take a moment to examine the comments of some of the early church fathers regarding the nature of the State. By no means do I place these writings on the same level of authority as the Bible itself. However, it is fascinating material, and it gives us further confirmation that the understanding of taxation as a form of conquering aggression was ubiquitous in the ancient world. Reading the comments of the church fathers helps us to read the New Testament with the full context of cultural background.

Ireneaus (*Against Heresies*) – The Impossibility of a "Christian King"

Irenaeus wrote his great work *Against Heresies* around AD 180. *Against Heresies* is primarily a denunciation of a family of related cults called "Gnosticism". Irenaeus apparently wrote in Greek, although our available manuscripts of *Against Heresies* are a Latin translation. Irenaeus was a disciple of Polycarp, who was himself a disciple of the apostle John. Irenaeus is therefore a very important source of post-Apostolic Christian doctrine. *Against Heresies* even includes what I believe to be a prototypical form of what we now call the Apostles' Creed[16]. In summary, Irenaeus is writing as a Greek-speaking Christian in a very early period of church history. His theology is extremely orthodox, even by the standards of much later church councils, which had the benefit of more time to reflect on Scripture. Ultimately, we have good reason to believe that Irenaeus' background beliefs about daily life are not at all far removed from those of the apostles themselves. Here is what Irenaeus says in passing about the nature of the State.

> For since man, by departing from God, reached such a pitch of fury as even to look upon his brother as his enemy, and engaged without fear in every kind of restless conduct, and murder, and avarice; God imposed upon mankind the fear of

---

16 Irenaeus, *Against Heresies*, Book 1 Chapter 10.

man, as they did not acknowledge the fear of God, in order that, being subjected to the authority of men, and kept under restraint by their laws, they might attain to some degree of justice, and exercise mutual forbearance through dread of the sword suspended full in their view, as the apostle says: "For he beareth not the sword in vain; for he is the minister of God, the avenger for wrath upon him who does evil." ... Earthly rule, therefore, has been appointed by God for the benefit of nations, not by the devil, who is never at rest at all, nay, who does not love to see even nations conducting themselves after a quiet manner, so that under the fear of human rule, men may not eat each other up like fishes; but that, by means of the establishment of laws, they may keep down an excess of wickedness among the nations. And considered from this point of view, those who exact tribute from us are "God's ministers, serving for this very purpose."

Against Heresies, V.24.2

What we see here is Irenaeus' own interpretation of Paul's words in Romans 13:1-7. For Irenaeus, God's purpose in raising up kings to conquer the nations is a response to the wickedness of the nations themselves. As the people of a nation reach the point where they are at risk of tearing themselves apart, God appoints a ruler to rise up over the nation. The ruler is not justified in doing this. He is a scoundrel seeking his own pomp and power, but God uses him to bring some degree of order to the society, which was in danger of being destroyed by its own chaos. In this way, the rulers, whom God sovereignly allows to rise to power, are simultaneously both a judgement upon humanity for our wickedness and also a mercy upon us to keep our sinfulness from completely destroying us. If we are unable to live peacefully as a society, if sin begins descending into chaos, then a ruler will rise up who is adept at bending that state of chaos to his own benefit and we will come under his rule.

Nevertheless, as Irenaeus goes on, it becomes clear that he sees these rulers as useful tools in God's hand but certainly not as people serving God in any kind of "sacred" occupation. Irenaeus continues:

> Just as if any one, *being an apostate*, and seizing in a hostile manner another man's territory, should harass the inhabitants of it, in order that he might claim for himself the glory of a king among those ignorant of his apostasy and robbery...
>
> *Against Heresies*, V.24.4

There are two stunning ideas mentioned here in passing. The first is that Irenaeus clearly regards the act of raising oneself up over the people of a territory and proclaiming oneself their "king" as being an act of "robbery". For Irenaeus, the nature of taxation is quite clear. It is taking people's wealth under threat of force, and this is nothing different than robbing them. But what is perhaps the even greater indictment of such an action is that Irenaeus assumes, simply as a matter of course, that no one could ever engage in such oppression unless they were an "apostate". For Irenaeus, the idea of a "Christian" king who expands his territory by conquering his neighbours is basically incoherent. How could someone who claims to be a servant of the Living God go out, conquer a nation, and become their robber and oppressor? He couldn't. He would first have to deny the faith and apostatise. Only then would such a course be open to him.

Does this mean that there is no place for Christians to work in any type of government employment? No, I do not believe that is the case. We will see more about that in a later chapter where we examine how the gospels speak about the office of "tax collectors". But the specific position of a conquering *king* is one which Irenaeus believed could only be held by a pagan. Now, as a matter of technicality, Irenaeus does seem to leave open the possibility that a king could exist, at least in theory, who is righteous and "in subjection to God." But he clearly does not believe that such a king could ever be justified in conquering people, expanding borders, and extracting tribute.

Tertullian (*The Apology*) – Tribute is the "Mark of Servitude"

Tertullian was a highly articulate, well-educated man living in Roman North Africa. He became a Christian as an adult after being shocked and impressed by the bravery of Christians who were being martyred at the hands of the Romans. He became an apologist for the Christian faith, writing a large body of work in Latin. He lived from around AD 155-240, still well before the legalising of Christianity in the empire.

The Apology, which is perhaps Tertullian's chief work, contains some very strong indictments of the pagan Romans, which also touch on Tertullian's view of kingship and taxation. In one passage, Tertullian is mocking the pagans for their worship of idols, these graven images made with human hands. He mocks them because they allow their "gods" to be sold at auction, as though mere humans had the right to buy and sell these deities, treating them as the property of men. In this section, Tertullian makes an analogy to lands and peoples:

> But indeed lands burdened with tribute are of less value; men under the assessment of a poll-tax are less noble; for these things are the marks of servitude.
>
> *The Apology*, Chapter XIII

What is clear from this passing comment is that Tertullian would agree with our basic thesis, that there is a strong connection between taxation and slavery. For Tertullian, tribute and taxes are the clear signs that people have been driven into servitude.

Tertullian goes on in a later chapter to claim that emperors must have an innate knowledge that God exists and that God is greater than they are. Tertullian claims that the very power afforded to emperors reveals to them that they are not all-powerful and that there must therefore be something more powerful than themselves in existence. In making this point, Tertullian sarcastically dares the emperors to challenge God for supremacy:

> [The emperors] reflect upon the extent of their power, and so they come to understand the highest; they acknowledge that they have all their might from Him against whom their might is nought. Let the emperor make war on heaven; let him lead heaven captive in his triumph; let him put guards on heaven; let him impose taxes on heaven! He cannot.
>
> *The Apology*, Chapter XXX

Once again, we see Tertullian strongly connect the idea of imposing taxes with the idea of conquering an area. For Tertullian, imposing a tax on heaven and conquering heaven would be synonymous ideas.

However, all of this is not necessarily to say that Tertullian is a radical revolutionary out to bring down the Roman Empire. Quite the reverse. Tertullian goes on to assure the reader that the emperors have nothing to fear from the Christians:

> Without ceasing, for all our emperors we offer prayer. We pray for life prolonged; for security to the empire; for protection to the imperial house; for brave armies, a faithful senate, a virtuous people, the world at rest, whatever, as man or Caesar, an emperor would wish.
>
> *The Apology*, Chapter XXX

At first glance, Tertullian appears to be taking a very positive view of Rome and the emperor. He claims that the Christians pray for the empire's security and so on. How does Tertullian reconcile this with the view that the empire is built on conquering, violence and enslavement?

The simple answer for Tertullian is that Christians pray for the emperor *because* the emperor is one of their greatest enemies, and loving enemies is a part of the Christian life.

But we merely, you say, flatter the emperor, and feign these prayers of ours to escape persecution. Thank you for your mistake, for you give us the opportunity of proving our allegations. Do you, then, who think that we care nothing for the welfare of Caesar, look into God's revelations, examine our sacred books, which we do not keep in hiding, and which many accidents put into the hands of those who are not of us. Learn from them that a large benevolence is enjoined upon us, even so far as to supplicate God for our enemies, and to beseech blessings on our persecutors. *Who, then, are greater enemies and persecutors of Christians, than the very parties with treason against whom we are charged?* Nay, even in terms, and most clearly, the Scripture says, "Pray for kings, and rulers, and powers, that all may be peace with you." For when there is disturbance in the empire, if the commotion is felt by its other members, surely we too, though we are not thought to be given to disorder, are to be found in some place or other which the calamity affects.

> *The Apology*, Chapter XXXI (emphasis added)

We see two elements here which will help us to understand Tertullian's mindset. First, Tertullian takes a very pacifistic approach to the State. In the face of this horrible enemy and persecutor, Tertullian considers benevolence to be an appropriate Christian response. He does not want to repay evil for evil, but to overcome evil with good (Romans 12:21).

On the other hand, Tertullian also has a very "conservative" approach to civil society. Even in spite of the horrors perpetrated by Rome, Tertullian still does not wish to "rock the boat". He fears that any large upheavals would be bad news for everyone in the empire, including the Christians. He would rather see the existing institutions remain in place but be reformed and made to act in justice and righteousness.

The interpretive position that I am taking in this book is not as radically pacifistic as that of Tertullian. The main reason for this is that I am trying to make interpretive room for the tax revolts that took place in the Old Testament under the judges. However, it is worth noting that Tertullian agrees, as yet another voice in the chorus, that taxation is fundamentally an act of slavery and conquest.

Augustine (*City of God*) – Kingdoms as "Great Robberies"

Moving forward a little in church history, we come to Augustine of Hippo. Augustine wrote the *City of God* in the early AD 400s (published some time around the year AD 426). Augustine was a bishop in North Africa, which at that time was a Latin-speaking part of the Western half of the Roman Empire (in contrast to the Greek-speaking Eastern half). This means that Augustine, in contrast to Irenaeus and Tertullian, is writing *after* Christianity has been made a legal religion, *after* the council of Nicea, and *after* the Roman Empire has had its first ostensibly Christian emperor (Constantine).

In the *City of God*, Augustine sees that the Roman Empire has been attacked and that Rome has been sacked by the Visigoths. Many Romans wonder if this is a judgement upon their civilisation from the pagan gods, brought on because so many Romans have turned from Roman paganism towards Christianity.

Augustine writes a sort of philosophical, theological history of the world, seeing history as an ongoing struggle between the kingdoms of men and the "City of God" (meaning the kingdom that includes all believers through history under the rule of God). In his reflections, Augustine shares some of his thoughts on the nature of kingship:

> Justice being taken away, then, what are kingdoms but great robberies? For what are robberies themselves, but little kingdoms? The band itself is made up of men; it is ruled by the authority of a prince, it is knit together by the pact of the confederacy; the booty is divided by the law agreed on. If, by the admittance of abandoned men, this evil increases to such a degree that it holds places, fixes abodes, takes possession of cities, and subdues peoples, it assumes the more plainly the name of a kingdom, because the reality is now manifestly conferred on it, not by the removal of covetousness, but by the addition of impunity. Indeed, that was an apt and true reply which was given to Alexander the Great by a pirate who had been seized. For when that king had asked the man what he meant by keeping hostile possession of the sea, he answered with bold pride, "What thou meanest by seizing the whole earth; but because I do it with a petty ship, I am called a robber, whilst

> thou who dost it with a great fleet art styled emperor."
>
> *City of God*, IV.4

As with Irenaeus, we see that Augustine's working assumption from start to finish is that a king or an emperor is nothing different than a robber. A "king" is simply the name he is given when his robbery and oppression of a group of people becomes a publicly acknowledged and regularised feature of their society. In this way, Augustine views Alexander the Great as being no different than a common pirate, except for the degree of Alexander's success in his wicked endeavours.

I said back in chapter 2 (Understanding Slavery in the Bible) that we could not be certain who had been the first human to levy a tax upon their neighbours. However, I did find a possible answer to that question in Augustine. Augustine makes reference to a historian named Justinus. Even from Augustine's perspective, Justinus is digging into the foggy depths of antiquity. But Justinus tells us how the practice of conquering neighbouring peoples may have first begun with an Assyrian king named "Ninus".

Justinus, who wrote Greek or rather foreign history in Latin, and briefly, like Trogus Pompeius whom he followed, begins his work thus: "In the beginning of the affairs of peoples and nations the government was in the hands of kings, who were raised to the height of this majesty not by courting the people, but by the knowledge good men had of their moderation. The people were held bound by no laws; the decisions of the princes were instead of laws. It was the custom to guard rather than to extend the boundaries of the empire; and kingdoms were kept within the bounds of each ruler's native land. Ninus king of the Assyrians first of all, through new lust of empire, changed the old and, as it were, ancestral custom of nations. He first made war on his neighbours, and wholly subdued as far as to the frontiers of Libya the nations as yet untrained to resist." And a little after he says: "Ninus established by constant possession the greatness of the authority he had gained. Having mastered his nearest neighbours, he went on to others, strengthened by the accession of forces, and by making each

> fresh victory the instrument of that which followed, subdued the nations of the whole East."
>
> ...
>
> But to make war on your neighbours, and thence to proceed to others, and through mere lust of dominion to crush and subdue people who do you no harm, what else is this to be called than great robbery?
>
> *City of God*, IV.6

It may be that Ninus, king of Assyria, really was the first to try and take over the whole world. As a further note of interest, I am deeply suspicious that this "Ninus", mentioned by Justinus and Augustine, may be closely connected to a character we meet in Genesis 10:8-12 named "Nimrod".

> Cush fathered Nimrod; he was the first on earth to be a mighty man. He was a mighty hunter before the LORD. Therefore it is said, "Like Nimrod a mighty hunter before the LORD." The beginning of his kingdom was Babel, Erech, Accad, and Calneh, in the land of Shinar. From that land he went into Assyria and built Nineveh, Rehoboth-

> Ir, Calah, and Resen between Nineveh and Calah; that is the great city.
>
> Genesis 10:8-12

Genesis 10 records the so-called "table of nations", the different clans that spread out over the earth after the Great Flood of Noah's day. Nimrod, we are told, was "the first on earth to be a mighty man." The Hebrew term translated here (using the ESV's rendering) as "mighty man" is a fairly broad term, sort of like calling someone "a great man" in English. But the context here makes the meaning clear. Nimrod was the first, according to Genesis, to raise himself up *over a kingdom*. Verse 10 informs us "The beginning of his kingdom was Babel, Erech, Accad and Calneh in the land of Shinar." For most readers, those names are likely unfamiliar. It will do for now to simply think of them as "places in the Middle East somewhere." What is interesting is where Nimrod goes after this. Verse 11-12, "From that land he went into *Assyria and built Nineveh...*"[17] Nimrod is the person who

---

17 Astute readers who compare various Bible versions may notice that the King James Version renders verse 11 slightly differently. The KJV renders verse 11 as "Out of that land went forth Asshur, and builded Nineveh..." "Asshur" is just the same word as "Assyria" (they are two different ways of representing the underlying Hebrew

first built up Nineveh, the capital city of the Assyrian empire (you may remember it as the wicked city that the prophet Jonah is sent to preach against). We're also told that Nimrod has a kingdom that spreads across several other regions of the Middle East. All in all, there is a good case that this "Ninus" mentioned by Justinus and

> word using English/Latin letters). The real difference is that the KJV understands the verse to be saying that *someone named* Asshur/Assyria went out and built Nineveh. The ESV, by contrast, takes the grammar to be indicating that the aforementioned Nimrod went *to the place called* Asshur/Assyria. Both appear theoretically possible from the grammar of the original Hebrew; however, I believe the context strongly favours the ESV's rendering. The argument for the KJV's rendering is that a few verses later, a person named Asshur is specifically mentioned as one of the sons of Shem (Genesis 10:22). Therefore, perhaps it makes the most sense to assume that the place called "Asshur" is in fact named after the person "Asshur" who likely was the first person to settle there. That may well be the true story of how the region first got its name, but that does not mean that we need to assume Asshur (the person) is being spoken of in verse 11. There is a clear order to the table of nations. The sons of Japheth are discussed first, then the sons of Ham, and then the sons of Shem. The KJV's rendering requires us to upset this order and backport a single individual from Shem's line back into the story of Ham's descendants. Instead, I think it makes much more sense if the story has a continuous flow, and we understand "the first mighty man" Nimrod to have gone into the place already called "Asshur" (because of Shem's son who first settled there), and have begun his infamous path to notoriety by taking that place over and building Nineveh, the foothold from which the Assyrian empire would come to dominate all of the surrounding nations.

Augustine either *is* Nimrod (being referred to with a version of his name more familiar to Greek or Latin speakers), or is perhaps a descendant of Nimrod who did a good enough job at extending Nimrod's empire that Justinus gives him credit for launching the whole enterprise.

At any rate, Augustine goes on to point out that Rome is not necessarily the kingdom to end all kingdoms, as some of its supporters may have believed. The Assyrian empire, Augustine points out, did not last forever, and it was an even greater empire than Rome, having lasted for an even longer period of time.

While these historical asides may be interesting, the important point for our purpose is that Augustine regards the whole practice of kingship and empire as a sinful activity, carried out in rebellion against God.

Taxation in the New Testament Epistles

By this point, it should be clear that understanding taxation as a form of slavery is not some novelty that I am pulling out of thin air. The idea did not arise with Enlightenment-era philosophers, nor from the catchphrases of modern libertarians. Taxation as slavery is the common view from the Old Testament period through to the days of the early church fathers.

Having seen these examples, I am sure that you have many questions. What about all those passages in the New Testament that look like they are instructing us to pay taxes as part of Christian living? How are we supposed to interpret those in light of these clear indications that taxation is slavery? Given that those who came before *and* after the New Testament writers clearly regarded taxation as slavery and robbery, we must assume that a similar view prevailed among the writers of the New Testament (at least until clear evidence to the contrary is presented).

But if, for example, the apostle Paul was steeped in this way of looking at things (being a good Jew, well versed in the Old Testament writings), then what did he mean when he told the Christians in Rome to pay their taxes? If Jesus understood Caesar as someone who was enslaving Israel, why did he tell them to "give to Caesar what is Caesar's"?

Let us begin by looking at the pastoral instructions given in the New Testament epistles on dealing with the government. We find specific instructions for how the church is to relate to the government in three New Testament letters, 1 Peter, Titus, and, of course, Romans. None of these cases appear in isolation. All of them come in the context of a progressive *sequence* of instructions.

In two of these cases (1 Peter and Titus), instructions on relating to civil government come in the immediate context of discussing relations between masters and slaves. The remaining case is Romans 13, which does not discuss masters and slaves in the immediate context. Rather, Romans 13 follows directly on from a progressive sequence in Romans 12, where we see ever-greater calls to love our enemies and to do good to those who hate us.

1 Peter 2 – Free People, Yet Slaves of God

> Be subject for the Lord's sake to every human institution, whether it be to the emperor as supreme, or to governors as sent by him to punish those who do evil

> and to praise those who do good. For this is the will of God, that by doing good you should put to silence the ignorance of foolish people. Live as people who are *free* [ελευθεροι, eleutheroi i.e., "people free from slavery"], not using your freedom as a cover-up for evil, but living as servants [δουλοι, douloi i.e., "slaves"] of God. Honour everyone. Love the brotherhood. Fear God. Honour the emperor.
>
> 1 Peter 2:13-17

Notice that even here, as Peter discusses the relationship between Christians and the Roman State, he uses the language of slavery and freedom. Why? Because he is acknowledging that, from a worldly perspective, they are unfortunately slaves to the emperor. Yet Peter tells them, because of the gospel, they are free in the way that really matters. They are free from sin and death and alive to God their Creator. So Peter tells them, in light of this gospel reality, live as people who consider yourselves free, even though the world may regard you as slaves. In Christ, you have been freed from the bondage of sin; therefore, use your freedom to do good to those who oppress you. Live not as slaves of the emperor but as slaves of God. And as

God's slaves, do His will by loving those who hold themselves over you, even to the point of showing honour to the emperor himself (conquering scoundrel though he may be).

Titus – Testifying to the Gospel by Godly Living

Paul writes to Titus with a series of practical instructions to pass on to the church in Crete. Towards the end of the letter, we find this:

> Remind them to be submissive to rulers and authorities, to be obedient, to be ready for every good work, to speak evil of no one, to avoid quarrelling, to be gentle, and to show perfect courtesy toward all
>
> Titus 3:1-2

At first glance, this appears to be a clear-cut passage. Paul is telling Titus and the church in Crete that they need to submit to the rulers and authorities. But let us examine the preceding context for a moment and understand where this instruction fits into the flow of Paul's thought. Only a few verses earlier, we read this:

> Show yourself in all respects to be a model of good works, and in your teaching show integrity, dignity, and sound speech that cannot be condemned, so that an opponent may be put to shame, having nothing evil to say about us. Slaves [δουλους] are to be submissive to their own masters in everything; they are to be well-pleasing, not argumentative, not pilfering, but showing all good faith, so that in everything they may adorn the doctrine of God our Saviour.
>
> Titus 2:7-10

We should note Paul's motivation for these commands. He wants Titus and the other believers to "adorn the doctrine of God our Saviour." He wants their opponents to be "put to shame, having nothing evil to say about us." This is what lies behind the instructions. Paul wants them to make the message of the gospel shine brightly to their opponents and even to their enemies and oppressors by the love and integrity that they display.

In light of that, we see Paul giving the instruction for slaves to be submissive to their own masters. What is interesting is that Paul does not bother at this point to make any distinction between slaves who are in slavery by the result of conquest versus slaves who are in slavery through a contract. He gives this instruction to "slaves" as a general category.

There are two possible reasons for this. The first is simply that Paul and his readers understand the distinction *implicitly*. They have a shared cultural understanding of the difference between conquest slavery and contract slavery, which does not need to be re-explained every time the word δουλος is used. But the second reason, which I think is more likely and important in the context, is that (for the purpose of this particular instruction) the origin of a person's slavery does not matter. It may be that there were both contract slaves and conquest slaves reading the original letter. Even if there were not, certainly both types of slaves would eventually come to read it. But the advice of Paul is the same for both: "be well-pleasing, not argumentative, not pilfering, but showing all good faith".

For those who are in the position of slavery by contract, this makes perfect sense. Paul is telling them to "show the glory of Christ by living with clear integrity to the contract by which you are bound."

For those in the position of slavery by conquest, it is a little more subtle. In the situation of slavery by conquest, we can further divide cases into those who had some realistic chance of escape and those who did not. While it is horrifying to contemplate, if a slave by conquest tried to flee from their master, they would most likely be treated as a fugitive. Their sad reality may have been that any attempt at escape would most likely end in horrible punishment or even death. What could Paul and Titus possibly say, pastorally speaking, to encourage someone in this position? The answer is just what they did say. Serve your (scoundrel of a) master with dignity, integrity and honesty. This is how you will express the freedom that you have in Christ and testify even to your wicked master what God has done for you. You will not be ruled by circumstance. You will not be coerced into bitterness. You will take your joy in God. You will know that the social stigma, the "shame" of your current position is taken away by the cross of Christ. You will know that in Christ, you are free, and with that freedom you are able to show goodness even to those who hate and wrong you.

This instruction is first given to individual slaves, those who are in immediate contact with their own specific masters. Only then does Paul go on to apply the same concept to the ambient slavery experienced by all of his readers at the hands of the Roman authorities:

> Remind them to be submissive to rulers and authorities, to be obedient, to be ready for every good work, to speak evil of no one, to avoid quarrelling, to be gentle, and to show perfect courtesy toward all people.
>
> Titus 3:1-2

With respect to the Roman Empire, all of Paul's readers were effectively slaves by conquest. They had no realistic hope of escape. When the tax collectors came knocking, demanding tribute for Caesar, where could they run to? They would either submit or else be crushed by the imperial legion. So Paul tells them they are to be submissive. They are to respond to this unfortunate situation by doing good and refusing to do evil to those who oppress them. This is the common path outlined in New Testament teaching on relations to the State.

Romans 13 – Love Your Enemies, Even the Emperor

Now we come to a critical passage. It is perhaps the single most-quoted passage on the issue of the church's relationship to the State. Romans 13:1-7.

> Let every person be subject to the governing authorities. For there is no authority except from God, and those that exist have been instituted by God. Therefore whoever resists the authorities resists what God has appointed, and those who resist will incur judgement. For rulers are not a terror to good conduct, but to bad. Would you have no fear of the one who is in authority? Then do what is good, and you will receive his approval, for he is God's servant for your good. But if you do wrong, be afraid, for he does not bear the sword in vain. For he is the servant of God, an avenger who carries out God's wrath on the wrongdoer. Therefore one must be in subjection, not only to avoid God's wrath but also for the sake of conscience. For the same reason you also pay taxes, for the authorities are ministers of God, attending to this very thing. Pay to all

> what is owed to them: taxes to whom
> taxes are owed, revenue to whom revenue
> is owed, respect to whom respect is owed,
> honour to whom honour is owed.
>
> Romans 13:1-7

This passage is more dense and has more for us to unpack than 1 Peter and Titus did. We will handle the issues one at a time. The first issue is, how does this passage connect with our thesis, that *taxation is slavery*? Slavery is not mentioned explicitly in the immediate context, as it is with the passages in 1 Peter and Titus. However, there is a principle of Christian living which drives the instructions to slaves in those passages. That principle is that believers who find themselves trapped in the unfortunate position of being slaves ought to be gracious and submissive to their masters and thereby make the gospel of Christ shine brightly.

This same *principle* is expounded in the immediate context of Romans 13. Romans 12 is a chapter on the essence of Christian living. Far too often we are distracted by the chapter divisions in our modern Bibles (which are not a part of the original text!). Because of this, we mistakenly think that each chapter deals with a distinct and separate idea. But notice how clearly the progression of thought flows when we let the end of Romans 12 lead into the beginning of Romans 13.

> Bless those who persecute you; bless and do not curse them. Rejoice with those who rejoice, weep with those who weep. Live in harmony with one another. Do not be haughty, but associate with the lowly. Never be conceited. Repay no one evil for evil, but give thought to do what is honourable in the sight of all. If possible, so far as it depends on you, live peaceably with all. Beloved, never avenge yourselves, but leave it to the wrath of God, for it is written, "Vengeance is mine, I will repay, says the Lord." To the contrary, if your enemy is hungry, feed him; if he is thirsty, give him something to drink; for by so doing you will heap burning coals on his head. Do not be overcome by evil, but overcome evil with good. Let every person be subject to the governing authorities...
>
> Romans 12:14-13:1

Now this passage is finally coming into focus. For many years, I thought of Romans 13 as nothing more than a proof text showing that Christians were supposed to obey the government and pay their taxes. In reality, it is the climactic, real-world application of gospel grace: loving our enemies.

Why does Paul *conclude* his string of ever-greater calls to radical grace by telling the Roman Christians to be subject to the authorities, showing them honour and paying their taxes? Is it because the authorities are some kind of praiseworthy class of self-sacrificial, public servants? Is it because the authorities have dedicated themselves to pursuing righteousness? No! In the context of chapter 12, that would make absolutely no sense. Clearly, the discussion of Christian relations to the State flows out of the call to love our enemies. This is because Paul recognised that the Roman State was among the greatest enemies of the church of Christ.

So even though slavery is not explicitly mentioned in Romans 12-13, the "show love to your enemies" principle, by which Paul calls slaves to be submissive to their masters, is the same principle at work when he calls the believers at Rome to be submissive to their own oppressor, the emperor of Rome. The enslavement of the Roman Christians is less direct and personal, but the fact remains that they are compelled by threat of violence to pay tribute to Caesar. The first-century Christians' relationship to Caesar was the same as the Moabites relationship to king David, when David made the Moabites his "slaves" by imposing a tribute (1 Chronicles 18:2). As a result, the ethical principles that drive the relationship of Christian slaves to their masters are also the principles which drive the relationship of subjugated Christians to the State which is over them.

Romans 13 cont. – How Does the Authority of Rulers Come from God?

There is a second question that arises out of Romans 13. What are we to make of the statement in Romans 13:2-3 that "there is no authority except from God, and those that exist have been instituted by God"? Doesn't this mean that God has given His blessing to the rule of the powers that be? Does this mean that God has sanctioned their holding of that position? This is certainly what John Calvin understood from this passage[18].

Yet it should be clear to us that no such thing is meant. Such an interpretation is absurd on its face. How could the God who led Gideon to throw off the yoke of the Midianites also say that the yoke of the Romans is righteous and must not be violated? To

---

18 John Calvin, *Institutes of the Christian Religion*, IV.20.4.

say such a thing is to accuse the Eternal God of being indecisive.

It makes much more sense to interpret this passage as saying that the yoke of the Romans is something that God has *allowed* to take place. It is a great irony that Calvin, being an iconic defender of the doctrine of God's sovereignty, should have missed this point. This same irony is amplified in Kuyper, whose whole intellectual framework was built on the foundation of God's sovereignty in all areas of life.

God does not "institute" the authorities that exist in the sense of giving them His blessing and approval. Rather, retaining His sovereign control over the flow of history, God brings about the situation in which wicked men rise up and conquer their neighbours. But why does God allow this? If Caesar really were such a villain, would God not prevent him from rising to power? Not according to biblical history.

Consider the times when Israel was conquered. Were the kings of Midian, Assyria or Babylon paragons of virtue, appointed by God for their fair-mindedness and devotion to dealing righteously with the people whom they ruled? No, certainly not. We are told clearly that God merely used the wickedness, conquering and pillaging of those kings in order to discipline Israel after they had strayed from the commands of the LORD.

> Therefore thus says the LORD of hosts: "Because you have not obeyed my words, behold, I will send for all the tribes of the north, declares the LORD, and for Nebuchadnezzar the king of Babylon, my servant, and I will bring them against this land and its inhabitants, and against all these surrounding nations. I will devote them to destruction, and make them a horror, a hissing, and an everlasting desolation. Moreover, I will banish from them the voice of mirth and the voice of gladness, the voice of the bridegroom and the voice of the bride, the grinding of the millstones and the light of the lamp. This whole land shall become a ruin and a waste, and these nations shall serve the king of Babylon seventy years. Then after seventy years are completed, I will punish the king of Babylon and that nation, the land of the Chaldeans, for their iniquity, declares the LORD, making the land an everlasting waste. I will bring upon that land all the words that I have uttered against it, everything written in this book,

> which Jeremiah prophesied against all the nations. For many nations and great kings shall make slaves even of them, and I will recompense them according to their deeds and the works of their hands.
>
> Jeremiah 25:8-14

We see here that on the one hand, God is perfectly happy to use Nebuchadnezzar, king of Babylon, as His tool for bringing judgement upon Israel. He even calls Nebuchadnezzar "my servant". But in the very next breath, God says that He will punish Nebuchadnezzar for all the evil that he does and Nebuchadnezzar himself will be conquered.

All this to say, it is not out of character for God to appoint a wicked king to come in and temporarily conquer Israel as a sign of judgement upon Israel's sin. God has used such wicked kings to execute His judgements in the past. All that is really being said in Romans 13:2-3 is that God is once again exercising His sovereignty over the rise and fall of empires, this time through Caesar. In this way, we see that Irenaeus was correct when he read Romans 13:1-7 as a statement that God uses oppression by wicked rulers both as a judgement against sinful nations *and* as a way to maintain some degree of order when a society threatens to tear itself apart through its own injustices. To that extent, we should note that even the worst of rulers are not *utterly* depraved. They do not seek to do as much evil with as much intensity as they possibly can with their span of life. For example, even the worst rulers still tend to make a point of punishing murderers within their dominion. It is right for us to be grateful for that. We ought to give thanks to God for the punishment of those genuine evildoers whom even a wicked ruler may see fit to condemn, because in that way they function as "the servant of God, an avenger who carries out God's wrath on the wrongdoer" (Romans 13:4).

Romans 13 cont. – Why Then Do We Pay Taxes?

How then are we to understand Paul's statement in Romans 13:6 about the reason that we pay taxes? Paul tells his readers, "for the same reason, you also pay taxes, for the authorities are ministers of God, attending to this very thing." What is the "reason" that he is referring to?

I think the most consistent way to understand this verse is to see Caesar as fulfilling the role of the "avenger of blood" described in Deuteronomy.

> But if anyone hates his neighbour and lies in wait for him and attacks him and strikes him fatally so that he dies, and he flees into one of these cities, then the elders of his city shall send and take him from there, and hand him over to the avenger of blood, so that he may die. Your eye shall not pity him, but you shall purge the guilt of innocent blood from Israel, so that it may be well with you.
>
> Deuteronomy 19:11-13

In the context of this passage, the avenger of blood is not necessarily a person holding any type of political office. This passage is describing rules for the period before Israel ever had a king. But God is firm that someone must rise up and punish the murderer. God says that "your eye shall not pity him" (Deuteronomy 19:13) and that no ransom shall be accepted for the murderer's life (Numbers 35:31). The blood of the murderer must be shed (Numbers 35:33). These laws fulfil the mandate going back to Genesis 9:6 that "whoever sheds the blood of man, by man shall his blood be shed, for God made man in his own image".

When Caesar bears the sword and becomes "an avenger who carries out God's wrath on the wrongdoer" (Romans 13:4), this is the role that he is assuming. This punishment of evildoers by the avenger is a good thing, even a holy thing. That is why Paul uses priestly language to describe the authorities in Romans 13:6. Notice that while the emperor is called God's "servant" (διακονος, diakonos) in Romans 13:4, the authorities are instead called God's "ministers" (λειτουργοι, leitourgoi) in Romans 13:6. This Greek word "leitourgoi" is related to our English word "liturgy". It is a worship word. It is used of a person who performs service in the temple. Paul uses this same language to describe himself in Romans 15:16 where he calls himself "a minister (λειτουργον) of Christ Jesus to the Gentiles in the priestly service of the gospel of God".

Paul is saying that when Caesar performs the function of the avenger of blood in bringing God's wrath upon the evildoer, he is engaged in a holy act of service to God. That is not to say that all of Caesar's acts are holy. Nor is it to say that Caesar has entirely pure motives for performing the function of the avenger. But the act itself is to be respected. For that reason, we may take comfort that when Caesar unjustly exacts taxes from us, God is still using Caesar to accomplish something good. In that sense, Kuyper was partly right when he described taxes as a "sacred offering, given to God". Kuyper's mistake was in thinking that taxation itself was justified by the use that was made of the confiscated funds. That is not what Paul is saying. Rather, Caesar is wrong to impose his taxes on those whom he has conquered. But if we are unable to escape from the situation of being under Caesar's conquest, then we should take the peaceful path, submit to Caesar, pay his taxes, and be grateful to God for those instances where Caesar does do God's work as the avenger.

Conclusion: Tactical Pacifism

How then can we describe the teaching of 1 Peter, Titus and Romans on dealing with the State? Their advice can be summarised by the term "tactical pacifism". They are suggesting that when Christians are faced with an overwhelming State force, which they cannot realistically overthrow or escape, then they should take a pacifistic approach. The Christians should seek to overwhelm the evil of their enemies by doing good to them.

This approach has precedent in the Old Testament. We see Daniel and Nehemiah, both enslaved to foreign kings. They both enter humbly before their conquerors and serve them diligently. Both of them, when they come before their masters, wish them long life and prosperity. Daniel brings the interpretation of an ominous dream to Nebuchadnezzar but opens by saying, "My lord, may the dream be for those who hate you, and the interpretation for your enemies!" (Daniel 4:19). Nehemiah, likewise, when he goes before King Artaxerxes, begins his remarks by saying, "Let the king live forever!" (Nehemiah 2:3).

The core teaching of the New Testament epistles is that this course of action is to be commended to believers. It is in keeping with the gospel of grace, it points the attention of a wicked world towards Christ, and it follows a grand tradition of similar behaviour in the lives of the Old Testament saints.

The purpose of the New Testament teaching on taxation and the State is not to say that the government is righteous and holy or that living in a society with no ruler and no taxes would somehow be a sin. The point is simply that, given a situation where an unrighteous government is extorting money from you, the natural response of gospel-driven Christians is not to be overcome by that evil, but instead to overcome evil with good.

Now, this does not mean that the only Christian option is the total submission of a proverbial "doormat". The pacifistic response to State oppression recommended in the Bible is very nuanced, which is why I have called it "tactical" pacifism. Clearly, Ehud and Gideon were practising no form of pacifism at all when they led violent revolts against their Moabite and Midianite rulers. Likewise, the New Testament ethic does not require that we embrace slavery, even in cases where we are capable of escaping. Consider this passage from 1 Corinthians 7.

> Were you a slave when called [by God]? Do not be concerned about it. But if you can gain your freedom, avail yourself of the opportunity. For he who was called in the Lord as a slave is a freedman of the Lord. Likewise he who was free when called is a slave of Christ. You were bought with a price; do not become slaves of men.
>
> 1 Corinthians 7:21-23

On the one hand, Paul advises believers in Corinth who are slaves not to be distressed about their situation. The circumstances of their earthly life do not need to dominate their worries all day long. They can rightly regard themselves as free in God and take joy in that. Nevertheless, Paul clearly regards their enslavement as an evil. He tells them that if they see a chance to gain their freedom, then they should take it. He finishes with the direct instruction that a Christian should never *seek* to become a slave of their fellow man. Why? Because we have been bought at a price (the blood of Christ, shed in our place), and we belong to God, not to a man.

All of this to say, the New Testament clearly recognises that living under a tax-levying state is a form of slavery. However, the New Testament is also very nuanced on how a Christian should respond to that reality. A pacifist course, in which we deliberately do good to our oppressors, is entirely valid and commendable as a way to give honour to God. If we are trapped in our slavery, we should pursue that course. But it is also entirely permissible to strive to be released from slavery and gain our freedom. If that option is open to us, we are encouraged to take it. The main issue is that we regard ourselves first and foremost as free in Christ, belonging properly to God, so that we live in a way that brings Him glory.

Taxation in the Gospels

The New Testament epistles show us that our relationship to the State and its taxes should be understood in terms of loving our enemies. However, the epistles do not necessarily give us much detail on certain practical issues. How are we to interact with the State on a day-to-day basis? If taxation is an expression of slavery, does that mean that a Christian must never accept any type of government employment? If our roads are built with the proceeds of taxation, are we then obliged to boycott the roads?

These are questions that must be answered if we are to have a robust understanding of our relationship to the State. Fortunately, there are passages in the gospels where specific ethical scenarios involving the State are discussed.

Matthew 22:15-22 – Give to Caesar What is Caesar's

Perhaps the second-most quoted passage on the Christian's relationship to the State is Matthew 22:15-22. In this passage, a group of Pharisees and Herodians come to Jesus to try and trick him into saying something that will get him in trouble.

> Then the Pharisees went and plotted how to entangle him in his talk. And they sent their disciples to him, along with the Herodians, saying, "Teacher, we know that you are true and teach the way of God truthfully, and you do not care about anyone's opinion, for you are not swayed by appearances. Tell us, then, what you think. Is it lawful to pay taxes to Caesar, or not?" But Jesus, aware of their malice, said, "Why put me to the test, you hypocrites? Show me the coin for the tax." And they brought him a denarius. And Jesus said to them, "Whose likeness and inscription is this?" They said, "Caesar's." Then he said to them, "Therefore render to Caesar the things that are Caesar's, and to God the things that are God's." When they
>
> Matthew 22:15-22

The first step we must take is to correct a common misinterpretation of this passage. McCumber provides a typical example of the way this passage is handled by modern commentators[19]:

---

19 William E. McCumber, *Matthew*, Beacon Bible Expositions (Kansas City, Mo: Nazarene Publishing House, 1975), 172.

> The Pharisees put a loaded question to Jesus. "Yes" will be interpreted as traitorous, for the Jews hate to give tax support to the Romans. "No" will be translated as seditious, a precipitate of rebellion against Rome. They have Jesus in a dilemma, so they think...
>
> ... The answer recognises Caesar's rights. Benefits and services from government should be paid for by taxation. But the answer also delimited Caesar's authority. Man is stamped with God's likeness (cf. Gen 1:27f.). Human life, therefore, is to be governed by God's will. If God and Caesar issue counter commands, men should obey God, whatever the cost (cf. Acts 5:29).

This interpretation is simple enough and sits very neatly with the usual "limited government" view that was described earlier. However, this interpretation also creates some grave difficulties. If we are to give to Caesar what is Caesar's, then what *is* Caesar's? The formulation that we must obey the government right up until the point where they command something directly contradictory to God's own command simply will not do. If taxation is indeed an expression of conquest slavery (as has been quite thoroughly demonstrated), then the conquering State is a totally illegitimate entity. Every penny that the State extracts from its conquered subjects is an act of rebellion against God. Where then could we possibly draw the line? If Jesus intended to preach the legitimacy of Caesar's rule but only up to certain boundaries, then he is making a break with the consistent view of the Old Testament. This would be a very strange thing for Jesus to do in the context of the question that was asked. The question was about how Torah-observant Jews should apply the Old Testament law. The question posed to Jesus was, "Is it *lawful* to pay taxes to Caesar?" An interpretation that requires Jesus to make a radical departure from Old Testament precedent is a non starter. We will need to find a more satisfying answer.

Hauerwas takes Jesus' answer to be a direct condemnation of the idolatry represented by the coin. The inscription on the denarius bore an image of Caesar and stated that Caesar was divine. For this reason, it could be argued that it was right for Jews to ship every single one of these coin-shaped "graven images" out of Israel and back to pagan Rome[20]. However, this raises an obvious

---

20 Stanley Hauerwas, *Matthew*, Brazos Theological Commentary on the Bible (Grand Rapids, Mich: Brazos Press, 2006), 190.

contextual question. If the point was to trap Jesus in his words and Jesus was responding with an outright condemnation of the emperor, would this not have been enough to have him arrested? Yet Jesus' questioners do not immediately accuse him of insurrection, but rather, they are amazed at his answer. Therefore, the pure-condemnation interpretation seems highly unlikely.

Turner's answer comes closer to walking this subtle line. Turner believes that the brilliance of the answer lies in the fact that it simultaneously reminds the anti-Rome Pharisees to pay the tax, since God's sovereignty has brought them under the emperor's rule, while also reminding the pro-Rome Herodians that their devotion to God should supersede their devotion to any human ruler[21]. This is getting much nearer to our "tactical pacifism" paradigm found in the epistles and to the legacy inherited from Old Testament examples like Daniel and Nehemiah.

Reframing the Question: Is It *Lawful* to Pay Taxes?

While Turner's answer is helpful, it also leaves out an important aspect of the dialogue. The question brought to Jesus is not, "*Are we obliged* to

---

[21] David L. Turner, *Matthew*, Baker Exegetical Commentary on the New Testament (Grand Rapids, Mich: Baker Academic, 2008), 528.

pay taxes to Caesar?" Not at all. It is taken for granted that Caesar is a conquering scoundrel who has no right to rule Israel whatsoever. Instead, the question that was actually asked was, "Is it *lawful* to pay taxes to Caesar?" That is, for a Torah-observant Jew, is paying the tax to Caesar even *permissible?* Or are pious Jews required to abstain from paying it?

This is a very different way of understanding the question. Typically, a modern Christian will read this passage and ask, "Do I have to pay taxes?" I am suggesting that in Jesus' day, the real question being asked was, "*May I* pay taxes?" Everyone recognised that Caesar was a horrible tyrant. Everyone also recognised that they would be punished severely if they refused to pay the tax. For most people, in most places, life is simply easier if they pay their taxes without resistance. What these people are asking Jesus is, "Do they have permission to take that easy way out?"

In the past, there have been people and groups who attempted to withhold taxes from the government as a form of protest against policies they disliked. One example was people refusing to pay certain taxes in the USA as a protest against the Vietnam War. That is the sort of action that is being discussed in this passage. The questioners know that Caesar is wicked. If they pay their taxes, they will be helping to fund Caesar's imperial war machine, the same war machine that is oppressing their own people. So perhaps they should refuse to pay? On the other hand, they do not appear to have any real hope of standing up to the Roman army. Maybe it is better to just "pay up" so that Rome will leave them alone and they can get on with their lives? Still, they wonder, is it a selfish strategy, simply resigning themselves to the taxes in order to avoid trouble?

Seen through this lens, Jesus' answer becomes clear. "Give to Caesar what is Caesar's, and to God what is God's." This simply means, give Caesar what he demands, but do not be devoted to him. In sum, Jesus is saying that it is *not* a sin to be the victim of conquest, but it *is* a sin to worship Caesar as a god. Submitting to your conquerors and paying their taxes under duress does not make you morally complicit in their actions. But at the same time, you must not become devoted to your conquerors so that you are led to participate in their sin. Keep your devotion directed towards the Living God, where it belongs.

Bitcoin – The Separation of Money and State

Before making his famous statement, "Give to Caesar what is Caesar's", Jesus calls his hearers' attention to the fact that Caesar's face is engraved upon the coin.

You may occasionally have heard someone point out a parallel here between Caesar's image on the coin and God's image in man. Douglas Wilson gives us an interpretation along these lines[22]:

> They were trying to trap Jesus with a question of tax policy, and Jesus answered by pointing to two different kinds of coin. One coin had the image of Caesar on it, and it was therefore lawful in principle to give that back to Caesar. That which has Washington's image on it may be sent back to Washington. That which has "Federal Reserve Note" printed on it may be mailed back to the Federal Reserve. But Jesus did not just say that they should render Caesar's image back to him—He said that something should be rendered back to God and not to Caesar. What would that be? The answer is that we are a coin from God's mint. We are created in the image of God, and are therefore forbidden to render ourselves to Caesar.

Similar things have been said by pastors in my own country, where the coins all have a picture of

---

22 Douglas Wilson, *Rules for Reformers*, Section 3.

Queen Elizabeth II on them. We should not dismiss this interpretation completely. It is at least half correct. Yes, we are made in God's image, and therefore, no, we are not permitted to give our devotion to Caesar. Nevertheless, it is very strange to imagine that Caesar's claim to ownership over our wealth would become legitimate simply because he forces us to use a currency with his picture on it. This point could be argued from an abstract theological foundation. However, the modern world gives us an interesting way to quickly expose the inconsistency.

To be consistent, Wilson and others would need to say that if we *do not* use Washington's or Elizabeth's or Caesar's currency, then we do not owe them any taxes. Would most pastors be prepared to take that position? I seriously doubt it. Yet that would be the logical implication, if the ruler's ownership claim is indeed derived from us using their currency.

When I was a child, doing business without using the government's preferred currency would have sounded crazy and impossible. The days of circulating gold and silver coins were long gone, and it seemed like government-issued paper money would never go away. But that is no longer the case. For the first time in a long time, we genuinely have the option to do business with a currency that is not issued by *any* government. We have entered the age of *cryptocurrency*.

Suppose that 50 or 100 years from now, Bitcoin (or some other cryptocurrency[23]) has become the most commonly used medium for market exchanges. Would Wilson still be able to argue from this passage that there was some intrinsic connection between the government and the money supply? Clearly he could not. By design, Bitcoin does not have the face of any president or king upon it at all. It is a "stateless" form of money.

Now, let us ask a practical question. If using Bitcoin in daily commerce becomes as "normal" as using dollars, euros or yen, do you believe that your own government will let it go *untaxed*? Will

---

23 I mention "Bitcoin" here because it is the cryptocurrency most likely to be recognisable to readers who are unfamiliar with the broader cryptocurrency space. As a practical matter, my personal opinion is that Bitcoin (BTC) is actually somewhat ill-suited to become a global currency for the average person. There are other cryptocurrencies which I personally believe are better suited to function as peer-to-peer cash. In particular, I keep up to date on the development of Bitcoin Cash (BCH), Nano (XRB) and Monero (XMR). Each one has different strengths and weaknesses and to my mind each one has legitimate potential to become the preferred peer-to-peer cash of the world. But I will quickly point out that this footnote is included for the sake of interest only and should not be construed as "investment" advice. What is most important is that *none* of these aforementioned cryptocurrencies has the image of a president or a king stamped upon them!

your government officials say, "Our hands are tied. The Queen's face is not on your Bitcoin, so we have no right to take it from you. We did not make the Bitcoin, nor did we grow the vegetables that you are buying with it. We had nothing to do with any part of that transaction, so we cannot justify imposing a sales tax."

Of course no government will take that position. In my country, accepting cryptocurrency for goods and services already requires you to pay income and sales tax *as if* you were accepting Australian dollars. When the State thinks about levying taxes, it never enters their minds that the taxes are justified because they are denominated in a currency connected to the President or the Queen. They levy their taxes, not because some imprint on the currency gives them the right to do so, but simply because they wish to take wealth for their own purposes from someone else's pocket.

The sooner we let go of the delusion that money must come from the State, the better off all of us will be. State-issued money allows the State to tax the whole population by stealth, through *inflation* of the money supply[24]. State-issued money also

---

24 Describing all the evils of inflating the money supply is beyond the scope of this book. I recommend Gary North's book "Honest Money" (freely available online), where he describes the consequences of inflation, and argues at length that printing money is a systematic violation of God's command that we should use "equal weights and

helps the State to maintain the illusion that society would not be able to function if the State did not exist.

As the portion of the global economy that uses non-State money continues to grow, the State loses more and more of its power because it loses its inflation-based revenue. By this mechanism, cryptocurrency gives us an opportunity to live out a biblical ideal: seceding from the rule of our overlords through a strategy of non-violence.

Luke 3:10-14 – Bureaucrats and Police

Once we understand the State as an institution of society-wide slavery, this passage in Luke comes into clearer focus. In the ancient framework, slaves do not merely serve as individuals, they serve as part of a "household". The head of a household could have many slaves, whether by contract or conquest, and not all of them would perform the same task. Indeed, as a household became larger, and as the available slave labour increased, it was necessary to appoint managers and foremen to oversee the operation. But those managers were still part of the overall household slavery system. This is what happened to Joseph when he was sold into slavery in Egypt. Although he remained a

---

measures" (Deuteronomy 25:15).

slave, he ultimately rose to a position of substantial authority within Pharaoh's house (Genesis 41:41). Over the centuries, many people living in slavery have nevertheless found themselves in a position of authority over their fellow slaves. Some have been conquered by an invading nation, only to find themselves in high-up positions within that nation's bureaucracy (like Joseph and Daniel). Others have taken up relatively-minor, functionary positions (like the common tax-collectors of Jesus' day). When this type of situation arises, the question is, How is this power to be handled?

In Luke 3, we see John the Baptist preparing the way for the coming of Christ, calling Israel to repent and to turn back to the Lord. In the midst of this, we read of particular people coming to him and asking "what does repentance look like for our specific circumstance?" In all three cases where people ask John a specific question, the question has to do with how they should live in a context where they are enslaved by Rome.

> And the crowds asked him, "What then shall we do?" And he answered them, "Whoever has two tunics is to share with him who has none, and whoever has food is to do likewise." Tax collectors also came to be baptised and said to him, "Teacher,

> what shall we do?" And he said to them, "Collect no more than you are authorised to do." Soldiers also asked him, "And we, what shall we do?" And he said to them, "Do not extort money from anyone by threats or by false accusation, and be content with your wages."
>
> Luke 3:10-14

To The Crowds: Voluntary Charity

In this brief dialogue, we get a lot of helpful instruction on how we are to interact with both society and the State. The first group that comes to John is only referred to as "the crowds". John's advice to them is simple "if you have plenty of food and clothing, share it with those who do not have enough." Doubtless, someone, somewhere, has read this verse as a confirmation that a Christian society ought to embrace socialism. "The rich must share with the poor" they would have said. But such phrasing leaves out a lot of important detail.

First, notice what John is *not* advocating for here. John is not telling them that they must give until they themselves are in need. The suggestion is not "whoever has *one* tunic must give it away, and be cold and naked himself, for the sake of another person." The suggestion is, the person who has enough for themselves and also some left over should share with the person who does not have enough. He who has *two* tunics should give to him who has *none*. That is not to say that there is anything wrong with making genuine sacrifices in order to help someone else. Certainly not. Indeed, doing so would mean following the example of Christ himself, the servant king who washed his disciple's feet and died in their place. However, as regards the good ordering of society, the ideal presented here is not that every single person should be in poverty, lest they enjoy some pleasure that someone else cannot afford. The ideal is only that people genuinely in need should not starve in a society where others have the capacity to help them. If you are greedy, if you are amassing wealth and failing to be generous with it, John does not let you off the hook. Yes, he says, you do need to share some of it around to those who are struggling.

Now, having established that, the question becomes, By what mechanism are we to achieve this goal? John's firm answer is that it is to be achieved voluntarily, *not* by the apparatus of the taxing State. This is clear from the immediately following context. The next two inquiries that come to John are from exactly the two groups of people who would be in charge of collecting the taxes: the bureaucrats and the police. John tells both of these groups that they need to restrain themselves in such matters.

To The Tax Collectors: Do Not Be a Part of The Problem

In verse 12, we read that tax collectors come to John to be baptised and ask him what repentance should look like for them. John's simple answer is, "Collect no more than you are authorised to do."

Now, this immediately raises a question. We have established that taxation is a mechanism of slavery. Furthermore, in the context of this passage, we are definitely talking about conquest slavery, for we are talking about the Roman imperial forces that had conquered Israel. So then, why does John not simply tell them to resign and refuse to collect *any* taxes at all?

The answer is similar to the one that Jesus gave to the Pharisees and Herodians who asked him whether it was "lawful" to pay taxes to Caesar. Jesus indicated that, yes, it is permissible to submit to your conquerors and pay the tax. Doing so does not make you complicit in their crimes. Here the question is turned around. What if the State is ordering you to go around and collect the tax that they have imposed? That is a step beyond merely paying the tax. If you act as a tax collector, does that make you complicit in the State's oppression?

Many Jews in Jesus' day clearly thought so. Tax collectors were a hated group, and not just because nobody enjoys having to pay bills. Tax collectors were typically seen as collaborating with the Romans and were therefore to be despised by good, patriotic Jews. However, the practice that likely drew the most scorn from their countrymen was the tax collectors' tendency to overcharge their neighbours and keep the extra money for themselves. If Rome ordered a $100 tax, the tax collector might demand $120 from their neighbours for a $20 profit in their pocket. For this reason, people would literally bid against one another to buy the tax collection duties for a region[25]. For people who did not mind ripping off their neighbours and becoming a lackey of Rome, this was a very profitable business opportunity.

So, given that background, what is the point of John's answer? "Collect no more than you are authorised to do." Clearly, what this means is that a repentant tax collector is not required to resign from that job. What they *are* required to do is to stop being complicit in the oppression of their neighbours. This has very practical implications for Christians living in the modern world. For many believers today, there is scarcely an inch within the

---

25 Wyndy Corbin-Reuschling, "Zacchaeus's Converson: To Be or Not to Be a Tax Collector (Luke 19:1-10)," *Ex Auditu* 25 (2009): 72.

economy of their home country which is not subject to some kind of State intervention. One way or another, some part of their wages probably comes from a government grant, a government salary, or some other tax-derived source. For many people, the bureaucracy seems inescapable. The question is, How can a Christian interact righteously with the bureaucracy of the State? John's sympathetic answer is that it *is* lawful to submit to the existence of a State bureaucracy, even to the point of being employed within that structure.

This is a practical case where saying that taxation is "slavery" is subtly distinguished from the more catchy variant that taxation is "theft". Speaking biblically, because taxation is a form of slavery, we have an ethical framework for understanding the role of bureaucrats. A country enslaved by a taxing State is ultimately in the same ethical position as a group of slaves operating within a single large household. When the slave master of a household appoints one of the slaves to be in charge of recording the produce that comes in from the fields, that slave has become an administrative "bureaucrat" within the household. They are still a slave like all the rest, but they have been given a specific task to perform. Suppose the slave master, from all the wealth generated by his slaves, sets aside a portion to be used for the slaves' food, clothing and shelter. That does not mean that he is being "generous" towards them. On the contrary, he is still stealing away the fruit of their labour for himself. However, if he wants to get slave labour out of them for a longer period of time, then he needs to provide them with enough resources so that they do not starve or become desperate enough to start a revolt.

Now, suppose the master appoints one of the slaves to ensure that all the rest are receiving their appropriate rations. That slave who is in charge of the distribution has not automatically become complicit in the master's crimes. In reality, they are still a slave themselves.

Likewise, it is the State which levies taxes upon the citizens of a country. If a person takes a job within a government department, working for that department is not in itself immoral, even though they receive rations from the slave master State. Having said that, there may be certain government jobs which *do* explicitly require them to commit acts of wickedness. Such jobs should obviously be avoided. For example, someone who works for the government as a spy may be asked to kill several innocent people while pretending to be from another country, in order to frame the government of that other country and create a pretext for an invasion. This would be murder and malicious deception. Those actions do not become any less of a crime just because they are ordered by a government. On the other hand, suppose the State in your country maintains a forced monopoly over the issuing of driver's licenses. You may prefer a society in which private businesses competed to offer high-quality certifications to drivers. You may regard the State's enforced monopoly on this business as immoral. But you are not doing something immoral by accepting a job where you process forms in the government's licensing centre. You are merely accepting and submitting to the State enslavement under which you have found yourself.

Let us return then to the tax collectors who asked John what they should do in order to demonstrate repentance. In their case, it was the Roman State that was actually taxing the people. By adding a little extra on top of the official Roman tax, they were effectively committing the same wicked act as the Roman State. Just like their overlords, they were taking for themselves something which was not theirs to take. That is the action from which they needed to repent. But they did *not* need to repent of allowing themselves to function as State employees.

To The Soldiers: Do Not Engage in Extortion

Finally, in verse 14, some soldiers come to John and ask how they should express their repentance. Again, John's answer to them is simple: "Do not extort money from anyone by threats or by false accusation, and be content with your wages."

Functionally, this is the same answer that was given to the tax collectors. The soldiers are to regard themselves as slaves, carrying out a task within the household of the Roman State. They are to provide security services and keep the peace in exchange for the rations (wages) given by the slave master State. But, like the tax collectors, they must not allow themselves to become complicit in the crimes of the State. They must not use the threat of force to extort money from people. It is easy to see how this could be a temptation for a soldier in the pay of an occupying State, just as it would have been for a tax collector. A soldier could easily threaten a random peasant, saying either that they would physically harm them or that they would accuse them of crimes against the State if the peasant did not give them money.

In practice, this is exactly what the State itself does when it levies taxes. The person who refuses to pay the tax is threatened with physical abduction and imprisonment if they refuse to pay.

Police today are routinely guilty of similar immoral acts. Some countries have a reputation for police corruption. In my own country of Australia, many people take holidays to the Indonesian island of Bali. It is widely understood by Australians that in the course of their holiday, a Balinese police officer will probably try to shake them down for a bribe. They account for this expense in their travel plans and regard it as simply an expected part of the Balinese experience. Taking bribes has a much larger negative stigma in Australia than it appears to have in Bali. As a result, most Australians do not think of our own police as being "corrupt". However, police in Australia still routinely use false accusations as a tool of their trade. I myself have heard officers laughing about times when they have written tickets for made-up infractions as a way of punishing people who spoke to them disrespectfully. The truth is that police in most countries today, like those Roman soldiers, have plenty of scope to bully the public with impunity.

John's command to the soldiers is that it is not a crime to take a job in a State security organisation. However, you must not give in to the temptation to engage in extortion and thereby engage in the very crimes which the State itself commits.

If you, dear reader, are currently employed by an agency of the State, you need to ask yourself how your role fits into the State's overall pattern of enslaving the nation. Are you merely accepting rations in exchange for performing a particular service? Or are you yourself actively engaged in the oppression of your neighbours? If it is the former, rest assured, it is no sin to take a government job. Joseph, Daniel and Nehemiah all took jobs in the bureaucracies of their slave masters. But if your job has led you to become complicit in the State's theft, extortion, murder or other crimes, then you need to remove yourself immediately from that situation and cry out to the Lord for forgiveness.

Matthew 17:24-27 – Not Giving Offence

Let us finish our tour of taxation in the gospels by briefly revisiting Matthew 17. In this passage, we find Jesus and Peter at the temple. The collectors of the half-shekel temple tax ask Peter what Jesus will do.

> When they came to Capernaum, the collectors of the half-shekel tax went up to Peter and said, "Does your teacher not pay the tax?" He said, "Yes." And when he came into the house, Jesus spoke to him

> first, saying, "What do you think, Simon? From whom do kings of the earth take toll or tax? From their sons or from others?" And when he said, "From others," Jesus said to him, "Then the sons are free. However, not to give offence to them, go to the sea and cast a hook and take the first fish that comes up, and when you open its mouth you will find a shekel. Take that and give it to them for me and for yourself."
>
> Matthew 17:24-27

As we noted previously, Jesus uses the language of "freedom" here to refer to the sons, those who do not have to pay the tax. But it is important that we also witness Jesus' personal behaviour. Jesus, despite being under no obligation, *chooses* to pay the temple tax. Why does he do this? In his own words, he does this "not to give offence". Again, this fits in very nicely with our "tactical pacifism" model for interacting with those who levy taxes against us.

Jesus has just declared that he would be well within his rights *not* to pay. However, for the sake of having peace with them, he chooses in this instance to simply waive his own rights. Given that Jesus himself did this, then clearly it is acceptable for a Christian to do likewise if it seems wise in their own context.

A Systematic Theology of Property Rights

Having taken an introductory look at what Scripture says about taxation, our next step is to develop these ideas into a systematic framework. If our interpretation of Scripture leads to contradictory ideas, then it cannot be correct. Therefore, a Christian view of economics, politics and the State must have a robust, logical foundation. We will begin by developing a theological framework for the origin of property rights. Once that is done, we will bring our theological framework back to the text and see where we may further sharpen our understanding of God's word.

Where Does "Property" Come From?

What is "property"? Where does it come from? In common usage, "property" means anything that it is possible for a person to "own". But this is almost a tautology. What does it mean to "own" something? To "own" something means to have a moral right to decide how that thing ought to be used.

If someone says that they "own" the pair of boots they are wearing, we understand that to mean that they are claiming to have the moral right to decide who should be allowed to use those boots. As the "owner" of the boots, they are entitled to put them on and take them off at any time they wish. But if someone else wishes to wear those same boots, that other person may only do so if they have the consent of the one who "owns" the boots.

This seems simple enough. The more difficult question is, How does a human person *initially* come to "own" something? Is there a fundamental reason to say that a particular pair of boots belongs to Alice rather than belonging to Bob? Or are all such "ownership" claims fundamentally arbitrary? Is the statement that "I own this pair of boots" merely an expression of my own *subjective* impressions about my relationship to the boots (which others are free to disregard)? Or is it a statement about an *objective* reality, which others are morally required to recognise and respect?

Having Scripture as our guide, we can quickly plant at least one intellectual peg in the ground. In the eighth commandment given to Moses, God speaks to Israel, saying, *"You shall not steal."* (Exodus 20:15). For this verse to mean anything at all, it must mean that it is possible, at least in some cases, for someone to own *some* property. If no property was owned by anyone, in any sense at all, then the command not to "steal" would have had no meaning whatsoever. But the commandment stands there in God's word, so we can be assured that God (whose opinion is the definition of truth) regards at least *some* claims to "ownership" as valid[26].

Ownership as a Feature of Human Law

A second critical insight which we can gain from Scripture is that God expects humans to be capable of recognising specific, valid ownership claims *without* the need for ongoing divine revelation. Consider this passage from Leviticus:

> The LORD spoke to Moses, saying, "If anyone sins and commits a breach of faith against the LORD by deceiving his neighbour in a matter of deposit or security, or through robbery, or if he has oppressed his neighbour or has found something lost and lied about it, swearing falsely—in any of all the things that people

---

26 Wayne A Grudem, "The Eighth Commandment as the Moral Foundation for Property Rights, Human Flourishing, and Careers in Business," Themelios 41.1 (2016): 77.

> do and sin thereby— if he has sinned and has realised his guilt and will restore what he took by robbery or what he got by oppression or the deposit that was committed to him or the lost thing that he found or anything about which he has sworn falsely, he shall restore it in full and shall add a fifth to it, and give it to him to whom it belongs on the day he realises his
>
> Leviticus 6:1-5

In this passage, God gives Moses a precedent by which Moses should judge disputes among people in the newly liberated nation of Israel. God instructs Moses that if an Israelite has robbed his neighbour of some property, then he must return it with 20% interest ("a fifth"). There are two important implications here. First, God is expecting Moses (and eventually, Moses' successors) to be able to carry out this instruction. God does *not* say, "Moses, when someone claims to have been robbed, you will not have any way of determining whether that is true, so pray and inquire of me and I will reveal directly to you who is in the wrong and how much they must pay for restitution." Rather, God expects Moses to be able to do this without further assistance. God expects that the

Israelite society will be able to recognise, without any supernatural intervention, when a valid ownership claim has been transgressed. The second important implication is that God expects them not only to be able to recognise the transgression, but to *accurately quantify it*. God expects that when a person is robbed or defrauded, Moses or another judge will be able to determine with reasonable precision how much was taken and properly calculate the 20% interest that must be paid.

What this means is that when God hands down the commandment that "you shall not steal", He is expecting this commandment to become a feature of the commonly recognised laws of Israelite society. It is to become a part of the "common law" which humans judge and administer among themselves. Therefore, the commandment not to steal implies that there is such a thing as *recognisable* human ownership.

Divine Ownership and Human Ownership

Before we try to discover a basis for human ownership of property, we would be wise to begin with an understanding of divine ownership. To understand God's ownership of property, we begin from a more fundamental doctrine, the doctrine of

God's *sovereignty*. As both Calvin and Kuyper rightly understood, a proper theology must recognise that God both claims and exercises sovereignty over everything that exists. God alone possesses the power to create *ex nihilo*, "out of nothing" (Genesis 1:1, Romans 4:17). God alone is in control of the flow of all history and holds the very hearts of kings and the fates of nations in His hands (Exodus 9:16, Proverbs 21:1). God alone does whatever He pleases to do, both in heaven and on earth and in the seas and all deeps (Psalm 135:6).

Now, it would be possible for God to simply assert His great power over all other things that exist. He alone is omnipotent, and, therefore, He alone is able to exercise ultimate control over all things. But if this assertion had no moral component, if it was merely a naked act of power, then it would not be what we call "ownership". After all, if I wrestle you to the ground, take your boots from off your feet, and then put them on my own feet, this does not mean that I "own" the boots. My mere act of exerting power over them does not make them "mine". I may have taken the boots from you, but I have not taken away your *moral right* to exercise control over the boots. Forcibly denying you the ability to exercise that moral right does not prove that you ought not to have it.

So then, the question becomes, Does God have a *moral right* to exercise His sovereign power over all things? At this point, we could enter into a deep discussion of the source of morality within a theistic worldview[27]. However, this book is written primarily for the benefit of readers who already agree that the Bible is the Word of God. So we will simply observe that, according to the Bible, God does have a moral claim to exercise His sovereignty however He sees fit. God says plainly to Job:

> Who has first given to me, that I should repay him? Whatever is under the whole heaven is mine.
>
> Job 41:11

Or as God says again through the Psalmist:

---

[27] If you want to dip your toe into a more abstract, philosophical discussion about the source of morality in Christian theism, then I would recommend material from modern Christian philosophers like Ravi Zacharias or William Lane Craig. If you feel like you're ready to dive in head first, I would recommend you start by reading "The God Who Is There" by Francis Schaeffer or "Defending Your Faith" by R.C. Sproul.

> For every beast of the forest is mine, the cattle on a thousand hills. I know all the birds of the hills, and all that moves in the field is mine. If I were hungry, I would not tell you, for the world and its fullness are mine.
>
> Psalm 50:10

According to God Himself, there is nothing in the whole world that a human can claim to own over and against God's claim to ownership. No one can ever say "God owes me X", because God is actually the rightful, moral owner of X, whatever X may be.

As Kuyper so poetically put it, "There is not a square inch in the whole domain of our human existence over which Christ, who is Sovereign over all, does not cry: 'Mine!'"[28]

We are therefore faced with a serious dilemma. On the one hand, we do affirm God's rightful claim to legitimate ownership over all things everywhere. On the other hand, we see that God expects us, as a matter of everyday life, to recognise legitimate *human* claims to ownership when we see them. How can we reconcile these

---

28 *Abraham Kuyper: A Centennial Reader*, ed. James D. Bratt (Eerdmans, 1998), 488.

two ideas? They both stand before us in the Word of God, plain as day. So we must necessarily conclude that it is possible for property to simultaneously belong, in one sense, to God, and at the same time, in another sense, to particular human owners.

Now, God's ownership of all things must be a far higher and more potent ownership claim than any human claim. Things do not pass into and out of God's ownership the way that they do with human ownership. God gives nothing away, barters nothing, and receives nothing. He owns everything that ever exists for the full duration of its existence.

Human ownership, in contrast, is dramatically more finite, limited and provisional. We must therefore conclude that any human claim to ownership is not a claim to *total* ownership, but is rather a claim to *delegated* ownership. In order for a human to be the rightful owner of property, God must delegate that right to them, and their ownership must be derived somehow from God's ownership.

But if all human ownership claims are delegated and God expects human society to recognise legitimate ownership claims without continual divine revelation, then one more thing is clear. There must be some *principled mechanism* by which we can recognise the delegation of an ownership right by God to a human person. God must have provided us with a way, through the exercise of our reason, to know which property He has delegated and to whom.

Two Schools of Thought on Delegated Human Ownership (Locke versus Aquinas)

What then is this mechanism? After attempting to read a large number of Christian thinkers down through the centuries, I have concluded that their views are basically reducible to two major schools of thought. One school of thought sees human ownership and property rights as a feature of "positive law". The other school of thought sees human ownership and property rights as a feature of "natural law". Both schools have a long list of representatives, many of whom would differ with each other on a variety of nuances. But in each school, the common thread is their belief that property rights are either "posited" by a human agent or are "natural" and independent of human proclamations. That is the fundamental difference. Once a person has decided which of those two camps they fall into, the rest of their theory of property tends to follow fairly predictably. So then, we will examine these two schools of thought and try to determine which of them makes the most sense within a biblical worldview.

To give these two schools of thought an anchor point in Christian history, we will contrast the views of Thomas Aquinas (Positive Law) with the views of John Locke (Natural Law). Among proponents of the natural-law view, there seems to be a general consensus that John Locke made a critical contribution to that tradition. Subsequent followers often build self-consciously upon Locke's own insights. Because of that, Locke has naturally emerged as an iconic figure for this school. Thomas Aquinas on the other hand is anything but iconic for the positive-law view. In fact, those who are familiar with Aquinas will most likely be surprised to see him associated with "positive law" at all. Aquinas was in fact a great champion of *natural* law as a vital concept in philosophy and theology. However, the fact remains that Aquinas viewed property rights specifically as a feature of positive law, rather than natural law. This positive-law view of property rights was certainly not *established* by Aquinas. There is a long history of church fathers, monks, etc. who have held a similar, positive-law view. But Aquinas furnishes us with a clear, systematic exposition of this positive-law view (as opposed to more scattered remarks from earlier thinkers), and that is what is most helpful to us as we seek to understand these ideas.

Before we can properly contrast Aquinas' thought with Locke's thought, we must first define some terms.

Natural Law and Positive Law

The concepts of "natural law" and "positive law" come into play when we ask the question, "What is law?" This line of inquiry is what is known as "jurisprudence". At the most basic level, we all understand that a law is a statement about an action which you are either required to do or prohibited from doing. The question then becomes, What is the *source* of that requirement or prohibition?

Consider the following situation, which we will call "the Queensland bunny rabbit scenario". My own country, Australia, is made up of several smaller states. I have lived in two of those states, New South Wales (NSW) and Queensland (QLD). The different states here mostly have the same (federal) laws. But there are also differences between the states. In New South Wales, it is perfectly fine to keep a bunny rabbit in your backyard as a pet. But in Queensland, it is a crime. Rabbits are not a native species, they breed very rapidly, and they can damage farmland as they spread out. For this reason, they are considered a "pest", and the Queensland government has prohibited people from keeping them as pets. If you try to bring your pet bunny rabbit from New South Wales up north into Queensland, someone may tell you that it is "against the law" to do so. What do they mean by this statement? What does it mean for something to be "against the law"?

Next, let us consider a second situation, the "Nuremberg trial scenario". After World War II, high-ranking officials of the Nazi party were put on trial for "war crimes" in a city called Nuremberg. They were accused of being "war criminals", which is to say that in the course of the war, they had "broken the law." But what does it mean to "break the law" in that context? Is it something different than what "breaking the law" means in the Queensland bunny rabbit scenario? Or are they fundamentally the same thing?

We often use the same "breaking the law" language to describe both of these things, and so we are often confused about the distinction. But in fact, these two scenarios illustrate the difference between positive law on the one hand and natural law on the other.

If I say that it is "against the law" to have a bunny rabbit in Queensland, what I am really saying is that "the members of the Queensland government have agreed that there should be some punishment given to people who continue keeping pet bunny rabbits in Queensland." Therefore, if you have a pet bunny rabbit in Queensland, you are breaking a rule *created by* the members of the Queensland government. However, if you keep a pet bunny rabbit in New South Wales, there is no punishment for you. The government of New South Wales has decided not to have this law in their state[29]. In general, people in both New South Wales and Queensland respect this difference. There is no great outcry from one side of the border, claiming that the other side has committed some great moral atrocity because of their differing laws on bunny rabbits. The Queensland government simply recognises that if you are in New South Wales, you are not under the jurisdiction of the Queensland government, and Queensland's "no pet bunny rabbits" law is not binding upon you.

Contrast this with the Nuremberg trials. In that instance, members of the Nazi party were put on trial for the crimes that they had committed, they were convicted of those crimes, and ultimately they were sentenced to execution. But the crimes that they had committed were not against the laws of their *own* country. People from *another* country, with a different set of laws, crossed into Germany

---

29 For my international readers, please don't make the mistake of concluding from this anecdote that New South Wales is generally a more "libertarian" state than Queensland. Quite the contrary, in fact!

and put German people on trial for something that was not against German law. Somehow though, most of us would not see this as an intolerable "invasion". We instinctively realise that prosecuting the Nazi leaders was something that needed to be done.

If the Queensland police crossed over the border into New South Wales, began confiscating everyone's pet bunny rabbits, and issued the owners with fines, we would immediately cry out that they had no authority to impose Queensland's laws upon the citizens of New South Wales. Why then do we not feel the same way about Nuremberg? Why does it seem "right" to us that non-Germans should be able to cross into Germany and put Germans on trial for something that German law did not regard as a crime? How could they possibly have the authority to do such a thing?

The answer is that we instinctively recognise that the "no pet bunny rabbits" rule in Queensland is merely a feature of "positive law", while we regard the rule against committing genocide to be a feature of "natural law".

Now, this is *not* to say that the rule against genocide is a "real" law, while the rule against having pet bunny rabbits in Queensland is somehow "not real". Both are real laws. The distinction between them is the *source* of the law.

When we say that something is a part of the "natural law", what we are saying is that the *source* of that law is nature itself. For that reason, it is shared by all of humanity, it is objective, and it is unchanging. It is not something that any particular human being made up. Rather, it is simply an objective statement about "the way the world is".

In contrast, when we say that something is a feature of "positive law", we are saying that the source of that law is that it has been *posited* by someone (or by some group of people). That law has been "put forth" by them. It is a creation of conscious, human deliberation. It is a rule which someone has decided, for practical reasons, ought to be treated as part of "the law" in their own context.

For Bible-believing Christians then, what follows is that the "natural law" covers the rules that are given to all of humanity *by God*, even to those people who worship other gods, or who do not believe that God exists. God gives this law to humanity by weaving it into the very fabric of His creation. He sets up nature in such a way that these laws are an inescapable fact of our existence.

In contrast, "positive law" covers the rules that are not given by God at all but are products of a human mind. Now, in some cases, it is obviously true that positive law and natural law could say contradictory things. In these cases, natural law, because it is God's law, must prevail. We must always be prepared to let natural law critique the quality of any positive law that is instituted. But that is not to say that positive law is always invalid. An example will help. We may say that it is a feature of natural law that we ought to drive in such a way that we are not recklessly endangering the lives of others. God has set up the natural world and the laws of physics in such a way that reckless driving leads to injury and death, therefore we must not drive recklessly.

But should we drive on the left side of the road or on the right? Clearly, either option is valid. Various countries choose either one or the other, and neither choice seems to cause any great devastation. On that basis, we might argue that God has set up the natural world in such a way that it is perfectly acceptable to choose to drive on either the left side of the road or on the right. But if individuals all made this choice independently of one another, this would obviously be a mistake. We are all better off if humans exercise their wisdom and rationality and invent a positive-law rule, demanding that we drive only on one side of the road in a particular area. In this way, natural law gives us fundamental information about right and wrong based on the way the world objectively is. Positive law, in contrast, exists to serve society by codifying useful *conventions* within the boundaries of natural law.

To return to the Nuremburg example, "you shall not commit genocide" would be an example of a rule from the natural law. Because of this, it was not within the power of the German government to simply "decide" that they would make genocide allowable within their own jurisdiction. The Nazis had egregiously violated natural law by mass murdering Jews, and so it was right that they should be brought to account for that violation by others who were also under that same natural law. But the "no pet bunny rabbits" rule is only a feature of *positive* law. For the moment, let us sidestep the larger issue of whether the Queensland government has the legitimate authority to make such a positive law for that state. For the sake of argument, let us assume that they do have that authority. Because it is only a positive law, they should not be allowed to enforce this rule outside of their own jurisdiction. The Queensland government does not have the authority to enforce its *posited* laws outside of Queensland's borders.

So then, we see that natural law and positive law are not enemies, nor are they necessarily incompatible with one another. Positive law exists to aid in the concrete implementation of natural law, and natural law retains the authority to critique positive law[30]. In this way, both have their place in a well-ordered society.

For our purposes then, the important question is whether property rights are a feature of positive law (and therefore able to be adjusted for pragmatic reasons) or a feature of the natural law (and therefore immutable and unable to be modified by any human legislation).

Thomas Aquinas: Property Rights are a Feature of *Positive* Law

Let us first examine Aquinas' view that specific property rights are a feature merely of positive law, rather than of the natural law. In Aquinas' view, God has given the whole natural world to mankind in common. Therefore, the natural world belongs to us all, and the natural law does not prescribe that it should be divided up among individuals in any particular way. For this reason, Aquinas writes[31]:

> In this respect man ought to possess external things, not as his own, but as

---

30 Aquinas himself argues that Isaiah 10:1 ("Woe to those who decree iniquitous decrees") proves the possibility of critiquing positive law in the light of natural law. *Summa Theologica* II-II, Q. 57, Art. 2
31 Aquinas, *Summa Theologica* II-II, Q. 66, Art. 2.

> common, so that, to wit, he is ready to communicate them to others in their need. Hence the Apostle says (1 Timothy 7:17-18): "Charge the rich of this world... to give easily, to communicate to others"

While Aquinas thinks that it is valid for people to regard specific things as "their own", he is careful to remind them that ultimately all of these resources are owned by mankind in common. For that reason, he argues that people should at all times be ready to renounce their individual claims to property ownership and allow that property to be distributed to whomever has need of it. This makes sense, because in Aquinas' view, at a natural-law level, the person in need is fundamentally just as much an owner of that property as the person who is currently claiming the property right.

However, this does not by any means indicate that Aquinas rejects individual property rights completely. Rather, Aquinas affirms the necessity of individual property rights for the good ordering of society. In Aquinas' thinking, these individual property rights are purely the product of human reason in pursuit of some larger goal. For Aquinas, the justification for individuals holding private property is only pragmatic and utilitarian. The economist Milton Friedman was fond of saying that government spending is typically wasteful because "nobody spends someone else's money as carefully as they spend their own". Aquinas, anticipating Friedman by many centuries, gave a similar reason for why he thought it was prudent for individual property rights to be included in positive law. Aquinas writes[32]:

> Moreover [individual property rights are] necessary to human life for three reasons. First because every man is more careful to procure what is for himself alone than that which is common to many or to all: since each one would shirk the labor and leave to another that which concerns the community, as happens when there is a great number of servants. Secondly, because human affairs are conducted in a more orderly fashion if each man is charged with taking care of some particular thing himself, whereas there would be confusion if everyone had to look after any one thing indeterminately. Thirdly, because a more peaceful state is ensured to man if each one is contented

---

32 Aquinas, *Summa Theologica* II-II, Q. 66, Art. 2.

> with his own. Hence it is to be observed that quarrels arise more frequently where there is no division of the things possessed.

Aquinas is here describing what we have come to call "the tragedy of the commons". This is the phenomenon where property that is thought to be owned by "everybody" ends up in a state of disarray and disrepair, because everybody is trying to leave the burden of maintaining it on everyone else. Aquinas argues that things are better cared for overall if the people who do the work to care for them have a reasonable expectation of gaining more benefit from them than do their neighbours. Therefore, including individual property rights as a feature of positive law benefits society because people are thereby given an incentive to cultivate their property more diligently.

Implications of this Positive-Law View

Understanding property rights the way that Thomas Aquinas does leads to some interesting implications for the way society operates. The most important implication is that it becomes possible (and necessary) to experiment with a variety of different arrangements for who will "own" all the stuff. If property rights are *not* a feature of natural law, then there is no single, absolutely correct way that property should be allocated. We are no longer trying to conform our distribution of property to an objective, ideal standard. Instead, we are experimenting with different arrangements to try and discover empirically which one will yield the distribution of property that we find most desirable.

In this system, if our legislature enacts a series of rules about who owns what and after a couple of years we decide that some people have "too much" while others have "too little", then the legislature is completely free to alter its policy and redistribute society's property however it sees fit. It might do this by tweaking the day-to-day rules, or it might get there by just doing arbitrary redistributions from time to time. Both of these options are fine. There is no "correct" allocation of property rights baked into the created order. It is up to us to determine how we will measure one system of allocation as "better" or "worse" than another, and then to try to optimise our legal code so that we end up at the best arrangement possible.

On a moment's reflection, it should be easy to see that most countries' legal systems today *assume* that this positive-law view of ownership is correct. Individual politicians, lawyers and judges may not have thought it all the way through, but most of them behave as if they believe this positive-law view to be the right one. Just think about the sort of debates that come up around our elections, regarding the economy. Should we raise taxes or lower them? Should we have five income tax brackets or six? Will it be good for the housing sector if we give out a $50,000 grant to first-home buyers? Should interest paid on the mortgage for an investment property be tax deductible? These kinds of questions only make sense if we *assume* that the legislature has the right to decide who will be given ownership rights over all the stuff in society. If the legislature does not have that right, then how can they presume to decide that property should be taken from one person and given to another?

If the positive-law view is correct, then some very extreme possibilities are legitimately on the table. As I write this, Elizabeth Warren is running for president of the United States. Part of her platform is introducing a "wealth tax". That proposal goes a step further than an income tax, which takes a percentage of what you *get*. A wealth tax takes a slice of whatever you *have*. Even if you have owned your property for years, free and clear, you would now have to start giving a chunk of it to Warren's government. Some people will think that this is a great idea, because (allegedly) it will help even things out and reduce "inequality". But to propose it seriously means one of two things. Either (a) Warren is simply a thief who is proposing that the government should confiscate property through naked power; or else (b) she is assuming that the elected government genuinely has the authority to transfer ownership rights to property from one person to another by decree. Furthermore, there is no real limit to this. A system where the tax rate is 100% is just as valid as a system where the tax rate is 50%, 20% or 0%. Whatever system the government can dream up, they are free to try it if they wish.

Have Christians done this? Absolutely. Dwight Porter Bliss, a self-described "Christian Socialist" favoured a system in which individuals only had private property rights over consumption goods that they personally used. Anything that was a capital good (a good that was not consumed directly but was used as an input for some process of production) was not to be owned by an individual on his view but should be owned collectively (which in practice means owned by the government)[33]. Incidentally, this is essentially the same thing that was proposed by Marx and Engels in the Communist Manifesto[34].

---

33 William Dwight Porter Bliss, *What Is Christian Socialism?* (Boston: The Society of Christian Socialists, 1890), 5.

Now, most people would not want to enact such an extreme proposal as that of Bliss or Marx and Engels (most Western countries have systems far less extreme than that at present). But the point is that, on a positive-law view of property rights, there is nothing *inherently* wrong with such a proposal. The only way to argue against it is by arguing that some other arrangement would provide more desirable results.

John Locke: Property Rights are a Feature of *Natural* Law

The alternative possibility is that property rights are a feature of *natural* law. On this view, there does exist some absolute standard as to who owns what. While there are secular forms of this view, any Christian form will certainly go a step further and say that this absolute standard is woven into the created order by God. That is to say, the naturally emerging allocation of property rights, simply arising by things being what they are, is something deliberately chosen by God. When God was deciding that there would be seven colours in the rainbow, that grass would be softer than rocks and that chilli would taste spicy, He also decided at that time how to build a world in which it was possible for us to "own" things.

---

34 Karl Marx and Friedrich Engels, *The Communist Manifesto* (Charleston, SC: Filiquarian Publishing, 2010), 24-25.

John Locke not only held this view but also proposed a way for us to *know* who was the rightful owner of various pieces of property according to natural law. This was very important because a natural-law view is not much good to us unless we can discern, from nature around us, who actually owns things. If no examination of the natural world can yield these answers, then the natural law gives us no more information about the allocation of property than we had before. In that case, all we could do in practice would be to fall back on a positive-law view.

Locke's proposal was simple. Locke proposed that initially, all the resources that God has put into the world are in a "state of nature". That is, they have not been changed by any human agent; they are completely in the state in which God left them for us when He created the natural world. Locke suggested that any objects in this "state of nature" were not owned by any human person but could be freely used by any human person who wanted them. However, by the very act of taking them and using them, the person who did so caused a change. They caused the object which they had taken to transition out of the "state of nature" and instead to become a *cultivated* resource. By doing so, they caused the object to pass *from* being commonly available to all people *into* a state of being their own personal property. The example that Locke gave was about apples on a tree[35]. If we were to discover a wild apple tree in the forest, the apples growing on it would belong to no one, and they would be perfectly fine for anyone to pick. However, if a person came along, picked a basketful of those apples and took them home, then that basketful of apples would have been removed from the "state of nature". That basketful of apples would now have become the rightful property of the person who picked them. If I were to go into that person's house and take an apple from the basket, I would now be stealing. I'm free to take an apple from the *wild* apple tree, those apples are still "unowned". But I cannot take one of these apples from the basketful that now belongs to my neighbour.

This process of removing something from the "state of nature" and thereby converting it into privately owned property is called "homesteading". Now, we could see (at least in theory) how this homesteading principle might be applied to just about anything. Imagine I find an area of land that no one else has ever set foot on, I clear the rocks off it, I plough the ground, and I plant some apple seeds there. To whom does that land belong? And when the apple trees have grown, to whom will they belong? The clear answer is that they belong to me. They do not belong to someone else who

---

35 John Locke, *Second Treatise on Government*, Chapter 5.

comes along after I have done all that work and starts picking apples off the trees in my orchard. The trees in my new orchard are not in a "state of nature" like the wild apple tree. Instead, they are the product of my focused will and effort to transform the natural state of that land which they were planted on. By ploughing the ground and so on, I have effectively "homesteaded" the soil, and the crops that grow there are now mine too.

Locke's reason for seeing property rights this way is that he sees it as a natural mechanism which God has woven into creation. That is, the world is set up in such a way that once I have removed something from a state of nature, it is recognisably different than it was before I had done so. There is an imprint of myself now inseparably embedded into that resource. In the world that God has made, there is a distinct difference between a "garden" and a "forest". A forest exists in nature without any human effort, but a garden requires active cultivation by a human agent[36].

---

36 Christians who are familiar with the debate over creation and evolution will already have been exposed to a fairly robust theory of "intelligent design". Out of necessity for the debate over origins, many Christians have already thought at length about how one would go about detecting the imprint of intelligence upon a natural resource. This means that the Lockean theory of ownership through "homesteading" is actually a surprisingly natural fit for us.

Because this is simply the way the world is, no matter how any of us feels about it, the natural law has implicitly dictated that cultivating a natural resource always causes that resource to become the private property of the cultivator. Therefore, there is an objective standard for the correct configuration of property rights. The property available in society has been allocated to its correct and rightful owners only when it is in the possession of either (a) the person who first transformed it from the state of nature; or (b) the person to whom that first cultivator has *transferred* their ownership rights, either through a gift or a voluntary exchange.

Implications of this Natural-Law View

If it is true that property rights *are* in fact a feature of natural law, that would also have some drastic implications for the ordering of society. If property rights are a feature of natural law, then it is *not* permissible for legislators to enact various sets of experimental schemes for redistributing property in whichever way they please. Neither the will of a king nor of a parliament nor of a democratic majority can simply "decide" who the rightful owner of a piece of property ought to be. The property has an *objective* rightful owner, regardless of anyone's opinion or preference.

As Murray Rothbard pointed out, this way of looking at property rights as *objective* means that there is a fixed standard by which the current distribution of property in society can (and should) be evaluated. Accepting a natural-law theory of property rights implies a radical scrutiny of the status quo[37]. Through this scrutiny, many of the present positive-law rules about the distribution of property would likely be revealed as *unjust*.

Suppose that the legislature of a community enacted a rule, stating that only white males would be permitted to own houses. Furthermore, they may declare that if anybody bequeaths a house to a black man or if a woman builds herself a house, those houses will be regarded as the property of the government and will be auctioned off to the highest-bidding white male.

On a positive-law view of property rights, there would be no *objective* reason to criticise this arrangement. *Subjectively*, many people may complain that they find this state of affairs distasteful. They may even suggest that it violates the "spirit" of certain non-property-related commands given to us by God. However, on a purely positive-law view of property rights, they would have to admit that the legislature did in fact have the *authority* to enact this policy. If the

---

37 Rothbard, *Ethics of Liberty*, 17.

legislature were persuaded that a whites-only property law would be helpful somehow, then they would be within their rights to implement it.

By contrast, the natural-law view entails a strong mandate to loudly criticise a race-based distribution of property, to call out that injustice for what it is, and to see it overturned with all haste. On a natural-law view, it would not matter what reason was given for a whites-only property law. It would not matter if a majority of voters were persuaded that the policy would somehow benefit society. None of that would matter because the policy *itself* would be a violation of natural law. The house gifted to the black man belongs to the black man, the house built by the woman belongs to the woman, regardless of any politician's opinion.

Biblical Examples of Acquired Ownership

Having described these two schools of thought about how property rights might come to be delegated to individual people, we are faced with the task deciding which of them is more biblical. Is the positive-law view correct, and is it our biblical mandate to experiment with various laws and schemes until we arrive at the distribution of property that we find to be the most desirable? Or is the natural-law view correct, and our mandate biblically is to uphold the property rights of people who have acquired their property through the natural-law mechanism of homesteading?

I knew that if I was going to settle this question in my own mind, I would need to have biblical grounds for preferring one of these two positions to the other. I turned to the Bible, looking for any instances I could find where a piece of property passed from being "unowned" into a state of specific human ownership. I expected this task to be difficult. After all, in the vast majority of cases, people tend to live on land that was already owned by someone else before they got there. We are usually born into towns and cities that already exist. But to my surprise, I did find some examples of biblical figures out on the frontier, forging into new areas. In fact, there are several *clear* examples of the homesteading principle being applied in biblical history.

Abraham

Abraham lived for a significant portion of his life as a wandering nomad. By the standards of the ancient world, he was a wealthy man. His "household" was made up of over 300 people[38], including his actual relatives and his servants.

---

38 Genesis 14:14.

They moved around from place to place, setting up camp wherever it seemed to make sense for them. At some points, they set up camp within the territory of an existing State[39], but at other times they were simply pitching their tents on unclaimed land[40].

Scripture records a particular event in Abraham's life in which the principle is assumed that the person who homesteads a piece of land is its rightful owner. In Genesis 21:25-31, we read of a dispute between Abraham and Abimelech, the king of that region, over a particular well.

> When Abraham reproved Abimelech about a well of water that Abimelech's servants had seized, Abimelech said, "I do not know who has done this thing; you did not tell me, and I have not heard of it until today." So Abraham took sheep and oxen and gave them to Abimelech, and the two men made a covenant. Abraham set seven ewe lambs of the flock apart. And Abimelech said to Abraham, "What is the meaning of these seven ewe lambs that

---

39 For example, when they "sojourned" in the territory of Abimelech, king of Gerar (Genesis 20:1-2).

40 Abraham is referred to several times as dwelling "by the oaks of Mamre" rather than in some particular king's domain (e.g. Genesis 13:18).

> you have set apart?" He said, "These seven ewe lambs you will take from my hand, that this may be a witness for me that I dug this well." Therefore that place was called Beersheba, because there both of them swore an oath.
>
> Genesis 21:25-31

Abraham had dug the well, but then Abimelech's servants had come along and seized it for their own use. Abraham appeals to Abimelech that this is unjust and that Abraham ought to be recognised as the true owner of the well. Now, there is a transaction that takes place here with livestock, but it does not amount to Abraham "buying" the well. Rather, Abraham appears to be giving these animals to Abimelech in exchange for Abimelech's assurance that Abraham's rightful title will be recognised in perpetuity. That is, he is asking Abimelech to act as a witness to his property title. But the basis by which Abraham claims to *possess* that title is simple: it was Abraham who dug the well. He dug it, and therefore he owns it, regardless of what Abimelech or Abimelech's servants or anyone else might think. As a practical matter, he offers payment to Abimelech in exchange for

Abimelech's services as a reputable witness in case a similar dispute occurs in the future.

Isaac

We gain a further insight into the nature of acquired property rights by observing what happens with these same wells a generation later. Abraham's son Isaac eventually comes to settle in Gerar as well, in the same area where Abraham had dug these wells. Since the time when Abraham had lived there, we read that the wells had been filled in (Genesis 26:15).

When Isaac's household begins to grow large with servants and flocks, Abimelech requests that Isaac move his clan a little further away. Isaac obliges and decides to set up camp in Gerar and to re-dig the wells that Abraham had dug a generation earlier. However, we read that when Isaac does this, a dispute breaks out:

> So Isaac departed from there and encamped in the valley of Gerar and settled there. And Isaac dug again the wells of water that had been dug in the days of Abraham his father, which the Philistines had stopped after the death of Abraham. And he gave them the names

> that his father had given them. But when Isaac's servants dug in the valley and found there a well of spring water, the herdsmen of Gerar quarrelled with Isaac's herdsmen, saying, "The water is ours." So he called the name of the well Esek, because they contended with him. Then they dug another well, and they quarreled over that also, so he called its name Sitnah. And he moved from there and dug another well, and they did not quarrel over it. So he called its name Rehoboth, saying, "For now the LORD has made room for us, and we shall be fruitful in the land."
>
> Genesis 26:17-22

It is possible that Isaac may have been able to enter into a formal dispute here. Perhaps he could have asked Abimelech to fulfil his agreement with Abraham and to bear witness to the title over these wells (naming Isaac as the heir who should inherit them). Isaac evidently decides not to do this, though the reason why is not entirely clear. A good guess is that Isaac has just had a run-in with Abimelech where Isaac lied about Rebekah being his sister rather than his wife. Abimelech feared that God's wrath would have come upon his people if this deceit had led to one of them sleeping with Rebekah. Additionally, we read that the reason Abimelech wanted Isaac to move his clan away was because they were becoming somewhat strong and numerous. There was a fear that Isaac's clan would be able to overpower Abimelech's people if it came to a fight. Only later in this chapter, after Isaac has moved away (Genesis 26:26-31), does Abimelech come with Phicol (the commander of his army) to make a covenant of peace with Isaac. All this to say, there appears to have been some tension in the relationship between Isaac and Abimelech. It is probable that Isaac realised that pressuring Abimelech to recognise his title over the wells would be unwise and may even have provoked a battle.

So instead, Isaac decides to simply surrender the ground and move further out. He does so and digs another well, which is also contested, so he moves again. It is only when Isaac digs a well that goes uncontested that we get an insight into his thinking. At this point Isaac says, "For now the LORD has made room for us."

Note the implication of this. It is not that God had spoken explicitly to Isaac and told him, "I have given you this land and the well at Rehoboth." Rather, Isaac regards his title to the well at

Rehoboth as having been given to him by the LORD precisely because he dug it himself and it went uncontested.

That is, in Isaac's thinking recorded for us in Scripture, when someone homesteads a piece of property that was previously unowned (and hence, uncontested), this means that *the LORD* has therefore bestowed the title on the one who did the homesteading.

Homesteading by Animals

These passages about Abraham and Isaac homesteading property are of course interesting, but the argument may be raised that they are "isolated" or "culturally derived". Perhaps this homesteading principle for property acquisition was simply a custom of the ancient Near East, and construing it as a feature of God's natural law is reading too much into the text.

Unfortunately, it is difficult to find many other examples in Scripture that are as explicit about the origin of new property rights as these two.

There are other parts of the Bible where people clearly move into unowned territory, but they tend to be focused on more of the big-picture details rather than giving us a detailed account of how the division of property titles took place. For example, when Noah's family comes off the ark, we read that

Noah "began to be a man of the soil, and he planted a vineyard." Based on our understanding of homesteading, we might reasonably conclude that this made Noah the owner of the vineyard, but that is not explicitly spelled out for us in the text.

However, there is at least one more passage which deserves careful consideration. In Matthew 6:25-26, Jesus is teaching a lesson about faith and anxiety. He tells his hearers not to be anxious about what tomorrow holds, but instead to trust God to provide for their needs. Jesus tells us that we should observe the birds of the air, noticing that God continuously looks after them and provides for their needs. From that observation, we should learn the lesson that God will also provide for us. We should exercise faith in God's provision as the cure for our anxiety. That lesson may seem simple enough, but what is incredibly interesting, once it dawns on us to see it, is how Jesus describes the process of God's provision. Jesus simply says this:

> Look at the birds of the air: they neither sow nor reap nor gather into barns, and yet your heavenly Father feeds them. Are you not of more value than they?
>
> Matthew 6:26

What does it mean that God the Father "feeds" the birds? Evidently, it does not mean that God puts out seed into bird-feeding boxes at the same time each day so that the birds have no work to do. We can see with our own eyes how God's provision comes to the birds. God's provision of food comes to them through unclaimed, natural resources. That is, God has ordered the world in such a way that there are worms in the ground and fruit on the trees and seeds in the fruit and so on. Animals in the wild do not naturally possess these things. Gathering their food requires effort. The bird that does not go out searching for worms will still go hungry, but this is not due to a lack of God's provision for that bird. I am indebted to Pastor John MacArthur for this point, which he raised in a wonderful book called "Anxious for Nothing"[41]. It is precisely when the bird "homesteads" a worm, which it finds in the ground, that it has received God's provision. What we observe among the birds is similar to a person appropriating an apple from Locke's proverbial apple tree. Since the homesteading principle applies to animals as well as to people, the homesteading principle cannot be construed merely as a vestige of ancient Near Eastern culture. It must be a feature "built in" to God's creation.

---

41 John MacArthur, *Anxious for Nothing: God's Cure for the Cares of Your Soul*, 3rd ed. (Colorado Springs, Colo: David C Cook, 2012), 23.

Taxation is Slavery

The Doctrine of Creation and Economics

So far, we have been dealing with ownership as it is experienced by a single individual. Our next step is to consider how our view of ownership affects our understanding of the social interactions between people.

We began this book by looking at Abraham Kuyper and his doctrine of "sphere sovereignty". Kuyper proposed that the creation is fundamentally good. It is damaged in many ways, as a result of the Fall, but it's central goodness still remains. Science, the practice of investigating nature, still glorifies God. Art, expressing creativity, still glorifies God. Business, providing for the needs of consumers, still glorifies God. This positive view of God's creation is central in Kuyper's thought. However, as we saw earlier, Kuyper falters when he tries to accommodate the "mechanical" sphere of the State into his account of sphere sovereignty. Legitimising the function of the taxing State, even seeing the State as a positive good, leads to all sorts of difficulties and contradictions.

So then, how can we retain the most helpful parts of Kuyper's thought while also resolving these lingering problems? I found the answer to that question in the writings of a French economist and politician from the mid-1800s, a man named Frédéric Bastiat.

Bastiat's Doctrine of Economic Harmony

Reading Bastiat, it became apparent that Kuyper had fallen short of his own goal. In many ways, Bastiat is like Kuyper, only far more radical. Both believed that the world God created is a good world. But Kuyper thought that it was still necessary to impose the unnatural authority of the State in order to make the creation work properly. Bastiat, on the other hand, wants no such inconsistency. For Bastiat, any system which called for men to impose their rule upon their neighbours was doomed from the outset. Because God is good, Bastiat expected a world that would function most effectively when people treated their neighbours righteously.

Bastiat realised that a view which required some men to rule over others by force could not possibly be correct. To say such things is ultimately to say that "in order to do good, we must do evil." That statement is absurd because God is sovereign and God is good. Why would a good and sovereign God create a world in which righteous societies tend towards poverty while unrighteous societies tend towards prosperity?

God would not do that. The world that God has made must surely be a world in which things work best when we obey God's commands. That is to say, a world made by God is a world intended for *harmony*.

Harmony does not simply mean that if individuals act righteously, then those particular individuals will tend to prosper. It is much more than that. A creation intended for harmony means that the best interests of God's creatures are *not in conflict* with one another. A creation intended for harmony means that the best interests of every creature are compatible with the best interests of all the others. In a world made by a good God, it is not required that one creature must be impoverished if another creature is to be enriched. We should expect that, when economic activity is conducted righteously, the natural result is an improvement of life for *everyone* involved. If you grow apples and I grow wheat and we mutually agree to exchange them between us, then we both benefit, and – crucially – *no one else is hurt by this*. I had more wheat than I needed, but not enough apples. Now I have a useful amount of both. My situation has improved. You had extra apples, but not enough wheat. You also are made better off by the trade. Working and trading with one another are both righteous activities, and as such, they tend to improve living conditions for all parties.

It is right to expect the created world to be harmonious because it originates in the rational mind of a loving Creator. Therefore, we should expect that the best outcomes will occur when we do not interfere with other people's righteous pursuit of their own inclinations and desires. We should let them be free so that they might do the good things which God has prepared in advance for them to do. As Bastiat put it:

> God has given to men all that is necessary for them to accomplish their destinies. He has provided a social form as well as a human form. And these social organs of persons are so constituted that they will develop themselves harmoniously in the clean air of liberty.
>
> Frédéric Bastiat, *The Law*

The created order, in Bastiat's view, is already ordered such that the best outcomes arise when people work hard, trade honestly, and cooperate together. Doing so will make all of them richer. Because of this, any attempt to *meddle* with the natural outcome of such free activity is necessarily a bad idea. Every time the State intervenes and uses the threat of violence to change people's behaviour, they are working against the natural harmony of the created order. A free man will always work more productively than a slave. The reason for this is simple. Freedom is the natural state of man, it is what he was made for. In his natural state of freedom, man has the incentive to work hard and enjoy the fruits of his own labour. But slavery is an unnatural state for man. It is a deviation from the natural harmony of the creation. It is working against God's good design and will therefore tend towards inefficiency and misery. The man has no incentive to work hard, because the fruits of his labour go to someone else and so his productivity falls.

For this reason, Bastiat argued that the State should not confiscate the wealth of its citizens, no matter what strange label they affixed to that practice. Whether taxes or tariffs or levies or duties or tributes or whatever other name they might dream up, Bastiat rightly grouped this whole family of activities under the name of "legal plunder". No intervention or meddling in human nature is necessary, declared Bastiat, for God has already made men precisely the type of creatures that they need to be in order to flourish in the world that He has made for them. In Bastiat's view, it is only the *pride* of government officials that leads them to believe that they can improve society by forcibly restructuring the economy.

This insight is what was missing from Kuyper. This is the key to a biblical understanding of economics. God has made man the type of creature who can cultivate natural resources and possess private property. God has made the world in such a way that cultivating resources, respecting property rights, and trading with others leads to prosperity. When one man says to another, "I have grown wheat and you have grown apples. Come, let us trade together", then both will prosper. But when one man says, "I will conquer these people, I will demand tribute from them under threat of violence, and I will live off the hard work of others", that is what leads a society into poverty. As the Teacher wrote:

> The fallow ground of the poor would yield much food, but it is swept away by injustice.
>
> Proverbs 13:23

The lesson in all this is simple. A Bible-believing, God-honouring view of economics will reject all forms of legal plunder and will instead embrace the *free market*.

How Free Markets Work

One goal of this book is to make a biblical defence of truly *free* markets. In order to make that defence, I need to give at least a basic definition of what the free market is. For many people, when they hear the words "free market", they may take that to mean "whatever happens when right-wingers are in power." Sadly, this is far from the truth. In reality, most Western, English-speaking countries today hardly look any different from one election cycle to the next. Even under so-called "right-wing" presidents, prime-ministers and legislators, we still seem to have taxes, minimum wages, price controls, tariffs and government-imposed monopolies. The government seems to have an endless supply of ideas for how they might intervene into the free market and make it less free.

In essence, the "free market" is simply what happens when legitimate property rights are respected. The "free market" is what occurs when there is no stealing and no conquest. It is what happens when people only acquire property by cultivating it from nature or by receiving it through a gift or a voluntary exchange.

Conceived of this way, it becomes obvious that the free market must *necessarily* be a biblical ideal. The free market is what happens when everyone is obeying the eighth commandment: "you shall not steal". It is nothing more or less than that.

In that sense, any interference in the free market represents someone's attempt to improve society by *breaking God's law*. For any thinking Christian, it should be obvious that this cannot possibly work. Breaking God's law can never be a wise or effective way to improve the world.

But is this practical? Many economists and politicians, even those who seem to have their hearts in the right place, say that the market needs to be managed and regulated. They say that without such interference, the rich will get richer while the poor get poorer. As Christians, we certainly do not want to promote a system which makes life worse for the poorest people among us.

In these next sections, we will think through how the free market works in practice. We will see how the market arranges the prices of the things we buy, how the market allows us to use the gifts that God has given us, and how the market enables people to earn interest on their savings. In each case, we will see that when we refrain from interfering, the individual interests of the people in the market all come together so that everyone benefits, both rich and poor.

Market Prices

The first crucial step in understanding the free market is to understand the role of prices. Fundamentally, prices are a system for *coordinating* the economy. There are certain resources in our world that have lots of different uses, but they cannot be used for all of those purposes at once.

Let us take apples as a simple example. An apple can be used for many different things. It can be made into a glass of apple juice, or it can be baked into an apple pie. An apple can be fomented to make alcoholic cider. Apple shavings can be an ingredient in herbal tea. There are many uses for an apple. But the same apple cannot be used for all of these purposes at once. If you bake an apple into a pie, you will not be able to turn that same apple into juice or cider.

Now, suppose that we have a small apple orchard. Our orchard grows 100,000 apples every harvest season. How many of those apples should we use to make apple pies? How many should we use for apple juice? How many apples should be turned into alcoholic cider?

Some people want to consume them as juice, while others want them as pies. Even more complicated, some people want both juice *and* pie, but if they can only have one, they will choose juice. Other people also want both, but if they have to choose, they will choose the pie. We want to figure out the best way to use each apple so that the people who consume them will get the maximum possible enjoyment. This is the purpose of *prices*.

Instead of trying to predict how many people will want pies, cider or whatever other apple products, we simply sell our apples for whatever *price* we can get for them. We let our neighbours come over and bargain with us, bidding against each other to see who will offer the highest price for the apples. Whoever is willing to give us the most in exchange for each apple is the one who will get it. If the price is too high, lots of customers will go shopping for different fruits. If we ask them for $100 per apple, people will make banana pies or orange juice instead. That is not good for us, because we cannot make a profit on apples that we do not sell. But if we set the price too low, then there will be people who want to buy our apples but cannot because we will quickly run out. If we sell our apples for 1 cent each, many orange-juice drinkers will switch to apple juice because it is cheaper. These new apple-juice drinkers will buy up all the apples, leaving no apples left to make pies. How do we avoid these two extremes? Simple. We negotiate with people and move the price up and down until we find the point where we are getting the most money we can for all of our apples.

When we find that tipping point, that means every apple we sold has gone to the person who valued it the most. Some of our neighbours will want apples for pies, others will want them for tea, others for cider, still others for juice, and so on. It would take us far too much time and energy to actually interview all of our customers and find out about every reason they may want an apple. They may want pie today but change their mind and want cider tomorrow. If we had to plan out how every apple would get used before we sold any, there would be far too much information to digest, and we would just be creating work for ourselves. By negotiating for the best price on each apple, we actually end up with the best result anyway. The people who value apples the most get them, and the people who do not value apples that much are encouraged to look for other options.

Suppose that Fred has a business baking apple pies, while Bob has a business selling herbal tea with apple shavings. If more customers want to consume pies, then Fred will bid more for our apples. If more customers want to drink herbal tea, then Bob will bid more. If a bunch of people decide to try gluten-free diets, then Fred will lose some pie customers. Fred will see that his sales of pies are dropping, and he will buy fewer apples the next week so that he does not waste money on ingredients for pies that he cannot sell. As the orchard owners, we do not have to know anything about gluten-free diets or *why* pie sales are down. All we need to know is that Fred needs less apples this week. We see that some apples are not getting sold any more, so we lower our apple price. When the apple price drops, some people who were previously going to brew beer decide to take advantage of the cheap apples and use them to brew some apple cider instead. Again, we do not have to know anything about consumer preferences for beer over cider. All we have to do is put the price up and down until we sell all of our apples for the best possible price. This naturally encourages people to direct the apples to wherever consumers desire them most. The price system saves us from having to try and predict all of those consumers' choices in advance.

Still, the problem of distributing apples may not sound totally impossible at first. If you put your mind to it, perhaps you think you could come up with a decent, rational plan that does not require people to pay different prices and bid against each other. But what happens when you try to do it with something a little more complex?

What about computer chips? Lots of things have computer chips in them now. Phones, laptop computers, desktop computers, servers in a data centre, TVs, maybe even your fridge. All of these devices need different types of computer chips. All of those different chips take a lot of expensive materials and labour time to put together. How could you ever work out, on a global scale, whether you should allocate more silicon and copper toward building chips for laptop computers or for smart fridges? If you make a mistake, maybe you make 10% too many fridges and 10% too few laptop computers compared to what people actually want to use. Globally, that is an incredible amount of wasted effort and material. But the problem is worse than that. How many different types of laptop are there? Probably thousands? Some are built to have more computing power, while some are built to run slower but have a longer battery life. How are you going to decide how many high-power laptop chips to build compared to the number of longer-battery-life chips?

There is simply no way for you to know all of the information you would need to know in order to make even a semi-reasonable estimate. You could never do enough personal interviews to really know what balance of speed and power consumption every person needs in their computing devices. Even if you did interview a million people around the world, they may not be able to give you accurate answers ahead of time. They might not know exactly what type of laptop they want until they actually see it. They might not know, until they see several of their friends try it, whether they need a laptop at all or whether a smart phone is all they need.

By letting people freely negotiate prices, all of that information can be passed around effectively so that resources go to where they are most valued. Consumers buy what they want in the store. The store sees which products sell more volume and which sell less. The store also sees which products will sell much more volume if they are put on sale. The store communicates all of this back to their suppliers by ordering more of the high-selling products to fill their shelves. The factories see all of this sales data and use it to determine how much of the raw materials (silicon, copper, etc.) to buy from the miners who are digging it out of the ground. Everything gets to where it needs to go, but the miners who find the raw copper never need to know that more people started buying laptops with longer battery life this year because rising fuel prices meant that more people took the train to work, which meant they spent more time working on their laptops. The vast complexities of why people prefer one product to another do not have to be understood by every person who does any work in the process. All of that information simply gets distilled into a single number: the price.

A "socialist" society is one where the government claims ownership over all the capital goods in the society and then has government experts try to plan the economy and allocate all of the resources from the top down. In theory, the goal of this planning is to keep people from becoming poor. However, the economist Ludwig von Mises saw that this attempt to plan the economy means that the government planners no longer have access to any pricing information. They can no longer see what people would buy or how much they would pay if they were free to make their own choices. The resulting lack of information causes big problems for a socialist economy. Precisely because it does not have freely negotiated prices, a socialist society simply cannot be as efficient as a capitalist society when it comes to providing for people's wants and needs. Mises wrote[42]:

> ... No single man, be he the greatest genius ever born, has an intellect capable of deciding the relative importance of each

---

42 Mises, *Socialism*, 117.

> one of an infinite number of goods of higher orders. No individual could so discriminate between the infinite number of alternative methods of production that he could make direct judgments of their relative value without auxiliary calculations[43].

Whenever the government steps in and tries to forcibly change the price of something, they are disrupting the flow of information in the economy. They tax one thing, subsidise another, and put regulations on yet another. Each time they take these sorts of actions, they distort the individual choices that people would have made if they could spend their money on what they really wanted. This creates inefficiencies. The people who produce goods and services end up producing too much or too little of things compared to what the consumers actually want and need. This inefficiency causes everything in the economy to become more expensive. This helps no one, least of all the poor. When basics like food, clothing, shelter and electricity become more costly, it is the poor, not the rich, who suffer the most.

---

43 In context, "auxiliary calculations" refers to being able to assign accurate prices to things, so that we can mathematically evaluate their relative value.

As the government interferes with prices more and more, you eventually end up at full socialism, where they try to plan out the whole economy. What follows is a series of planning failures and corruption scandals, leading the socialist nation into poverty.

Division of Labour

The next distinctive feature of a free market is that it embraces the "division of labour". That means that the free market encourages people to become especially good at doing one particular job. They may be the kind of person who has lots of hobbies outside of their day job. Or perhaps they will train in a secondary skill, just in case the demand for their primary skill dries up. But the point is that they do *not* try to become a master in every possible area. Instead, they specialise. Because the free market has a price system, people can try different jobs and figure out which one will bring them the most benefit. Part of the benefit will probably be higher wages, but it might also be things like a shorter commute time or a sense of doing something good in the world. The point is that people will freely choose to focus their time and energy on whichever tasks bring them the greatest satisfaction. This has three important effects.

First, getting people to specialise makes the economy much more efficient. If John understands cars better than Terry, then more customers will want to pay John to fix their car. Terry knows how to do an oil change and replace a fan belt, but beyond that he does not find cars all that interesting. However, Terry is terrific at painting houses; he has the steadiest painting hand in town. To some extent, John and Terry can both fix cars, and they can both hold a paint brush. But it does not make sense for them both to try to be a mechanic half the week and a house painter for the other half. Everyone in their town will be better off if John and Terry focus on the thing they do best. John will be able to fix more cars if he does that all week long than John and Terry would be able to fix together if they tried to share the mechanic job. Terry will get more houses painted with a smoother finish than John and Terry would be able to do if they tried painting together. By specialising, both of them get more and better work done and both are able to earn more money. When you multiply this out across thousands or millions of people, it is clear that much more productive work will get done when people specialise. The result is that everyone in the society will have a higher standard of living when people focus on the thing that they do the best.

The second key effect of this division of labour is that it creates harmony and cooperation between people. The more people specialise in what they do, the more they have to interact with one another in order to make things that the final consumer actually wants to buy. If you imagine a solitary man on an island, you understand that he has to make everything that he needs by himself. If he wants food, he has to hunt wild game, plant crops, go fishing, etc. If he wants a house, then he has to sharpen a rock into an axe, cut down some trees, and find a way to fashion the wood into beams. But there are certain things that he will simply never be able to make for himself without help. For example, he will never be able to make himself a bicycle to help him get around the island. Even if we assume that the island has all the raw materials that he needs, he would never be able to learn all the skills that would be necessary in order to convert those raw materials into a bicycle. He would need to learn enough chemistry to produce the rubber for the tires. He would need to mine multiple different metals (after first producing any required machinery). He would then need to learn enough metallurgy to merge them together into a steel alloy that was light and sturdy enough to be a good bicycle frame. He would need to develop the tools that he needed in order to precisely shape pieces of rubber and metal together into concentric cylinders with a valve seal, just to make a pump, just so that he could inflate the tyres. On and on it goes. Even if he tried to fashion a very basic bicycle, with no gears, no adjustable parts, and made of very heavy materials, it would still take him a huge amount of time and effort. Even if all of the raw materials were within walking distance and the island had a library full of books that he could use to learn all of the necessary skills in metalwork and rubber chemistry, it would still take him years to develop all of these skills and to accomplish the task.

Now, consider how much it would cost you to go and *buy* a decent bicycle at a local store. Perhaps a few hundred dollars? Let us suppose that it costs you $400 to buy a decent bicycle, and you make $5/hour at your job (a very low wage in a first-world country). The bicycle only represents 80 hours (or two full-time weeks) of your effort. Why does a bicycle only cost you two weeks of effort or less when it would take years to build it for yourself? The answer is because a whole lot of other people have *specialised* in the processes required to build a bicycle. Some specialise in producing rubber tyres. Some specialise in producing steel. Some specialise in shaping that steel into a frame. Some specialise in making bells, seats, gears, lubricants, and so on. Because they specialise, they can do each of these things more efficiently than any one person could do them all. Because they are more efficient, they can sell these components to a bicycle manufacturer at a cheaper price. The bicycle manufacturer can buy these cheap components, which lets them provide a cheaper end product to you at the bike shop.

That all sounds great, but one aspect of the process we must not overlook is the relationships among the people who make all of these components. Because people are free to negotiate prices, they are able to coordinate all of their specialised activities to make sure that the right amount of rubber tyres are produced for all the world's bicycles. The people who first produce the rubber might live in a different country to the people who produce the steel. They might all speak a different language to the person who eventually buys the bicycle. However, because they are able to buy and sell freely, and because they are free to specialise in their work, they naturally begin to cooperate, which enables people around the world to make all kinds of great products as efficiently and cheaply as possible. This makes us all richer. Specialising and trading creates harmony between different people, and enables them to enrich one another's lives, even when they would normally struggle to communicate with each other. This is good and is pleasing to the God who made us.

This leads to the third benefit of the division of labour: it enables us to glorify God by exercising our gifts and expressing our individuality. God did not make us to all be exactly alike, with the same strengths and weaknesses, the same preferences, or the same talents. God, in his creativity, made us all unique and different. He gave us all gifts, and He wants us to use those gifts for the good of the world. By dividing labour amongst ourselves and specialising in what we are good at, we free each other up to make the best use of the gifts and talents with which God has blessed us. I might not be a good mechanic, but I can praise God that I know someone who is. They can help me fix my car, which leaves me free to focus on exercising the gifts that God has given me. I might not be a good musician, but I can praise God that I have friends with skills in that area. Those friends are free to focus on their music because the division of labour makes society sufficiently prosperous that we have disposable income to spend on musical entertainment. As a society, we function like one body with many different parts, and this is to the glory of God.

Capital Interest

The final distinctive feature of the free market that we need to grasp is that it allows people to earn interest on invested "capital". The word "capital" in this context refers to the money that is used to buy "capital goods". A capital good is a good that is used to produce the final "consumption good" that a customer will buy. An example of a consumption good would be an apple pie. An apple pie is not used for making anything else. The pie is simply made to be consumed directly by the person who bought it. An example of a "capital good" would be the oven that we used to bake the apple pie. No one wants an oven merely for the sake of having an oven. They want the oven so that they can eventually make the pie.

In the free market, people can increase their wealth by letting others make use of that wealth in their business. If you want to start making a living as a baker, you will need a high-quality industrial oven. The oven is quite expensive. You cannot afford to buy one for yourself, and it is far too difficult for you to go out, find the raw materials in nature, and make an oven from scratch. Instead, you go to a friend who has been working and saving up money for a few years. You propose a deal to them. If this friend will give you the money to buy the industrial oven, then you will give them a 20% ownership stake in the new bakery, meaning that they will get 20% of all the profits that are made. The friend agrees, and they give you $10,000 to buy an oven. Because the friend provides you with the necessary "capital" (money for the oven), the friend is what we call a "capitalist".

For the next year, you work hard in the bakery making pies. At the end of the year, you have made $100,000 in total profits. You keep $80,000 as your own wage, and you give $20,000 to the capitalist who paid for the oven. You have made $80,000 for yourself, where you would have made zero without your friend's help to buy an oven. Your friend has doubled their original investment of $10,000. Ultimately, both of you have come out very well in this deal.

Marxists famously object to arrangements like the one described above, claiming that the capitalist is "exploiting" the baker. In Marxist thinking, the baker is the one who actually does the work to make the pies, so the full profit should go to the baker. But the Marxist is simply confused. If the baker had really done *all* the work to make the pie, then they would not have needed to involve the capitalist at all. It was only because the baker could not produce the pie without the help of an oven that they proposed the arrangement in the first place. If the baker could have bought the oven for themselves, then they would have done that and been able to keep the extra profit. Indeed, once the baker has worked making pies for several years, the baker may well save up enough money to buy their own oven (or ask the capitalist to sell back their stake in the bakery). In that case, the baker would no longer have to share their profits with the capitalist. But at the beginning, the baker needs the contribution of the capitalist, just as much as the capitalist needs the baker. Both of them profit by partnering together.

Not only does this type of arrangement generate wealth for both people, it also creates the possibility of going into a self-funded "retirement". Ideally, after working for many years, an older person will have saved up a sufficient nest egg that they are able to begin living entirely off the income generated by their investments. Bastiat rightly argued that this process of people retiring from hands-on work and living off their invested capital is a part of God's good design for the world[44]. How else, Bastiat asked, could a person enjoy true leisure time? If they could not legitimately profit from their invested capital, then they would only have two other options. One option is that they would have to become a leech upon their children and grandchildren in their old age, continually consuming the fruit of their offspring's labour. The other option is that they would have to plunder and steal from their neighbours. We may hope that children and friends would generously give aid to

---

44 Bastiat, *Capital and Interest*, essay available at http://bastiat.org/en/capital_and_interest.html

older people in the event of a misfortune that leaves them poor in their old age. But this is surely not how God *intended* the world to be. No, in our good God's world, there is a means provided by which a parent and a grandparent can continue to be a blessing to their offspring, rather than a burden, even when they can no longer labour in the field. They can keep being a blessing by carefully investing their saved-up capital resources so that others in their community might undertake new projects, advance the economy, and increase everyone's standard of living.

Society without the State

Up to this point, we have painted a basic picture of how the free market works. We have seen, at least in principle, why a society based on a free market becomes prosperous. Still, the question inevitably arises, How far can we really extend this free-market principle? Are there limits? Are there cases where the free market must be restrained in order to protect vulnerable people or to bring about some particular good in society? Or is the free market truly a universal principle which should be implemented at all times and in all cases?

Can we have a peaceful and prosperous society without any need for the State?

The Nature of the State

To begin to answer that question, we must first come to understand the true nature of the State. We have already seen that, according to Scripture and the church fathers, the tyrants of the ancient world were nothing more than particularly successful pirates, bandits and enslavers. The truth is that the rulers of nations today are not ultimately any different.

The revenue of each State comes from wealth that the State takes from its subjects by force. The laws imposed by the State are either consistent with the Natural Law, which exists independently and therefore does not require the State, or they are against the Natural Law and exist only for the State's benefit. According to the Natural Law, people have the right to share their thoughts freely with anyone who wishes to listen. But this presents a problem for the State because when people are free to speak their minds, they might criticise the State. For this reason, States around the world consistently punish people who expose the State's injustices. This is such a common occurrence that we have given it a name. We call a person suffering such punishment a "political prisoner". This person has not committed any real crime but is being punished for spreading information and ideas not approved by the State.

Even nations that pride themselves on being "free" have governments that habitually tax and oppress them this way. The USA, perhaps more than any other nation, holds "freedom" as a part of its national identity. Yet it is the government of the USA that wields the greatest apparatus on Earth for spying on its own citizens (the NSA), which has built a war machine unparalleled in human history, and which has driven people like Edward Snowden and Julian Assange into the status of political prisoners for exposing the government's wickedness.

At all times, and in all nations, the long-run effect of the State has always been to preserve and increase its own power and wealth at the expense of the people it presumes to govern. Nevertheless, there are many people who believe that the State has some good role to play. There have been many politicians who genuinely believed that by seeking political office, they could be a blessing to their fellow men. Most likely, many people reading this book will feel the same way. Many readers will still hold out hope that a misbehaving State could be reorganised to make it into an instrument of good rather than of evil.

To see why this attempt to redeem the State is misguided, we need to understand at a theoretical level why it is that no State can avoid harming its citizens.

All Taxes Cause Disharmony and Class Warfare

For a long time, I believed that the biblical data pointed to the State being a necessity. If the State is a necessity, then I reasoned that we would need at least some taxes in order to fund it. Over the centuries, governments have invented a huge variety of different taxes. I spent a long time sifting through them, trying to figure out what methods of taxation were likely to be the most "fair". I considered property taxes, undeveloped-land taxes, income taxes, import-export tariffs, consumption taxes, travel tolls, and so on and so forth.

Eventually, I came to see that taxes *of any kind* will always have two major, harmful effects.

The first harmful effect is that taxes represent a forcible intervention into the free choices of people in the marketplace. If you tax people for doing particular things, they will have to do those things less than they would have liked. If you use that tax money to subsidise something else, that thing will get done more than people actually wanted. This creates distortions in consumer preferences and price information, making the economy less efficient at providing the things that consumers actually desire. In this way, taxes (like any other form of economic intervention) always do harm to the overall standard of living in the society.

The second negative effect is less about economics and more about ethics. All taxes, no matter what shape or form they take, always cause society to be divided into two classes. One class is those who are net consumers of the taxes; the other class is people who are net payers of the taxes. Whatever complicated accounting schemes we come up with, whatever deductions and concessions are made, whatever services are paid for with the tax money, none of it will change this simple fact. Taxes force some people (the net payers) to foot the bill for benefits enjoyed by others (the net consumers)[45].

How can a society ever live in harmony when one group is forced to yield the fruit of their labour to another? They cannot. The society is condemned to ongoing conflict between those who take and those who are forced to give.

At this point, someone may object that their own government is a wonderful government. In their mind, their government does so many good things with its tax revenue. The government sets up

---

[45] Rothbard, *Man, Economy and State with Power and Market*, 1063.

schools and hospitals for the poor who cannot otherwise afford education or healthcare. The government provides roads to drive on, police services, and many other things like that. What is more, it appears that even the people who are net payers of the taxes in this society recognise the goodness of their government. The net payers seem to wholeheartedly support the things on which the tax revenue is spent.

However, when we examine the concrete, real-world actions of those same net payers, we find a very different story. If it were true that the net payers of taxes were genuinely willing to give the money being taken from them to those same things on which the State ends up spending the money, then there would be no need to take it from them in the first place. If the givers were genuinely willing, then the directors of the schools, hospitals, road networks, etc. would only have to ask the public and the needed donations would quickly come. In reality, we find that there is a continual battle between taxpayers and the State. The State hires auditors and prosecutors to chase down "tax dodgers". The taxpayers themselves hire accountants and attorneys to protect themselves from the State's grubby paws. If the taxpayers are really so happy with the decisions that the State makes with their money, then why does this battle occur at all? Clearly, the idea of a "voluntary" tax is a contradiction in terms.

Because all taxes are involuntary by definition, it becomes clear that the State is necessarily an organisation based upon violent interventions against the free market. The State collects taxes by threatening people with imprisonment. The State uses these stolen funds to grant subsidies to its favoured allies and groups that will give it "votes" in exchange for their share of the bounty. These "votes" help the State to portray itself as legitimate and to further expand its own power. The State gives certain favoured businesses a monopoly over a particular industry by threatening violence against any competitors. All these violent interventions in the free market reduce economic harmony and impoverish the society.

Once we understand that the State is *defined* by these sorts of violent interventions, it becomes clear that the State is by nature an anti-social institution. Free exchange in the marketplace is able to improve the lives of everyone without anyone being hurt. But the State can only help some people by oppressing others. Therefore, wherever the State exists, there must always be conflict between those who are benefiting from the State's violence and those who are suffering from it.

Why then are so many people convinced that we must have the State? Why do so many people go to the voting booth or run for political office with a genuine hope that they can do something helpful for their neighbours? In my experience, the main reason is that they believe there is some service, some good thing, some great necessity for society which can only be provided by the State. They believe that the free market is great for some things but that there are particular benefits which the free market cannot give us. So if we are to defend the free market as a biblical ideal, it is necessary to answer some of these objections.

What About Infrastructure (Schools, Hospitals, Roads)?

In a society without a State, there are no tax-funded services and therefore no taxes. There is not a single service for which you are *forced* to pay. Everything that you want is paid for only *voluntarily* and only if you decide that you actually want it.

Now, many of us are accustomed to living in places where a large number of services are only provided by the government. As a result, we often mistakenly believe that the free market is not capable of providing these services once the government steps away. But if we will only pay attention, history and experience will be enough to show that we have been mistaken.

Many governments provide tax-funded schools, but those often exist alongside private schools which are paid for voluntarily. Many people fear that without a tax-funded option for school, only the children of relatively wealthy parents would get an education. But many private schools, especially religious ones, already have generous donors providing many scholarships to help needy students attend their institution. The free market is clearly capable of providing a fully functioning school system because that system already exists.

Many people are accustomed to believing that the government must provide health care, but private hospitals certainly do exist. Many people who could not afford the cost of a private hospital out of pocket are still able to use them because they have purchased a health *insurance* policy. This mechanism of spreading risk and uncertainty among willing participants enables people to afford expensive services that only a few of them will actually need.

We will have more to say about the specific case of the poor in a moment. What is important to see first is that the free market is entirely capable of producing the schools and hospitals that we wish to attend.

Lots of people suggest that the government must provide telecommunications and mail services. But again, private companies have repeatedly shown that they can and do provide this service more effectively. Most mobile phone carriers are private, and many courier companies routinely deliver physical mail. In my own country, private 5G infrastructure appears set to provide higher-quality service than the government-funded "National Broadband Network" (NBN) before the latter is even finished being rolled out.

How about roads? How could we have roads without the government to build them? Again, private roads exist right now. They can be funded either by tolls (pay per use) or by some sort of subscription service (pay a monthly fee for unlimited use) or they can be provided as a complementary good. A complementary good is one which becomes valuable in connection with something else. A road is a good example. If I develop some land into a shopping mall, it will greatly serve my interests to provide good roads towards that mall. The easier it is for customers to access the mall, the more appealing it will be for merchants to rent shop space from me so that they can sell to those customers. Therefore, in my own self-interest, I will fund the building of excellent roads to connect my mall to surrounding suburbs, and I will build the cost into the rental price that I charge to the merchants. Those merchants will then build that into the cost of whatever they sell to their customers. Because a good road is in the interest of the mall owner, the merchant and the customer, all of these people will naturally collaborate through the price system to pay for that service. The same is true for a residential area. If a property developer builds out a new suburb with housing, they will get a much better price for each house if the houses are connected by well-made streets. The purchase contract for the property might even include a provision to keep paying monthly fees for the upkeep of those streets, the collection of garbage, etc. through a body-corporate organisation.

All of these things can be done voluntarily under prices and terms agreed in advance through a contract. There is no requirement that these services must be provided by a local government, which outlaws competition from other road builders and garbage collectors and which may raise the level of taxes it demands for this "service" at any time.

What About Public Safety (Fire Departments, Certifying Doctors)?

In a society without a State, some people object that public safety would be at risk because we would neglect certain services that we do not need very often. Many of us have never lived in a house that caught on fire. With that sort of life experience, how many people would voluntarily fund a fire department? But if the fire department went unfunded, there would be much more property destroyed when a fire eventually did break out.

Again, the market reveals the harmony of all of our interests. Almost everyone who owns a house in the developed world will hold an insurance policy for that house. The house is a large investment, and the owner would be greatly harmed if it were to be lost in a fire. If they bought the house with a loan from the bank, the bank may even require that the house be insured as a contractual condition of the loan.

If an insurance company is going to insure the house against a fire, then the insurance company has a strong incentive to ensure that the house does not burn down. If the company insures a thousand houses in a town, it makes very good business sense for the insurance company to fund a fire department to protect those insured homes. If different houses in a single neighbourhood use different insurance companies, then it will make sense for all of those insurance companies to have contracts with a shared fire department service that can protect all the houses in the area.

The homeowner does not want their house to burn down. The bank does not want the collateral asset for their loan to be destroyed. The insurance company does not want to have to pay out a large insurance claim. All of these interests align and give everyone in the community a strong incentive to set up effective fire-prevention services that are competitively priced. No one needs to be forced to participate because participation is in everyone's harmonious self-interest. What harms everybody is if the State mandates that there can only be one fire department, that everyone must pay for it whether or not they are satisfied with it, and no competition should be allowed. This inevitably leads to a more expensive and less effective fire service.

This same mechanism applies to all manner of public safety issues. For example, if we had no State, who would mandate that tall buildings must have handrails on their balconies? Well, the people who live in the tall buildings do not want to fall to their death. If the people who live there purchase life insurance policies, then their life insurance company may also require that they install handrails to minimise the risk of accidental death.

If we had no State, who would certify that surgeons were well trained and knew how to properly handle a scalpel? Well, a person who does not want to die on the operating table would only see a surgeon who they knew had been insured by a reputable medical malpractice insurer. In order to obtain that insurance, the surgeon would have to prove to the insurer that they were competent, perhaps by passing some sort of rigorous exam. No one wants to die on the operating table, no surgeon wants to be sued for malpractice by a grieving family, and no malpractice insurer wants to pay out an expensive legal settlement. All of these harmonious interests come together to ensure that people take safety seriously.

What About Handling a Virus Epidemic?

While this book was being written, the world went into lockdown over the spread of COVID-19, a highly infectious disease. Nations closed their borders; governments ordered that schools, churches and clubs must close their doors; and people were urged to stay at home rather than go to work. The thinking was that the less contact people had with one another during the crisis period, the slower the disease would be able to spread.

In a time of such crisis, it may seem that a society with no State would be helpless. How could the society implement such drastic measures if they did not have a central government to take the helm and issue authoritative commands?

It is true that a society with no State would be expected to be much more decentralised in its authority structures. This would make it difficult to ensure that blanket rules were applied to a large population. But this feature actually has many advantages in a crisis. Because there is no central authority, we avoid the problem of having to live with blanket rules that make sense in some areas but not others. In most countries, the COVID-19 crisis brought with it an order that all non-essential businesses must close their doors until the State authorised them to open again. This left vast numbers of people out of work and wondering how they would pay their bills.

In a society with no State, there would be no such central order. There would be no public property. In a Stateless society, every piece of land has a particular owner who has the authority to make the rules for their own property and to exclude anybody for any reason. This gives enormous scope for property owners to enact the policy that makes the most sense in their own context. An owner of a shopping mall, to avoid losing business, may provide a quarantine service for all staff and shoppers who wish to enter. To gain access to the shopping centre, a person would have to be tested for the disease. If they tested negative, then they would be permitted entry. Once you were on the premises of the shopping mall, you could be confident that every other person you met had also tested negative and was not going to infect you. Given the choice between a mall providing quarantine services and one that did not, cautious shoppers will lean towards the quarantined mall, and so competing malls will also be pressured to provide a similar service.

A Stateless society also allows property owners to go the other direction. A property owner could decide that their farmers' market will openly advertise that they do *not* do such quarantine checks and that there *is* a virus risk. If you are a person who has already caught the virus or has had the vaccine, you will have no problem shopping at such a location. If you wish to sell to such people, you still can, provided that you wear the proper protective clothing. Having no State allows property owners the flexibility to enact whatever policy best serves their customers and clients. Body-corporate organisations could use similar tactics, setting up quarantine checkpoints to enter or leave their neighbourhood. All of this would enable people to balance the risk of infection and the economic damage in the way that made the most sense in their own context, rather than being subject to sweeping rules without nuance.

What About Law and Order?

Among the more difficult questions that I sought to answer when considering a Stateless society was the question of a free-market justice system. John Locke proposed that, in the "state of nature", every man had the right to exact retributive justice upon every other man[46]. Bastiat proposed that the purpose of the government and its laws was simply to organise that individual right of self-defence into some orderly system[47]. I supposed that the only way that this could work is if there were a single legal system which was enforced equally upon everybody in the society. If there were multiple competing legal systems, would that not result in contradictory laws being passed? How could we resolve such a contradiction? Would not the competing law enforcement agencies end up going to battle against one another over these differences until one of them reigned supreme? I had begun to think that a single, government-monopolised legal system was inevitable.

---

46 Locke, *Second Treatise on Government*, Chapter 2, Point 11.
47 Bastiat, *The Law*, essay available at http://bastiat.org/en/the_law.html

Rothbard helpfully relieved me of this confusion by pointing out some facts about the real world. First of all, competing legal systems already *do* exist, and they do not cause the world to fall into chaos. Individual states in my home country of Australia have differences in their laws, but we do not go to war over them. Australia has different laws to the neighbouring country of New Zealand, but once again, there is no need for war. People travel between these places, live and work abroad, do business deals, import and export goods, and so on. None of that is prevented by the fact that the legal systems differ between these areas.

Second, Rothbard pointed out that there is no "world government" over these different countries which must step in every time a discrepancy is encountered between their legal codes. In reality, the nations of the world exist in a state of "anarchy" relative to one another[48].

Rothbard simply suggested that we extend this system down to gradually smaller and smaller areas. If New Zealand can have laws that are entirely independent of the laws in Australia, then why should not Queensland and New South Wales (two Australian states) also have entirely independent laws? Why should it be mandatory for a "federal" government to be over them and

---

48 Rothbard, *Ethics of Liberty*, 181.

impose a shared law on both states? One may argue that the geography of Australia gives it a definite, watery border and that the law should be uniform within that natural border. But of course, this is not the case for the vast majority of nations around the world. Alaska is under the national laws of the USA, but it is separated from the mainland of the USA by a stretch of *land* which is deemed to be under Canadian law. This situation does not result in continual legal battles or wars between the USA and Canada. So it is simply an empirical fact that a unified justice system is not a requirement in order to prevent chaos.

Having made this observation, the natural question that follows is, Why should we not extend the same principle down to ever smaller boundaries and groupings? If Canada may have a different legal code to the USA, then why could not Texas or California elect to have a legal code independent from the rest of the USA? If California could have different laws to the rest of the USA, then why could not San Diego and San Francisco decide to have different laws from one another? If two cities can do this, then why not two neighbourhoods within that city? Why not two households within the neighbourhood? Indeed, why may each individual not have the freedom to choose for themselves to whom they will go for police and judicial services?

Indeed, this is exactly what Rothbard proposes. He suggests that each individual should be free to patronise any one of a number of competing security and judicial firms on the free market. There are many strategies that companies on the free market might try in order to provide a service for which their customers are willing to pay. Here we will make a particular suggestion that seems plausible. Suppose there are a number of different private security agencies and private courts operating. If someone breaks into your house and steals your TV, you may call a private security service that you have been paying a subscription fee to that operates in your neighbourhood. They may track down the thief and attempt to retrieve the TV. If they generally do a good job at retrieving stolen goods, they will stay in business. If they usually *do not* find the culprit and get the goods back, then they will quickly lose subscribers and go out of business. Alternatively, you may sue the thief in a private court. If the court rules that you are correct, the person did in fact steal your TV, then the court may grant you permission to enter the thief's home and forcibly take the TV back (an action which you may outsource to a security company).

But suppose that the thief claims they are innocent. Suppose further that the thief sues you in a *different* private court, claiming that you have broken into the thief's home without reason and you are actually the guilty party in the whole affair. What then? Well, the court chosen by the thief will likely have a relationship with the court which you chose for yourself. Today's banking system exists in this way, as a network of connected businesses. When you give someone a cheque, it has the logo of *your* bank on it, but the way that they redeem the money is by taking it to *their own* bank. They expect that the two banks will communicate with each other in order to complete the transaction between the two accounts. Likewise, the thief's chosen court may choose to uphold the previous ruling handed down by your court, and then all would be synchronised and resolved. But suppose that the thief's court did *not* agree with your court's ruling? What then? Then the most likely resolution is that the two courts would enter into a contractual agreement to respect the decision of a mutually agreed upon third court as their court of appeal.

Once again, insurance companies would likely come into play and help to orchestrate the alignment of incentives. Suppose that you could pay a monthly fee for a "crime insurance" subscription. If someone breaks into your house and steals your TV, you would call your crime insurance company. They would have pre-arranged relationships with a private security agency and a network of courts. The courts in their network would likely have pre-arranged agreements about third-party courts to which they will appeal in the event of conflicting rulings. For the vast majority of customers and court companies, it would be in their best interest to subscribe to whichever court service they thought was the most fair and balanced. No one could know in advance whether they are more likely to be the plaintiff or the defendant. Some people may wish to subscribe to knowingly corrupt courts in the hopes of giving bribes so that rulings would go their way. But of course, if they get sued in that same court, that same corruption may very well work against them. To attract customers, courts would need to protect their reputation. Part of protecting their own reputation would be to repudiate and expel courts and judges from their network who are known to be corrupt.

There may be many different private court companies on the free market, each with subtle differences in their legal conventions and precedents. Each court would be free to establish its own legal code and patterns of rulings. Customers would choose the court in which they preferred to conduct their disputes. For example, Protestants and Catholics may have slightly different views on how the law should handle divorce settlements. Each individual would be free to conduct such a divorce settlement in whichever court system they preferred. If a Catholic and a Protestant were to be married and then seek a divorce, they may each choose a different court, and those two courts would likely refer any irreconcilable rulings to a pre-arranged court of appeal (or alternatively, if the scenario becomes common, the two courts may have pre-arranged a pattern of compromises they will enact in the event of such a conflict).

This system of free-market security, law and judicial services may seem like a lot of wishful and imaginative thinking. It may seem like a fairy-tale story of ivory tower academics. But again, it turns out to be an empirical fact of history that precisely these sorts of systems have existed and do exist today. As Rothbard points out[49]:

> [International] relations between *private citizens* of different countries have generally functioned quite smoothly, despite the lack of a single government over them. Thus, a contractual or a tort dispute between a citizen of North Dakota and of Manitoba is usually handled quite smoothly, typically with the plaintiff suing or placing charges in his court,

---

49 Rothbard, *Ethics of Liberty*, 181.

> and the court of the other country recognizing the result.

Contracts over international borders, crossing legal jurisdictions, are common in the modern world. And the legal institutions of the involved jurisdictions are entirely capable of resolving disputes as they happen. Of course, there are some difficult cases. Many Australians are well aware that the drug laws in neighbouring Indonesia are very different than they are in Australia. Drugs are readily available on the Indonesian island of Bali, and many Australians on holiday choose to partake of them. The Indonesian government has very harsh penalties for those who are caught. However, Australians are aware that if they are caught, then they are very likely to be able to bribe the police officers who arrest them into letting them go. Indeed, the necessary bribe is apparently a small enough sum of money that many Australians simply go ahead and take the risk. Nevertheless, there have been some high-profile cases where the Indonesian authorities have called for the death penalty for Australians caught with drugs in Bali. The international legal disputes that have followed have not been simple to resolve. But this by no means proves that a system of multiple jurisdictions *cannot* work. For of course, it is possible for a long, drawn out legal dispute to take place even within a single jurisdiction. So occasional difficult cases do not invalidate the multiple-jurisdiction concept as a whole.

In addition to the international examples before our eyes today, we also have the interesting example of decentralised judicial services in pre-monarchical Israel. We will examine that case in more detail later.

What About Negative Externalities (Pollution)?

Having thought through a free-market legal system, we are now able to ask about a difficult legal question that arises in a Stateless society. Without a State, how would a society handle the problem of "negative externalities"? In economics, the term "negative externality" refers to a case where some activity causes a cost to be imposed upon people who were not involved in the activity themselves. A classic example would be air pollution. Suppose that there is a factory that emits a lot of smog in order to manufacture its products. The smog from the factory slowly drifts towards a nearby town, where it slightly damages people's clothes, damages their health, etc. The factory has to pay for its raw materials, for its workers' wages, for its machinery and so on. But in most countries, the factory does not pay any money to the people in the town who are affected by the air pollution. Those people do not get compensated, and they are forced to bear the cost of that pollution without getting any of the profits earned by the factory.

One common suggestion for solving the problem of negative externalities is the so-called "Pigovian tax". A Pigovian tax is a tax that is designed to shift cost for a negative externality back onto the entity that is causing the damage. In our factory example, a government may levy a Pigovian tax on the factory owners based on the amount of smog that their factory emits. The proceeds from that tax could then (at least in theory) be used to offset the costs incurred by the people in the town. Additionally, this higher cost would incentivise the factory owners to change their production methods so that they produce less smog. The high-smog method may have been cheaper before (which is why the factory owners chose it). But the Pigovian "smog tax" would cause the high-smog method to become more expensive, which would motivate the factory owners to invest in making the change.

Of course, in practice, there are many problems with this sort of Pigovian tax. As a method, Pigovian taxation assumes that the government can accurately calculate how much extra cost is imposed upon the townspeople by the smog from the factory. In reality, this is very difficult to estimate, and the government is very likely to get it wrong. Some of the townspeople might prefer for the goods coming out of the factory to be cheaper, even if there is some slight damage to their property, because the factory's output is critical to their lives. They would prefer a lower Pigovian tax. Others might be totally uninterested in what is coming out of the factory and would like the tax to be very high so that the pollution goes down as much as possible. But the Pigovian tax is not a market price, where individuals can each decide for themselves whether they would like to pay for the service or would prefer to keep their money. Everyone will have to live with the results of the tax, no matter what their preferences are. Therefore, the government simply has to "guess" at the correct level for the Pigovian tax and hope for the best. But since there can be no proof either way, since the decision is somewhat arbitrary, everyone in the town is incentivised to lobby the government to try and get the Pigovian tax level set where they would like it. Politicians will end up setting the tax at whatever level is preferred by their friends, the people who will donate to their re-election campaign. If the factory owners are known to be strong supporters of an opposing political party, then they will get slapped with the highest Pigovian tax possible to make sure that they are less able to fund that opposing party at the next election. Despite its hopeful intentions, the Pigovian tax is still a tax. It is a demand for an arbitrary amount of money, backed by the threat of violence if the money is not forthcoming.

In society with no State, all actions are supposed to be voluntary. Therefore, such a society rejects *all* forms of taxation, including Pigovian taxes. But if this is so, how then could the problem of negative externalities be solved in the Stateless society? The two major mechanisms for solving this issue in the Stateless society would be an efficient system of "tort" law and private property titles to "easements".

Tort Law

As we have already seen, a society with no State would be expected to develop a system of competing private courts. Because these courts are competing with one another to be selected for hearing cases, the courts have a strong incentive to keep costs low for their customers, the plaintiff and the defendant. In the court system of most countries, where court services are a State-run monopoly, disputes often take months to resolve and cost tens or hundreds of thousands of dollars. Because of this, a dispute must involve very large damages in order to be worth taking to court at all. If a person has been defrauded of $10,000, they may wish to take the guilty party to court. But if it will cost the person $11,000 in legal fees to have the case pursued, then the innocent party is better off if they simply walk away.

Likewise, a group of people affected by a "negative externality", such as pollution from a factory, are unlikely to successfully sue the factory owners in a monopolised court system. The factory owners have much more to lose if their business is interrupted than the plaintiffs have to lose individually. For that reason, the factory owners would have every incentive to financially support the election campaign of politicians who will then pass laws helping to protect the factory owners from prosecution. For example, the factory owners may lobby the government to outlaw class action lawsuits entirely. The government may save face by claiming that they are outlawing this sort of action against the polluting factory in the name of "progress" or "removing roadblocks to develop the local economy". But in reality, they will simply be protecting the interests of their donors and simultaneously preventing the townspeople from exercising their natural right to protect their own lives and property.

By contrast, in a society where there is no State to hold a monopoly on judicial services, the most successful courts will be the ones that provide the most streamlined and efficient system for disputes. It is entirely possible that a pollution dispute could be handled, in a specialised tort-law court, in a matter of days or even hours, at a tiny fraction of the cost of a State-monopoly court. If it were clearly demonstrated to this efficient tort-law court that the factory was directly responsible for specific damages suffered by the townspeople, the court then would order the factory to pay damages to the plaintiffs (with interest), and that would be that.

Knowing that this would be likely to happen, the factory would be incentivised from the outset to avoid getting into the situation where they are likely to be sued. They will then be more likely to reduce their pollution before the need to sue them ever arises.

Property Titles to Easements

The second major mechanism that would exist for dealing with negative externalities in a Stateless society is the recognition of property titles to "easements". An easement is essentially a right to use a piece of property, without actually "possessing" it. In our current society, local governments often maintain easement rights to homeowners' properties in order to access shared infrastructure for maintenance. A particular house in the neighbourhood may have a key access point for the local sewage network situated in the backyard. When someone buys that house, part of the sale contract is that they acknowledge the local government's entitlement to access that sewer entrance whenever they wish. The home owners own the land that makes up the backyard, but the local government had a prior arrangement with the property developer that they would retain an "easement" to access that particular portion of the land where the sewer access is located. This easement was a condition of the local government allowing the property developer to put houses on the land. The property developer therefore did not have the ability to hand this entitlement over to the new homeowners. Instead, the entitlement stays with the local government.

Easements in a Stateless society would work in a similar fashion. There would be no local government demanding arbitrary easements to access land that was not yet developed, but there would be a recognition that when people cultivated natural resources into private property, they were also cultivating the associated easement rights. This comes into play with an issue like noise pollution. Suppose that a house and a carpentry workshop are located right beside each other. The owner of the house may complain that the carpentry workshop makes an awful lot of noise cutting wood with its power tools. The owner of the house may complain that this noise infringes their right to enjoy peace and quiet in their own home. If the house owner sues the workshop owner and asks the court to order that the workshop must stop using noisy tools, how should the court rule?

It depends on who first "homesteaded" the right over the noise easement for that area. If the house was built first, then the owner of the house can rightly claim that they were able to enjoy the house in peace up until the workshop owner invaded their airspace with the noisy tools. However, if the workshop was built first, and only then was the house built beside it, then the workshop owner can rightly claim that they have the title to the noise easement for the area. The house owner knew there was a carpentry workshop there when they chose to build the house, they knew that the workshop owner would be making a lot of noise, and that the workshop owner had already cultivated that space specifically for noisy activities. Therefore, the house owner is not being deprived of a right to silence that they had previously enjoyed. The workshop owner is simply exercising their right to their justly acquired noise easement.

By these sorts of mechanisms, courts in the Stateless society would recognise private property boundaries and concern themselves with crafting fair and practical conventions for easily delineating the boundaries of private property in the event of a dispute. Knowing that this will happen, property owners will naturally choose to build their houses in areas where they will not be caused problems by things like noise and smog easements, which have been justly acquired for industrial purposes. They will build their houses in areas where there are mostly just other houses. Likewise, factory and workshop owners will naturally keep their industrial buildings away from areas where there are houses lest they get brought into court in a tort case and have to pay damages.

Again we see that the Stateless society can be expected to resolve these types of problems more easily and naturally than the State-run society. This is precisely because the Stateless society respects God's design of the world and allows the natural harmony between people's economic interests to play out.

What About the Poor?

Finally we come to the important question of the poor. A society with no State, by definition, has no taxes and therefore no tax-funded welfare system. Could such a society possibly be considered humane? The answer is yes, absolutely. In fact, we have great reason to expect that such a society would deal much more humanely with the poor than our present State-based societies do.

The first thing we need to understand about improving the lives of the poor is that it is a surprisingly difficult and complicated task. Simply giving someone money does not necessarily improve their life in the long run. It can easily lead them to become dependent upon a constant stream of such handouts. We witness this in our societies today by the existence of multi-generational welfare families, where parents spend most of their lives on welfare while raising children who grow up to do the same. There is also the issue that poverty is often the result of poor decision making. For example, if a person starts taking drugs recreationally and becomes addicted, they may struggle to hold down a job. As long as they continue using drugs, they will find it very difficult to advance their career and improve their situation. By simply providing them with money, we are potentially making it easy for them to obtain the drugs that they want while continuing to ignore the consequences.

This is not to say that everyone who finds themselves in a difficult financial situation has made poor decisions. Certainly some people are struck by genuine misfortune. Others are in poverty due to the wickedness or foolishness of other people (such as their parents), rather than any action of their own. An ideal social "safety net" ought to be compassionate to people who are genuine victims of circumstance. But at the same time, the social safety net must not enable and perpetuate ongoing cycles of poverty.

The State typically shows total incompetence in distinguishing between those who are poor because of tragedy or misfortune and those who are poor through their own doing. The State tries to provide a generic policy that covers all cases. Often everyone on welfare gets basically the same level of payment, regardless of how they are likely to spend it. State welfare also tends to be extraordinarily expensive, being underpinned by a massive bureaucracy that attempts to restrain the inevitable abuses of the system. Those bureaucrats all need to be paid salaries, and all of this drives up the total cost of actually helping those in need.

In reality, helping the poor takes a lot of skill and care. If your goal is merely to keep a person clothed and fed, simple but expensive solutions can work. But if your goal is to help someone break cycles of bad decisions, recover from abuse, gain employment, and become self-sufficient, then you are going to have to approach the challenge much more carefully.

The glory of private charities is precisely that they *can and do* discriminate in how they distribute their funds. Because charities rely on voluntary donations, not involuntary taxes, they must behave in a way that pleases their donors. If the donors feel that the charity is giving away money to people who could easily work but are simply being lazy, then the donations will begin to dry up. If the donors feel that the charity is enabling substance abuse, they will also stop donating. The charities that succeed will be exactly those charities that can demonstrate to their donors that they are using the donated funds most wisely. The successful charities will work hard to find worthy recipients who are genuinely helped by financial aid and not led into ongoing dependence. The risk of losing their donor base to competing charities is a strong motivator for charities to use their funds as wisely as possible. Because of that motivation, firms that have to compete for customers (donors) will always tend to do a better job for a cheaper price than a monopolised government department.

Furthermore, helping the poor through private charities means that the donors do not all need to *agree* on the best strategy. Some donors may prefer that a charity should make all welfare payments conditional on passing a regular drug test. Other donors may think that stigmatising drug use is counterproductive and would prefer a gentler and more understanding approach to helping people deal with drug addiction. It may be that some welfare recipients would benefit more from a hard-line approach while others genuinely do need compassion and understanding. The market allows for donors to give to whichever organisations they feel are best reflecting their own values and showing the most helpful results. By contrast, State-based welfare programs force everyone to pay for whatever policies the government chooses, whether they agree with them or not.

However, even if we agree that private charities will use funds more efficiently than the State, there is still another problem. If all donations are voluntary, then will the funds necessary to support the poor actually be given? If no one is forcing them, will donors reveal their underlying greed and refuse to give? Actually, we have good reason to think that donations would be plentiful. Many charities exist today that are quite well funded. This happens in spite of the fact that State-based welfare exists. With the existence of State-based welfare, it would be easy for wealthy donors to say, "I have already given quite enough to the poor through my taxes, why should I give more?" In reality, there are large numbers of donors supporting charities today, desperately trying to make up for the failings of the State-based welfare system. The existence of private charities in a world that already has State welfare is good evidence that the desire to help the poor is not lacking. A world where the income of the wealthiest donors has doubled or tripled (due to the abolition of taxes) would be a world where the best charities are extremely well resourced.

The Stateless society is one in which private charities are free to put biblical principles for helping the poor into practice. On the one hand we are told, "Blessed is he who is generous to the poor" (Proverbs 14:21) and, "Whoever is generous to the poor lends to the Lord" (Proverbs 19:17). On the other hand, we are warned against enabling bad behaviour in the name of charity. Paul writes that the policy of the church should be that "if anyone is not willing to work, let him not eat." Instead, those who have been lazy are urged to repent, to do their work quietly, and to "earn their own living." (2 Thessalonians 3:10-12).

Free Markets are an Expression of Faith in God

Hopefully this has been a helpful sketch of what a society might look like without a State. Many more books have been filled considering how such mechanisms would work, but my hope is that this sampling has helped you to consider some new possibilities. I have tried to show that a society with no State is not a total fantasy land. Many elements of it already exist today in varying forms. Some people have said that communism is an unrealistic utopia. They speak as though a fully socialist society, where all property is owned by the government, would work just fine if only the people in it did not sin against one another. Some people have said the same thing about a fully free-market society with no State. They say that it is a fine idea, but that it can only work if no one sins against one another. In fact, *both* statements are false.

Socialism and communism fail, not because the people living within the socialist or communist system are sinners, but because the system of socialism and communism *is itself sinful*. Socialism is an institutionalised, regularised program of violating property rights. It is a system based on continually breaking the commandment that "you shall not steal" (Exodus 20:15). It is an attempt to live in God's world while violating God's law. That is why it does not work. It also does not help to claim that a socialist system would work if only it were "fully" implemented, with no half-measures. Not at all. Each and every incremental element of socialist policy added to a society will make that society worse off, as violations of God's law must always do. The 20th and 21st centuries give ample empirical demonstrations of this process.

In contrast, a fully capitalist system is marked by its capacity to make its inhabitants consistently better off. That is because the Stateless, capitalist society is committed to *refraining* from violating the commandment not to steal. We see for ourselves that wherever free markets are allowed to operate, the society in which they operate will be made incrementally better off. If a society were to abolish the State completely and the bulk of its citizens refused to tolerate any attempts by would-be dictators to re-establish a State apparatus, then we would see a beacon of *relative* peace and blessing. It would not be perfect. There would still be sinners within it. There would still be a market for security and judicial services. But where these services were free and non-coercive, God would be glorified in the economic harmony that would prevail.

Douglas Wilson wrote that "[it] is not possible to understand the gospel of free grace intelligently if it does not lead to a love for free markets. Free grace creates free men, and free men trade in free markets"[50]. I think those words are truer than even Wilson supposed them to be (Wilson himself is an explicit Kuyperian and still sees a role for a limited State).

Wilson would not go so far as to label himself a libertarian, and yet the statement above is a brilliant, Christian exposition of the libertarian ideal. If we wish to glorify God in the political sphere, the best thing that we can do is to move our

---

50 Wilson, *Rules for Reformers*, Part 1, Subsection "Alinsky Redux".

society as close as we can to the point of being totally Stateless. The best thing that we can do is to allow all people to cultivate the natural resources that God has provided and to exchange freely with one another. We must encourage people to do the good things which God has laid out for them to do, and to do them with all of their might. For we were bought with a price, and therefore we refuse to become slaves of men (1 Corinthians 7:23), even of men calling themselves a "government". This takes courage. More than that, it takes *faith*. It is a scary thing to leave the State behind. The State is a false god, one which many of us have worshipped for far too long. But the State is a created thing, born of man's desire to dominate his neighbour. It is not our Creator. We may fear what would happen in the unfamiliar realm of a truly free society. But we can pursue it and push closer to it, knowing that our Sovereign God will by no means allow a society committed to following God's commands to be ruined by their pursuit of obedience.

Embracing the market, instead of the sword, is an act of faith in the goodness of God. It means living out the conviction that our God has ordered the world in such a way that righteousness is wiser than wickedness and diligent work bears better fruit than robbing our neighbours.

Intelligent Design Theory and Economics

Having defined what we mean by "economic harmony" and seen that a Christian doctrine of creation leads us to expect economic harmony, we are now ready to make that position more rigorous. This leads us to the fascinating subject of Intelligent Design.

Intelligent Design is a theory usually associated with questions of the origin of life and of the various species that exist on the earth. Intelligent Design stands in opposition to the orthodox, neo-Darwinian view that all life on earth descended from a single common ancestor, which itself arose spontaneously from non-living matter. Proponents of Intelligent Design argue that this Darwinian hypothesis is ultimately infeasible. In their view, living organisms display characteristics which cannot be explained by a series of successive steps, where each incomplete step along the way must confer a distinct survival advantage. Because these structures cannot confer a survival advantage by progressive small steps, they conclude that these structures require the forethought of a rational designer in order to be produced.

While this argument began in the realm of biology, it has led to a more generalised theory about detecting the presence of intelligence in a dataset. For example, if you open up a book that is written in a foreign language, then you are *not* able to read it. But you would also not be able to read a book that contains a random jumble of letters. Both are unable to be read, but one of them has meaning (to the person who knows the language) while the other is nonsense (no matter what language you speak). The question is, If you cannot read either book, is there any way to tell the difference between them? Is there some way to tell whether the arrangement of letters on a page is *random* or *deliberate*, even if the full meaning is not known?

As it turns out, the answer is "yes". It is possible to discern the presence of intelligence in the way that something is arranged, even when we cannot precisely interpret the meaning of the arrangement. Various researchers in the field of information theory and computer science have developed quite rigorous theories of how this detection can be done[51,52]. From a Christian perspective, the idea of Intelligent Design is a part of our biblical worldview. Scripture calls us to

---

51 Werner Gitt's book, *Without Excuse*, is a key work in this space by an overt, biblical creationist.
52 Dembski and Marks' "Evolutionary Informatics Lab" has published many academic papers on intelligent design theory from a secular and empirical perspective (https://evoinfo.org/publications.html).

behold the creation with awe and wonder, because in it God has revealed Himself as our Creator (Psalm 19:1-6, Romans 1:91-20).

But intelligent design theory has further applications beyond biology and computer science. Intelligent design theory also turns out to be a very useful tool for clarifying certain issues in economics and libertarian legal theory.

Intelligent Design Explains Why Economic Harmony Exists

Intelligent design theory gives us some excellent foundational principles for explaining exactly why economic harmony emerges from the seeming disorder of the free market. In order to explain the relationship between intelligent design theory and economic harmony, we are going to begin with an overview of what intelligent design theory contributes to the sciences in general.

The essence of intelligent design theory is that "information" is a fundamental entity in the universe which needs to be taken into consideration in order to fully understand our world. In the physical sciences (chemistry, physics, etc.), it is common to think primarily in terms of the two fundamental entities: *matter* and *energy*. Everything in our world that you can see, taste, or touch is either some kind of matter or some kind of energy. However, if we believed that matter and energy could totally explain our world, we would draw false conclusions. To understand things properly, we must also account for the third fundamental entity, in addition to matter and energy, which is *information.*

Information is about the specific arrangement of matter and energy within space and time. Information is the reason that we are usually willing to pay more for a book than we are for a sheet of blank paper and a pot of ink. In both cases, we are still getting paper and ink for our money, but the arrangement of that ink into the formation of letters and words in the book is what gives it the extra value.

It is a well-known law from the physical sciences that matter and energy can be converted into different forms, but they cannot be created or destroyed[53]. This is not the case with information. Information *can* be created and destroyed. If you tear a book into tiny pieces, you may have "destroyed" the book, but you still have the same quantity of paper and ink sitting in front of you. That is, you have destroyed the information, the specific arrangement of the materials, but you have not destroyed the materials themselves. A cornerstone of Christian theology is that only God

---

53 This is the 1st law of thermodynamics.

can create matter *ex nihilo* ("out of nothing"). Human beings are not able to do that. When we speak of a human "creating" something, we only mean that they are rearranging pre-existing matter and energy into a more valuable, more useful configuration. When a person forms a clay pot, they do not "create" new clay. They only take existing clay and *arrange* it into the useful shape of a pot.

The same is true of all creative acts that are done by people. Suppose that I want to build a house for shelter. If I set out to "create" a house, I do not actually cause any new wood to exist. I cut up wood from a tree, then I shape it into beams, a door, floorboards and so on. I fasten these together, and now I have a house.

Ultimately, cultivating resources is always an act of expending *energy* to impose *information* upon *matter*.

So what does this have to do with economic harmony? Well, simply put, it means that all cultivation of natural resources is ultimately an exercise in *creating information*. If you plough a field, plant seeds and water them in order to grow an orchard, you are not creating any matter that did not already exist. The dirt existed, the seeds existed, the water existed. All of the nutrients that those seeds needed so that they might grow into a tree were already present in the soil. All of the solar energy that the tree needed was already available. These things were not brought into existence by the person who cultivated the field. All that the person did was to "move stuff around" into a more useful configuration so that it would then become easier to pick fruit from the trees for consumption.

It should be obvious that the person who has ploughed their field, planted seeds and watered them is *more wealthy* than they were before they did the ploughing, planting and watering. Their property is more valuable to them now that they have arranged the materials this way, even though the particular materials that are present have not changed. As we reflect on this, we see that *all wealth* is ultimately information imposed upon matter.

Bastiat argued that the great disagreement in his day between socialists and supporters of the free market could ultimately be reduced to one key idea. Socialists, according to Bastiat, believe that a person can only increase their wealth if the wealth of another person is decreased. Whatever one gains, another must lose. In response, Bastiat argued that God has designed the world such that the economic interests of individuals are in harmony with one another, and one person's gain does not require another person's loss. Intelligent design theory gives us a foundational explanation for why Bastiat was right and the socialists were wrong. How can it be that our labour increases the amount of wealth that we have without diminishing the wealth of anyone else? The reason is because our wealth is not ultimately the *material* objects that we possess; it is the *information* that has been imposed upon that material. As long as we can create new information, we can increase the total wealth that is available to mankind. Because our efforts and labours are about imposing information upon matter, information that previously did not exist anywhere, we are capable of *creating new wealth* without having to take anything away from our neighbour.

Intelligent Design Explains Why Landowners Don't Control Everything

The second contribution of intelligent design theory is that it firmly explains why landowners do not dominate our economy. One of the common objections that I have heard to a society based completely on private property is the fear that a group of elites would accumulate all of the wealth of the society. If a small number of wealthy people were simply allowed to get richer and richer, with no government stepping in to tax away their wealth and redistribute it, would the rest of us eventually become their functional slaves? What if they gradually purchased all of the land in the society so that all of us were forced to pay them rent simply in order to live *anywhere*?

The answer to this objection has two parts. The first part is simply to contemplate how radically difficult it would be for anyone to accumulate such a share of the world's wealth that they were able to charge everybody inescapable rent. Several incredible obstacles naturally stand in the way of such a feat. First, we have seen that the normal pattern for exchanges is for both parties to become wealthier through the exchange. There are cases where two people agree to make a trade, but one of them later comes to regret it. However, those events have a natural limit. If a used-car salesman sells too many "lemons" (vehicles that appear okay but turn out to have serious defects), he will quickly develop a reputation for dishonesty. If that happens, he will lose many customers to the honest dealerships, and there will not be much likelihood of him rising to incredible wealth. But for the honest dealer, the pattern of their exchanges involves enriching their customers by providing them with reliable transportation. This allows their customers to engage in more productive pursuits and gain wealth for themselves, which tends to immunise them from the risk of being too poor to escape a wealthy rent seeker. The point is, for an individual to gain such wealth that they would be in a position to dominate their fellow man by imposing inescapable rents, it would require an incredibly implausible series of events in which the great mass of people *all* make a series of extremely unwise exchanges to favour the aspiring aristocrat. So the danger of this happening in a free market is extraordinarily low. In general, monopolies occur precisely *because* the government intervenes and grants unjustified privileges to particular people and corporations (such as giving one phone company the exclusive right to provide phone service and outlawing competitors).

But suppose for the sake of argument that such an aristocrat did rise up. Suppose that an individual, without depending on any special government favours, managed to become fantastically wealthy and decided to try and buy up all of the residential land in an area. This area would have to be somewhat large so that it would be difficult for people to simply travel outside the borders of this aristocrat's property. But the market puts a natural limit on how big it could possibly be. As I write this, the wealthiest man on the planet is apparently Jeff Bezos, the founder of Amazon. His estimated net worth is somewhere around $150 billion. In reality, his functional net worth is a lot less than that, because if he tried to liquidate all of his holdings, he would drive down the price of the assets he holds. But for the sake of argument, let us suppose that he can actually liquidate his entire net worth and be left with $150 billion in cash.

Next, let us suppose that Bezos wants to try and spend his entire net worth on real estate. He wants to try and buy a whole city so that he can start charging exorbitant rents to everyone who lives there. How much does $150 billion buy him? If the average price of a home is $200,000 (a very low estimate[54]), then $150 billion will buy 750,000 homes. If there are an average of five people living in each of those homes, then that amounts to 3.75 million people. That is a city population about ¾ the size of Sydney (or about the size of metropolitan Seattle).

Now, as I write this, there is an ongoing phenomenon in Australia that large numbers of people are moving out of Sydney because real estate is so much more expensive there compared to smaller, regional cities. So it turns out that many people are prepared to move if the price of housing noticeably increases in their area. If Bezos starts trying to buy all the real estate in Sydney, he will rapidly drive up the asking price for those houses.

---

54 In fact, the median house price in Sydney is currently over $1 million.

In all likelihood, before Bezos gets done with buying even *one tenth* of Sydney's real estate, he will have driven the price up so high that even his enormous fortune will be exhausted. In the meantime, he will have driven so many people away that "controlling" the city would no longer seem very impressive. Many people will move to cheaper areas, thus removing themselves from Bezos' control. For those determined to stay, many investors and builders will be incentivised by the high prices to build more houses in and around Sydney, which will dilute the percentage of Sydney land that Bezos owns. If the richest man on the planet cannot obtain a meaningful monopoly over a single city by simply purchasing land, then it is not really a problem worth worrying about. The people whose monopolies *actually* cause problems are the ones who get the government to enact their monopoly into law. It is only State-enforced monopolies that have the advantage of the police coming to arrest any would-be market competitors.

On top of this, intelligent design gives us a second safeguard against this scenario. Remember what wealth really is. Wealth is the presence of useful *information* within material things. It will do the landlord no good to have land and property but have no one to work it. Not only will they need people to farm the land and grow things for them to eat, the landlord will also have demand for a thousand other services. They will need a doctor to take care of them if they get sick; they will wish for domestic staff to cook and clean for them; they will wish for a teacher to educate their children; they will desire engineers and mechanics to build them a car and keep it serviced; they will desire the services of artists to entertain them. All of these occupations can be engaged in with little to no property initially owned by the person who does the job, but many of them are generally paid quite well. Over time, these well-paid positions will enable the people doing them to accumulate capital of their own, and their wealth will grow relative to the wealth of the landlord.

We see this in practice. If land and capital were the main ingredient in wealth, then farmers would generally be the wealthiest people in society. The farmer usually owns a large area of land, many acres in fact, but that land is usually not very well developed. It may have a fence here or a dam there, but for the most part a farm is not radically different from the state that nature left these resources in. Contrast this with a doctor or lawyer's office in a city. The doctor or lawyer probably earns much more money than the farmer, yet their little office may take less than 1% of the land area of the farm. In that office, the lawyer pours over complicated documents (information) and makes even more complicated arguments about their contents (more information). The doctor applies years of study of the human body, carefully attempting to *reorganise* parts of a patient's body which have fallen into *disorder*. Both of these are *information-intensive* occupations rather than *land-intensive* occupations, like farming. It is precisely because wealth is found in the *information* that we add to material things that these information-intensive occupations attract such a high price in the marketplace.

However much land a person buys, they cannot buy your body. From the moment you are born, you gain control over your two hands, your two feet, your two eyes, your tongue, and so on. God gives us all a baseline of material property in our body, with all the tools necessary to take the thoughts of our mind and transmit them into various material mediums. Everything that we need in order to invent a story or diagnose a disease or wash someone's dishes is our own mind and body. Everything that we need to begin imposing information upon matter (that is, to begin generating wealth) is given to us by our own Intelligent Designer so that we might practice intelligent design ourselves. It is precisely by this practice that we enrich both ourselves and our neighbours.

Intelligent Design Clarifies Private Property Boundaries

The third area where intelligent design theory greatly improves our understanding of property rights is in the discernment of property borders. In a previous chapter, we discussed the Lockean concept of "homesteading", which is when a person converts a natural resource into their own private property by being the first person to cultivate it. We also saw some biblical examples of this taking place with Abraham and Isaac. But this naturally raises a question: Where do we consider the borders of someone's homesteaded property to *end*? If a person steps into a vast wilderness and begins planting seeds for an orchard, where would we say the boundary of their property lies? Can they claim the whole vast wilderness as their own? Probably not. We would surely want to draw a line *somewhere* and say, "This part is no different to the state in which it was left by nature, so you cannot claim it as your own property." But if we took this too far, it would get ridiculous. Would we really want to say that the trees that grow in this orchard are the property of the homesteader, but the thinnest layer of dirt around the roots of the tree is *not* a part of their property? That would be quite impractical. Realistically, the orchard farmer needs to be able to regard some area of the ground around their trees as their own.

So, just how far should the boundary of the cultivator's property extend? How much land should they be able to claim from the base of their trees?

The first thing to note is that this decision would be made by a body of conventions determined in court cases, which then become part of the common law. But how would the court go about deciding on a reasonable boundary line for the orchard? Surely there will be some parts of the land that are essentially "the same" as they were before the orchard was there. For example, the person planting the seeds may try to leave three feet of space between each tree in the row, just to make sure that the ground is not overwhelmed. Should we consider those three feet of ground space to be "fair game" upon which someone can come and plant their own trees?

Through the lens of intelligent design, we could answer that even though that three feet of ground in between the trees is not particularly different than it was in its natural state, its state is now part of a larger scheme of *deliberate organisation*. That is, it has been left in its original state *on purpose*, not merely out of laziness or indifference. This was done so that the trees in the orchard might be positioned for optimal growth. Because it has been left in its state on purpose, in order to serve a larger project with specific goals and intentions, there is a real sense in which the orchard planter has homesteaded this ground and *chosen* to leave it as-is.

Operating on this principle, the courts would likely come up with some generally accepted, common-sense conventions about where property boundaries would be considered to end. For simplicity, perhaps they might adopt the convention that the homesteader could claim ownership to land within a set distance from the furthest clearly artificial element that they had built. Perhaps they would adopt slightly different conventions for land beside new trees (which are expected to grow and spread out roots) compared to new houses (which are not expected to grow or expand). Doubtless, some subtle edge-cases would crop up, but at least we can see what would be the rationale involved. It is possible to discern when resources have had a human intelligence applied to them. It is even possible to tell when the ground has been *explicitly* and *intentionally* left fallow and uncultivated.

If we extend this principle even further, it also explains how a privately owned nature reserve could exist. Suppose that we wanted to preserve the natural environment of a particular area with as little human influence as possible. Perhaps we want future generations to be able to see and appreciate the animals that are there and how they behave in their natural environment. If Lockean homesteading were the rule of society, we might struggle to come up with a reason why a person would not be allowed to come in, bulldoze the nature reserve, and turn it into parking lots and office blocks. However much we disliked it, we would still have to say that it was not "owned" by anyone since it was in a natural state and was therefore fair game.

However, if we can set up the nature reserve as an area which is clearly left in its natural state *on purpose*, then we would have reason to object to its being homesteaded by someone else. Suppose that we put clear markings around an area, then we added a few minimal hiking trails through it, then we add informational signs to help people understand what they are seeing as they walk through. Suppose we start charging admission to join a tour group that walks through the trails and observes the wilderness. It would be clear to anyone that this area had been sectioned off for this very purpose, that those who sectioned it off had deliberately foregone their clear opportunity to develop the land, and instead were choosing deliberately to *use* the marked out wilderness area for a particular purpose. In short, we would be able to detect the presence of *intelligent design* in setting up this nature reserve. Because of that insight, we would be justified in disallowing someone else from trying to homestead it. We could rightly say, "This area has already been homesteaded. Can you not see the deliberate intention behind its layout? It belongs to someone else."

Consider that large parks exist in the midst of major cities today, such as Central Park in New York City. You could point to a particular small area within Central Park and rightly say that it looks just the same as if nature had been left alone. There may be nothing in that small area but grass, rocks and trees. Yet the park as a whole is clearly there by design. The park has clearly been established *intentionally* to provide the pleasures of a natural setting in the midst of an otherwise bustling metropolis. This is enough for us to intuitively know that the area is not available for homesteading.

Intelligent design provides a rational basis for courts to hand down common-law rulings which accord with our intuitions about where property boundaries ought to be identified in a society that respects homesteading.

Property and Politics in Old Testament Israel

In the preceding chapters, we developed a theoretical framework for understanding economics and property rights. Having done that theoretical work, we now want to come back to the text of Scripture itself. We do this for two reasons. First, to let the word of God critique our reasoning. Second, to see where our theoretical work enables us to understand the things we find in Scripture more deeply. To that end, we are going to examine the economics and political philosophy given implicitly by God when He established the nation of Israel.

If we want to understand the laws and customs of Old Testament Israel, then we must start by understanding Israel's national identity. What does it mean to be an Israelite? In the Old Testament, and especially in the Mosaic law, there is one key event that Israel repeatedly looks back upon in order to understand who they are and where they have come from: the Exodus.

Israel is continuously reminded that the LORD is their God, who brought them up out of the land of Egypt. The national identity of Israel is that they are the people who *used to be slaves*. They are the people who were enslaved in Egypt until the LORD freed them from their bondage and brought them into the promised land of Canaan.

This national identity as former slaves comes up repeatedly in the Mosaic law. It appears, not just as a reminder of history but as a rationale for many of the laws which God will give to this new nation through Moses. When God gives them the commandment to rest on the Sabbath, He gives it in two forms with different rationales. Both rationales are true, but they emphasise different reasons as to why the Sabbath is important for Israel. In the Ten Commandments, God grounds the Sabbath in the pattern of His own work in creation:

> Remember the Sabbath day, to keep it holy. Six days you shall labour, and do all your work, but the seventh day is a Sabbath to the Lord your God. On it you shall not do any work, you, or your son, or your daughter, your male servant, or your female servant, or your livestock, or the sojourner who is within your gates. *For in six days the Lord made heaven and earth, the sea, and all that is in them, and rested the seventh day.* Therefore the Lord blessed the Sabbath day and made it holy.
>
> Exodus 20:8-11 (emphasis added)

But when Moses is preparing Israel to enter the promised land, he presents the Sabbath commandment differently. In that context, Moses presents the command to them by using their national identity:

> Observe the Sabbath day, to keep it holy, as the Lord your God commanded you. Six days you shall labour and do all your work, but the seventh day is a Sabbath to the Lord your God. On it you shall not do any work, you or your son or your daughter *or your male slave or your female slave,* or your ox or your donkey or any of your livestock, or the sojourner who is within your gates, *that your male slave and your female slave may rest as well as you. You shall remember that you were a slave in the land of Egypt,* and the Lord your God brought you out from there with a mighty hand and an outstretched arm. Therefore the Lord your God commanded you to keep the Sabbath day.
>
> Deuteronomy 5:12-15 (emphasis added)

Israel needs to know two things about the Sabbath commandment. First, they need to know that God himself took a Sabbath rest to survey the good work which he had done in creation. For that reason, they too are to take Sabbath rest. Second, they are not to deny the pleasure of Sabbath rest to their slaves. They are to remember their national identity. They know what it is like to be slaves under a harsh slave master. Their own ancestors were once slaves to Pharaoh, king of Egypt. They will not treat their own slaves like that. Their slaves will get to enjoy Sabbath rest, just like everyone else.

This national identity as former slaves is central to the Mosaic law. Israelite parents are instructed to point to that identity when their children ask them where their laws have come from:

> When your son asks you in time to come, 'What is the meaning of the testimonies and the statutes and the rules that the Lord our God has commanded you?' then you shall say to your son, 'We were Pharaoh's slaves in Egypt. And the Lord brought us out of Egypt with a mighty hand. And the Lord showed signs and wonders, great and grievous, against Egypt and against Pharaoh and all his household, before our eyes. And he brought us out from there, that he might

> bring us in and give us the land that he swore to give to our fathers. And the Lord commanded us to do all these statutes, to fear the Lord our God, for our good always, that he might preserve us alive, as we are this day. And it will be righteousness for us, if we are careful to do all this commandment before the Lord our God, as he has commanded us.'
>
> Deuteronomy 6:20-25

While the connection between the Mosaic law and the Israelites' identity as former slaves is clear, it does raise a tough question. If the former-slave identity is so clear in the Israelite psyche, why do they tolerate slavery in their society at all?

This is a good point to refresh our memory about the range of meaning for the term "slavery" in the Bible.

Israelite Slaves versus Foreign Slaves

The Mosaic law has many rules and regulations around the institution of slavery. As we saw in a previous chapter, Israelites were required to give shelter to someone who had become a slave by conquest but who had then escaped from their master (Deuteronomy 23:15-16). Conquest slavery was always condemned as a monstrous evil.

But the Mosaic law did not forbid slavery through *contract*. It was permissible for a person to sell their services as a slave in order to pay off a debt or for reasons of financial hardship. Interestingly, the Mosaic law put certain restrictions on this practice, again pointing back to Israel's national identity. Consider the following regulations from Leviticus:

> If your brother becomes poor beside you and sells himself to you, you shall not make him serve as a slave: he shall be with you as a hired servant and as a sojourner. He shall serve with you until the year of the jubilee. Then he shall go out from you, he and his children with him, and go back to his own clan and return to the possession of his fathers. For they are my slaves, whom I brought out of the land of Egypt; they shall not be sold as slaves. You shall not rule over him ruthlessly but shall fear your God.
>
> As for your male and female slaves whom you may have: you may buy male and

> female slaves from among the nations that are around you. You may also buy from among the strangers who sojourn with you and their clans that are with you, who have been born in your land, and they may be your property. You may bequeath them to your sons after you to inherit as a possession forever. You may make slaves of them, but over your brothers the people of Israel you shall not rule, one over another ruthlessly.
>
> Leviticus 25:39-46

A distinction is made in this passage between Israelites and foreigners. Israelites are permitted to take foreigners as "full" slaves, whereas they cannot fully exercise a master-slave relationship over a fellow Israelite. A fellow Israelite can only sell themselves into slavery temporarily. An Israelite must be released at the Year of Jubilee (verse 40), but a foreigner does not have to be released. The foreigner can remain a slave forever (verse 46). Why is this?

It may be tempting to jump to the conclusion that this ruling is a reflection of primitive tribalism. We may assume that the law of Moses is simply "racist", and a reflection of a harsh, unenlightened culture (Rothbard made this very mistake[55]). But this misses the rationale that is given in verse 42. God says that Israelites shall not be sold as slaves because "they are my slaves". God himself exercises the "property rights" over the Israelites, since it was God who redeemed them out of their slavery in Egypt. As the legitimate master, God allows the services of an Israelite in his possession to be "leased" for a limited time (until the Year of Jubilee). But the reason that lease must come to an end is because ownership of that Israelite's services must revert to the rightful possessor, which is God.

By contrast, foreigners are not God's slaves in the sense that the Israelites are. God does not assert the same claim of ownership over foreigners, and, for that reason, their services as contract slaves may be freely bought and sold.

This is also the reason why Israelites are to pay a temple tax to God. As we have observed all the way through the biblical record, taxation is an expression of slavery. God levies a census tax on the Israelites precisely *because* they are his slaves.

---

55 Rothbard, *Economic Thought before Adam Smith*, 43.

> The LORD spoke to Moses, saying, "When you take a census of the children of Israel, according to those who are numbered among them, then each man shall give a ransom for his soul to the LORD, when you number them; that there be no plague among them when you number them. They shall give this, everyone who passes over to those who are numbered, half a shekel after the shekel of the sanctuary; (the shekel is twenty gerahs;) half a shekel for an offering to the LORD.
>
> Exodus 30:11-13

This is the same half-shekel tax that Jesus claimed he was not obligated to pay in Matthew 17:26. Jesus said he was not obligated to pay because he is God's Son and is therefore *free* (i.e. not a slave) in his Father's house.

So we see that throughout the Mosaic law, the overarching master-slave relationship between God and the Israelites is the basis for many of their customs and practices. It is the basis for them paying temple taxes, and also the reason why there are limitations on Israelites rendering contract-slave services to one another.

Capital, Labour and Interest in Mosaic Law

Having dealt with the issue of contract slavery, we now come to the broader question of commerce and markets in the Mosaic law. I am going to make the bold claim that the system of commerce described by Moses is rightly described as free-market capitalism. In a previous chapter, I have already explained that the term "free market" does not mean "whatever currently happens in allegedly capitalist America". Quite the reverse in fact. The USA has all kinds of taxes and regulations interfering with their markets. The term "free market" means a market in which no threats of violence are used in the process of trade and production. In a free market, people are free to sell their labour for money, people have individual property rights over capital resources, and people are free to earn a market rate of interest on capital that they invest.

Wages and Time Preference

In Mosaic law, we find a distinction between slaves and "hired workers". That is to say, not everybody who worked for someone else was a "slave". Some people hired themselves out as workers in other people's fields. We see this with Boaz in the book of Ruth. Boaz has many hired workers to help harvest his fields, because the window of time to harvest is too short and the fields are too big such that he cannot do it all himself. There are so many people working in his fields that he does not even manage them all directly. Instead, Boaz appoints a foreman to be in charge of the reapers and keep track of things (Ruth 2:4-7). We also see that Boaz has his wealth increased at the end of the book, as he acquires new land through his marriage to Ruth (Ruth 4:9-10).

But the Mosaic law sees the potential for trouble in this situation. A worker does not own the field that they are working in, and so part of the harvest will go to the owner, rather than the worker who did the harvesting. Knowing this, why would a labourer choose to work in someone else's field, rather than in their own? Well, first, it may be that the worker does not have their own fields (especially if they are a sojourner, rather than a native Israelite). Or it may be that their fields have not yielded a substantial crop in that harvest year (perhaps due to some sort of weather event that has damaged them). For some reason, the worker has seen that working their own land (if they have it) will be less profitable than hiring themselves out to work on someone else's land. The implication is that the hired worker is generally going to be poorer than the employer. For this reason, the Mosaic law gives a solemn warning to employers.

> "You shall not oppress a hired servant who is poor and needy, whether he is one of your brothers or one of the sojourners who are in your land within your towns. You shall give him his wages on the same day, before the sun sets (for he is poor and counts on it), lest he cry against you to the Lord, and you be guilty of sin.
>
> Deuteronomy 24:14-15

Notice two things here. First, we have a demonstration that the Mosaic law recognises the economic concept of "time preference" as the basis for wage labour. A key reason that a person may hire themselves out as a labourer is because they have a high time preference. That is, they need the fruits of their labour to be paid to them immediately, rather than waiting until the harvest is completed and the crops have been sold in the marketplace. Because they are poor, they cannot wait for a lengthy production process to be completed before they get paid. But because the hired servant is not waiting as long to receive the fruits of his labour, it is natural that the employer, who does have to wait and does run the risk of a low crop yield, would get a larger share of the profits as compensation.

Second, we must note that the Mosaic law demands that employers must recognise the validity of that worker's time-preference claim. If they wish to hire workers and pay those workers an agreed wage, rather than a share in the harvest, then the employer must accept the condition that the employee's wages will be paid very promptly (even before the sun sets each day). The employee has agreed to the wage rate precisely *because* they want to benefit from getting their share of the profits sooner than the employer does. Therefore, if the employer does not pay them on time, the employer is effectively reneging on the contract.

Returns on Capital Investment

This brings us to the issue of the employer gaining interest on their capital resources. Conducting a biblical discussion of interest and money lending is a difficult task, largely because imprecise terminology clouds the issues. In particular, we are accustomed to using the term "interest" with a dual meaning. When we invest money in a stock market mutual fund, we may refer to the annual rate of return on our investment as "interest". But when we buy a flat-screen TV using a credit card, we may also refer to the extra percentage which we pay to the bank as "interest". In reality, these are quite different arrangements. The distinction was rightly pointed out by Martin Luther in his "Treatise on Usury" (though the treatise also contains some serious economic blunders). What Luther correctly notes is that debt and investment differ in the location of *risk*.

When we buy shares in the stock market, we are taking a risk. The return on our investment is not guaranteed in advance. The return may be large, it may be small, or it may even be negative. On the other hand, when the bank loans us money via a credit card to buy our TV, the bank is not taking a "risk" in quite the same sense. There is technically a risk that we, the debtor, will default on the loan. But even if that happens, the bank will then be able to pursue us for payment of the debt. The bank can have our belongings repossessed by debt collectors, and the bank will get first dibs on a portion of our estate in the event of our death. Essentially, their claim over interest payments from us is *unconditional*. If we get fired from our job or if our business has a bad year, the bank does not need to worry about getting a smaller return on the loan that they gave us. By contrast, if we buy shares in a company but the company makes no profit in a given year, we as shareholders are *not* entitled to dip into the employees' pockets in order to get our desired returns. So it is important to make a distinction between returns on an *investment* (where the person providing the capital assumes the risk) versus returns on a *loan* (where the person receiving the capital assumes the risk).

On the topic of returns on an *investment*, the testimony of Scripture is consistently positive. We saw in the book of Ruth that Boaz both employs workers and also accumulates new fields, and he is regarded as a righteous man. We see that the glorious wife of Proverbs 31 is known for making good investments (she "considers a field, and buys it", Proverbs 31:16). Proverbs expects that the normal pattern of life will be for wise people to accumulate enough wealth over their lifetime to leave an inheritance to their children's children (Proverbs 13:22). When Jesus tells the parable of the ten minas in Luke 19:11-27, the servant is instructed by his master to use his master's money to engage in business until the master returns. The servant is judged "faithful" because the results of his trading bring back a large return on investment for the master (Luke 19:17).

Wisely investing capital resources (in the hope of a positive return) is a good and godly part of life. Yes, we need to be on guard against the love of money lest we let wealth become an idol for us. But there is nothing inherently sinful about productively investing our capital for a return. Indeed, as Bastiat pointed out, it is a feature of God's design in creation that we should be able to arrange some leisure for ourselves by saving and investing.

Lending Money at Interest

Next we come to the issue of loans. Interest on a loan is a little more complicated than returns on an investment. To understand what Scripture says about interest on loans, we have to understand the categories that Scripture uses to speak about interest. In short, Scripture regards interest on a loan as simply another form of *contract* slavery. Interest is not *conquest* slavery, and so it is not inherently immoral and deplorable. Rather, it is a contract freely entered into by both parties. Nevertheless, Scripture uses the language of "slavery" to talk about interest on loans.

The clearest statement of this connection is found in Proverbs:

> The rich rules over the poor, the borrower is the slave of the lender.
>
> Proverbs 22:7

We also see how this plays out in the Mosaic law. Back in Deuteronomy, we see that God places limitations on interest-bearing loans precisely because they are a type of slavery contract.

> You shall not charge interest on loans to your brother, interest on money, interest on food, interest on anything that is lent for interest. *You may charge a foreigner interest*, but you may not charge your brother interest, that the Lord your God may bless you in all that you undertake in the land that you are entering to take possession of it.
>
> Deuteronomy 23:19-20 (emphasis added)

Again we see that the Mosaic law has a distinction made between the Israelite and the foreigner. It is acceptable to charge interest to foreigners, because it is acceptable to enter into contract-slavery arrangements. However, because Israelites are fundamentally the LORD's slaves, the LORD reserves the right to set limits on the slavery contracts into which they may enter. What we see here is that it is ideal for people not to enter into any kind of contract-slavery arrangement at all. However, if contract slavery is the choice which people freely choose to make among themselves, then it is deemed acceptable. It is even a sign of God's blessing upon Israel that they are in a position to lend in this way:

> The Lord will open to you his good treasury, the heavens, to give the rain to your land in its season and to bless all the work of your hands. *And you shall lend to many nations, but you shall not borrow.* And the Lord will make you the head and not the tail, and you shall only go up and not down, if you obey the commandments of the Lord your God, which I command you today, being careful to do them...
>
> Deuteronomy 28:12-13 (emphasis added)

So we see that God only forbids the lending of money at interest to Israelites, and this is done so that their relationship to God as their true Lord and Master will remain intact. This does not mean that God forbids *interest-free* lending among Israelites. On the contrary, this is positively encouraged. Interest-free loans, along with the Jubilee year, are seen as a key method by which wealthier Israelites can provide a form of "welfare" to poorer Israelites.

At the end of every seven years you shall grant a release. And this is the manner of the release: every creditor shall release what he has lent to his neighbour. He shall not exact it of his neighbour, his brother, because the Lord's release has been proclaimed. *Of a foreigner you may exact it*, but whatever of yours is with your brother your hand shall release...

If among you, one of your brothers should become poor, in any of your towns within your land that the Lord your God is giving you, you shall not harden your heart or shut your hand against your poor brother, but you shall open your hand to him and *lend him sufficient for his need, whatever it may be*. Take care lest there be an unworthy thought in your heart and you say, 'The seventh year, the year of release is near,' and your eye look grudgingly on your poor brother, and you give him nothing, and he cry to the Lord against you, and you be guilty of sin.

Deuteronomy 15:1-3... 7-9 (emphasis added)

What we see here is that the Mosaic law assumes that deriving interest from loans and having no time limit on exacting repayment is the natural state of affairs. That is what natural justice would yield in the marketplace. But God asks the Israelites, in light of God's authority over them as their master, to go beyond mere justice and to be generous to their poor neighbour. What form does that generosity take? It comes in the form of interest-free loans, with a condition that repayment will be waived if the borrower is unable to pay it back by the time of the Jubilee year.

This is the distinction to keep in mind. Mosaic law does not consider interest on a monetary loan to be unjust *in itself*, which is why it is perfectly permissible to charge interest to foreigners. But it does consider contract slavery to be an undesirable state of affairs for Israelites, who are meant to recognise themselves as being primarily slaves of God. Therefore, contract slavery is subject to limitations when Israelites are involved, to reflect their national identity as those whom God freed from slavery in Egypt. Charging interest on a loan is not seen as the lender abusing the borrower, for of course, the borrower enters into the arrangement voluntarily (there is no violent conquest by the lender). However, *foregoing* interest on the loan is seen as an act of generosity, and, as their rightful Master, God obliges the Israelites to practice that generosity towards their Israelite kinsmen.

Land Boundaries in Ancient Israel

As we examine the regulations around commerce in the Mosaic law, it is worth taking a moment to consider the issue of land titles. In a previous chapter, we developed the idea of acquiring private property rights to land through "homesteading". We also saw examples where the homesteading principle was recognised in Scripture, particularly in the lives of Abraham and Isaac. Astute readers may well be asking how this homesteading theory fits in with the land allocations of ancient Israel. After all, the Israelites did not come into the promised land and then begin homesteading different areas. Rather, the boundaries of their tribal territories were defined for them in advance by God through the casting of lots.

This process goes on for many chapters in Joshua, describing in detail which cities of the Canaanites would be inherited by each Israelite tribe. But Joshua briefly summarises the process at one point:

> There remained among the people of Israel seven tribes whose inheritance had not yet been apportioned. So Joshua said to the people of Israel, "How long will you put off going in to take possession of the land, which the Lord, the God of your fathers, has given you? Provide three men from each tribe, and I will send them out that they may set out and go up and down the land. They shall write a description of it with a view to their inheritances, and then come to me. They shall divide it into seven portions. Judah shall continue in his territory on the south, and the house of Joseph shall continue in their territory on the north. And you shall describe the land in seven divisions and bring the description here to me. And I will cast lots for you here before the Lord our God.
>
> Joshua 18:2-6

Why is this done? Why should the land be divided up by lot, rather than being given to whomever among the people of Israel would homestead it first? The reason is because the land is not *unowned* and therefore not available for homesteading at all. Rather, in the same way that

God regards Israel as properly his own "slaves" and therefore disallows them from entering into open-ended slavery contracts, God also regards the land of Canaan as properly *His* land. This has two important implications. First, the land is not available for homesteading. It is land that is already owned and is being bequeathed as an "inheritance".

Second, the land is not able to be sold in perpetuity. Each tribe of Israel has been given its inheritance only in a provisional sense. The Israelites remain God's slaves, and the land remains fundamentally God's property. God has not transferred "full" property rights over the land to Israel, but rather, he retains ultimate ownership over it as their Master and, importantly, as their King.

This is why the LORD commands that the land should be returned to the tribe that inherited it at the time of each Jubilee year. It is not because there is anything inherently wrong with permanently selling land which was previously homesteaded. It is because in the specific case of the promised land of Canaan, the right to re-adjust the land distribution ultimately remains with God. The Israelites do not properly "own" the land, but they are sojourners within territory that is owned by God.

> The land shall not be sold in perpetuity, for the land is mine. For you are strangers and sojourners with me. And in all the country you possess, you shall allow a redemption of the land.
>
> Leviticus 25:23-24

Rejection of Class Warfare Between Rich and Poor

A final important element of the Mosaic law's view of property rights is the total rejection of "class warfare" between rich and poor. We saw above that wealthier Israelites were called to show generosity to their neighbours who had become poor. This was to be done by offering interest-free loans and by yielding to the LORD's year of Jubilee. But there is no hint that wealth was to be constantly redistributed as a matter of justice.

If we want a model for market interactions that meet the standard of "justice" (as opposed to generosity), the model that we should look to is found in the guidelines given to Israel for dealing with foreigners. It is foreigners whom they deal with in a strictly market-driven fashion. By contrast, their fellow Israelites are to be dealt with under the shared status of being God's slaves.

Foreigners, to whom only the laws of natural justice apply, could be charged a market rate of interest on loans and could be held in contract slavery indefinitely.

There is no call in the Mosaic law for the wealth of the rich to be confiscated simply because they are rich. Rather, the initial common-law guidelines absolutely forbid any judicial prejudice on the basis of wealth or poverty.

> You shall not fall in with the many to do evil, nor shall you bear witness in a lawsuit, siding with the many, so as to pervert justice, nor shall you be partial to a poor man in his lawsuit.
>
> Exodus 23:2-3

Then, a few verses later:

> You shall not pervert the justice due to your poor in his lawsuit.
>
> Exodus 23:6

Two forms of prejudice are forbidden here. First, in verse 2, Israelites are forbidden to side with the majority simply because they are the majority. The rules of natural justice do not change by majority vote. No matter how many people want a person to be convicted and punished, that person must still be judged fairly. This rules out any notion that one group of people can invalidate the property rights of another simply by majority vote. Stealing is stealing, no matter how many people vote for it.

Second, in verses 3 and 6, we see that a person being poor must not affect the outcome of their lawsuit, in *either* direction. It is a sin to hold back justice from a poor person. If a poor and weak person sues a rich and powerful person, it is precisely the purpose of the court to step in and defend the rights of the poor person where they cannot defend themselves. That is justice. But, at the same time, if the court gives unfair and preferential treatment to a poor person, then the court is acting wickedly. A rich person is not to lose any of their rights simply because they are rich. If they are innocent of the charges for which they have been sued, then they must be acquitted. It is a wicked thing for a court to arbitrarily favour a poor plaintiff or to lay fines or punishments upon a rich person due to resentment or envy.

According to the Mosaic law, it is not a sin to be rich, and it is not a sin to be poor. Rich and poor were both to treat each other as neighbours with an equal right to justice. Neither envy nor snobbery should influence the outcome of the case.

A Justice System Without a King

We next move on to consider the justice system that Moses set up for Israel as they came into the promised land. For our purposes, what is most fascinating about this judicial system is that it *did not depend on a central government*. In a previous chapter, you will recall that we discussed how a society could function when police and judicial services were provided on the free market like anything else. Libertarian theorists like Murray Rothbard and Bob Murphy[56] have written at length about how such a competitive court system might operate. There are some clear differences between the type of arrangements envisioned by such theorists and the judicial system of pre-monarchical Israel. However, it must be admitted that there is also a striking degree of overlap.

Open Right to Enact Retribution

The first thing that needs to be realised about the judicial system given in the Mosaic law is that

---

56 Murphy, *Chaos Theory*, https://mises.org/library/chaos-theory

the right to enact retribution was open to all. There was no privileged class of people who alone had the right to use force and execute justice. In his Second Treatise on Government, Locke described what he called the "state of nature" for mankind. The "state of nature" is the state in which man finds himself simply as a result of the way that God has created him to be. In the state of nature, men are not distinguished from each other by rank, status, class or office. Each is equal as regards their natural rights because all share in the common nature of mankind. Because of this, Locke argued that the right to enforce the natural law was open to anyone and everyone[57]:

> ... so that the law of nature that aims at the peace and preservation of all mankind may be obeyed, the enforcement of that law of nature (in the state of nature) is in every man's hands, so that everyone has a right to punish law-breakers as severely as is needed to hinder the violation of the law. For the law of nature, like every law concerning men in this world, would be futile if no-one had power to enforce it and thereby preserve the innocent and restrain offenders. And in the state of

---

57 Locke, *Second Treatise on Government*, chapter 2.

> nature if anyone may punish someone for something bad that he has done, then everyone may do so.

To modern readers from a Protestant tradition who are used to regarding the State and its official magistrates as a necessary requirement for law and order, this view may seem quite extreme. Most of us have been taught that Romans 13:4 establishes the principle that only government officials have the right to execute justice (that is, to "bear the sword"). Having always been taught that the government alone should have the authority to punish law breakers, we are uncomfortable extending that authority to other people. We fear that such a view might plunge the world into chaos. Can a system ever work in which private individuals are able to take action against law breakers, rather than some sort of government-ordained hierarchy? Yes, absolutely. In fact, this system of private individuals having the right to execute justice is precisely what God first gave to Israel. This appears most clearly in the explicit provision for an "avenger" to take the life of a murderer, wherever the murderer is found.

You shall set apart three cities for yourselves in the land that the Lord your God is giving you to possess. You shall measure the distances and divide into three parts the area of the land that the Lord your God gives you as a possession, so that any manslayer can flee to them. "This is the provision for the manslayer, who by fleeing there may save his life. If anyone kills his neighbour unintentionally without having hated him in the past— as when someone goes into the forest with his neighbour to cut wood, and his hand swings the axe to cut down a tree, and the head slips from the handle and strikes his neighbour so that he dies—he may flee to one of these cities and live, lest the avenger of blood in hot anger pursue the manslayer and overtake him, because the way is long, and strike him fatally, though the man did not deserve to die, since he had not hated his neighbour in the past...

[at this point, provision is given for the addition of extra cities of refuge in the future]

> "But if anyone hates his neighbour and lies in wait for him and attacks him and strikes him fatally so that he dies, and he flees into one of these cities, then the elders of his city shall send and take him from there, and hand him over to the avenger of blood, so that he may die.
>
> Deuteronomy 19:2-6, 11-12

We see here a provision for dealing with judging between murder and manslaughter. God directs the Israelites to set apart three cities to be cities of refuge, spaced evenly throughout their territory.

It is assumed from the outset that if a murder is committed, someone (the "avenger of blood") will come to exact justice by taking the life of the murderer. This is simply a given from the outset. There is no mention of any kind of arrest by police or submission to a specific court system. It is simply recognised that the life of a murderer is forfeit and may be justly taken by anyone. This is in keeping with what God had pronounced to Noah back in Genesis:

> Whoever sheds the blood of man,
> by man shall his blood be shed,
> for God made man in his own image.
>
> Genesis 9:6

Many Protestant commentators have jumped to the hasty conclusion that this verse in Genesis is only intended to legitimise the execution of capital punishment by the State[58]. But the Mosaic law's concrete implementation of the Genesis command shows that this is incorrect. The State is not implicit in Genesis, but rather, the right to exact retribution is given to all of mankind.

Because of this recognition of the natural, God-given right of any man to exact justice on a murderer, the Mosaic law also makes provision for the case of manslaughter (with the example given of an accidental death while chopping wood in the forest). It is recognised that there is a risk that the avenger will act too hastily (that is, "in hot anger", verse 6) when a loved one has been killed. The provision given is that the person who has committed manslaughter may flee to a city of

---

58 Sarfati, The Genesis Account, 602.
Stott, *The Message of Romans*, 345.
Kuyper, *Lectures on Calvinism*, 80.

refuge where he will be protected from any would-be avenger until the case can be heard.

We then see that the elders of the city are to be called to judge the case. If it is determined to be a case of manslaughter, then the one who has fled is to be kept safe in the city of refuge (out of reach of the avenger). However, if the case is determined to be one of deliberate murder, then the elders of the city are commanded to hand the guilty party over to the avenger so that the avenger may carry out retribution. Notice, it is not the elders of the city who execute the murderer. Rather, they simply hand the murderer over to the avenger, who is recognised as having the right carry out justice.

Multiple Independent Judges

We note that there were multiple cities of refuge to which a manslayer could flee. The primary motivation for this seems to have been sheer distance (the cities had to be spaced out so that one was never too far out of reach). However, there was also the side effect that multiple cities of refuge were available, which each had different city elders. If a person found themselves needing to flee to a city of refuge, and especially if they were near halfway between two of them, they would have the option of fleeing to whichever they thought was most likely to judge their case favourably.

Outside of the case of murder and manslaughter, Israel lived under a system of independent judges. While Moses remained alive, there was initially a clear chain of command. God had put Moses forward as an authoritative prophet. When Moses delegated the authority to judge disputes to a group of subordinates, it was recognised that difficult disputes, which they were unable to resolve themselves, would be referred up the chain to Moses.

> The next day Moses sat to judge the people, and the people stood around Moses from morning till evening. When Moses' father-in-law saw all that he was doing for the people, he said, "What is this that you are doing for the people? Why do you sit alone, and all the people stand around you from morning till evening?" And Moses said to his father-in-law, "Because the people come to me to inquire of God; when they have a dispute, they come to me and I decide between one person and another, and I make them know the statutes of God and his laws." Moses' father-in-law said to him, "What

> you are doing is not good. You and the people with you will certainly wear yourselves out, for the thing is too heavy for you. You are not able to do it alone...
>
> So Moses listened to the voice of his father-in-law and did all that he had said. Moses chose able men out of all Israel and made them heads over the people, chiefs of thousands, of hundreds, of fifties, and of tens. And they judged the people at all times. Any hard case they brought to Moses, but any small matter they decided themselves.
>
> Exodus 18:13-18... 24-26

However, after the death of Moses, this hierarchical system did not remain in place. There was no successor to Moses, in the sense of someone who claimed that same prophetic right of final judgement.

In the period of the judges, it is not clear exactly how the judicial system played out. There do not appear to be any cases recorded where a plaintiff or defendant is dissatisfied with a ruling and makes an "appeal" to a different judge. For the most part, it seems that judges organically rose to a position of respect and esteem, such that their judgements were broadly considered sufficient for finalising a matter. This happened multiple times, after a rescuer rose up and liberated Israel from invading foreigners. The liberating leader then typically went on to function as a judge until their death. This was the case with Othniel, Ehud, Gideon, etc.

But there is also a distinct possibility that judges' tenure could overlap in time, and that disputes were able to be taken to whichever judge the parties deemed most appropriate. For example, we see that when Samuel judged Israel, he did so by travelling in a circuit between three major cities, where people could bring their disputes to him:

> Samuel judged Israel all the days of his life. And he went on a circuit year by year to Bethel, Gilgal, and Mizpah. And he judged Israel in all these places. Then he would return to Ramah, for his home was there, and there also he judged Israel. And he built there an altar to the Lord.
>
> 1 Samuel 7:15-17

Samuel is held up as an example of a good judge who consistently renders just verdicts when people come to him. By contrast, when Samuel grows old and appoints his sons to take over the role of judging, they are seen as bad judges, perverting the course of justice:

> When Samuel became old, he made his sons judges over Israel. The name of his firstborn son was Joel, and the name of his second, Abijah; they were judges in Beersheba. Yet his sons did not walk in his ways but turned aside after gain. They took bribes and perverted justice.
>
> 1 Samuel 8:1-3

Part of what is interesting about this story is the geography. There are three cities in Samuel's judging circuit (Bethel, Gilgal and Mizpah), plus his home town of Ramah. Those three cities form a cozy triangle at the northwestern corner of the Dead Sea, with Ramah sitting right in the middle. It seems that Samuel generally confined his judging activities to a small area of Israel (roughly a 10km radius). By contrast, Samuel's sons are judges in Beersheba, which is around 100km away. This may explain in large part why Samuel is not held accountable for the poor behaviour of his sons the way that his predecessor Eli was (1 Samuel 2:27-36). In contrast to Eli, Samuel was living far away and not geographically available to hold his sons accountable.

This also means that when the people were fed up with the poor behaviour of Samuel's sons as judges, they had the option of trekking up toward Ramah and appealing their plight to Samuel there (1 Samuel 8:4).

What we see here is not precisely the system of market-competitive judicial services envisioned in a Rothbardian "Free Society". But then again, it is not so far removed either. The tribes and towns of Israel were each meant to have their own separate judges (Deuteronomy 16:18-20). If a case arose in the towns that the local judges could not resolve, then they were to refer the matter to the Levitical priests and the judge at the temple for a final decision (Deuteronomy 17:8-13). It seems that the Levitical priests were expected to have the most thorough and nuanced training in the Mosaic law since it was they who had to approve the copy of the Mosaic law copied out by each new human king (Deuteronomy 17:18). This provision for appealing to the temple judge is the one that the Israelites were exercising when they came to Samuel to complain about his sons (Samuel being a non-Levite judge who nevertheless served before the LORD at Shiloh[59]). Holding the Levitical priests and temple judge as the final court of appeal was not optional. Actively disobeying their final ruling carried the death penalty (Deuteronomy 17:12). To that extent, the final court of appeal was centralised (although it was still a joint decision among the Levitical priests and the temple judge, not a single dictator's rule).

Nevertheless, the overall legal system of Israel remained markedly *decentralised*. There was no central legislature that could simply decree new laws by fiat (as kings would often do). The law of the land was *only* the body of case law derived from the civil code given to Moses. Judges in each town were to interpret the Mosaic law, and there is no particular indication that they were compelled to synchronise the different case law rulings between towns.

Any Christian who claims that society cannot function without a State apparatus has to contend with the *distributed and non-taxing* legal system that prevailed in pre-monarchical Israel.

---

59 1 Samuel 1:24-28.

Was Pre-Monarchical Israel "Minarchist" or "Anarchist"?

Minarchism typically means the position that a "minimal" State is required for the provision of judicial services, security and national defence. Many libertarian and classical-liberal thinkers are rightly described as "minarchists", including Frederic Bastiat and Ludwig von Mises. In my own intellectual journey, I went through a brief phase where I considered myself a minarchist, though reading Rothbard pushed me to see that anarchism was ultimately the more consistent position.

Israel did have an apparent monopoly on the court of final appeals, that being the decision of the Levitical priests and the judge at the temple. Because of this, it could reasonably be argued that Israel in the period of the judges was actually a "minarchist" society, rather than an "anarchist" society. But if Israel was a minarchist society, then it was an *extreme* form of minarchism, much more extreme than that usually proposed by self-described minarchists. Israel's society may have had a monopoly on the final court of appeals, but there was not a monopoly among the lower-tier courts, and they had no monopoly on security or national defence. For such a radically decentralised society, "anarchy" seems to be the more natural description.

Common Law as a Pragmatic Approximation of Natural Law

As these judges roamed around Israel adjudicating disputes, what was the basis for their judgements? When two people came to a judge with a conflict and asked the judge to render a verdict, how did the judge decide what to do? Clearly, their starting point would be to look back at the laws given to Israel by God through Moses.

The Reformed tradition has historically recognised a division of the Mosaic law into three components: moral, ceremonial and civil. The moral component includes those precepts of God which are timeless and universal, such as the prohibition on murder. The ceremonial component includes those elements that were specifically concerned with the worship rituals of Judaism prior to their fulfilment in the person of Christ (such as the method by which a priest was to slaughter a lamb on the day of atonement). The remaining component, the civil law, is concerned with the specific legal rulings that would be used for ordering society in ancient Israel. When we ask how the judges were to make use of the Mosaic law, the component that concerns us is obviously the civil component.

But that raises a difficulty. It is plain to anyone who sits down and reads the Mosaic law that it is far from being a comprehensive legal framework. The Mosaic law is not a systematic treatise on ethics. It does not start with foundational principles and then logically derive rulings about particular cases. It contains rules about some incredibly obscure situations that would almost never be expected to arise. It also lacks rulings on some seemingly common events. How then were the judges supposed to keep everything straight?

Well, obviously if a case was clearly spelled out in the Mosaic law, then the judge could point to that passage and be done with it. However, if the case was that simple, the two people would hardly have bothered to bring it to the judge in the first place. If all that was required was to consult the Mosaic law directly, then people could do that for themselves or with the help of the elders in their town. Evidently, the point of the judges was that they would attempt to render a just verdict in cases which were *not* spelled out explicitly in the Mosaic law.

I submit that the civil laws outlined in the books of Moses are best understood as a foundational set of case law precedents intended to "jump-start" a system of common law in Israel. The reason that the civil law did not need to be systematic or exhaustive is that judges were primarily expected to recognise and implement *natural* law. Simply by being made in God's image with a rational mind and a conscience, the people were expected to know right from wrong in basic cases. It is only in the fine details of difficult cases that case law becomes a necessary guide. For example, if one man were to steal an animal from another, two consequences are simple and clear. First, the thief should be compelled to make restitution of the animal that was taken. Second, he should be forced to compensate the victim for the lost productivity which that animal *would have* given him. If an ox was stolen and slaughtered, then yes, of course the thief owes the victim at least one ox. But if the victim had not lost their ox, they may have used it to produce milk, to breed more oxen for their herd, to plough a field, and so on. What compensation should be given to cover those factors, since they are hypothetical and cannot be directly measured?

The Mosaic law provides specific case law to answer this question:

> If a man steals an ox or a sheep, and kills it or sells it, he shall repay five oxen for an ox, and four sheep for a sheep.
>
> Exodus 22:1

Now, not all oxen are created equal. A strong ox may have been able to plough a field in one day, but a weaker ox may have needed two days. The parties involved could argue to the judge for hours on end about the precise amount of restitution that should be due for that particular stolen ox. But it would be difficult for a judge to rightly understand every nuance of every case. In the interest of practicality, it is simpler to just assign rule-of-thumb values to different types of animals and leave it at that. Some oxen will be more productive than the five that are repaid, others will be less. The point is that five is not an unreasonable figure for damages, and by codifying this ratio ahead of time, there is less potential for bias and inconsistency on the part of the judge.

Over time, as more cases were brought to the judges, a body of further case law would develop. The case law given by Moses mentions oxen and sheep. But what about chickens? If a chicken was stolen, how many should be repaid? The judge would be expected to recognise, by use of his rational faculties, that there was an analogy between a stolen chicken and a stolen ox or sheep. He would also be expected to recognise that different classes of animals were more productive than others. On this basis, he would make a ruling which seems to match the overall precedent of sheep and oxen. He might determine that a chicken was a productive animal to own but was generally a less productive animal than a sheep, and would extend the Mosaic precedent by ruling that the stolen chicken must be replaced by only *three* new chickens.

In this way, the common law would gradually be refined as new cases arose and precedents were added. But at all times, the goal would be for the concrete applications of civil law to be a best-effort approximation of the natural laws that could be recognised in God's creation by use of the rational mind.

The Transition to Monarchy

This all brings us to the question of Israel's monarchy. If Israel after Moses was some kind of libertarian paradise where judges simply competed to give the fairest possible rulings on disputes, then why did Israel end up with a king? Indeed, how does Jesus fit into all of this? Jesus is supposed to be the ultimate King of the Jews. If kings are so bad, how can that possibly be squared with all of the good things that Scripture says about some of Israel's kings?

These are all fair questions. On the face of it, the Bible may appear to be very pro-monarchy. King David is certainly held up as a positive figure in the Bible, even as a servant of God. So how could we possibly say that a biblical view of politics would push us towards having *no* government at all? To understand where the Bible sits on the whole question of government, we need to go back and examine the roots of Israel's monarchy in detail.

Why Did the Monarchy Arise?

The first question is, Why did the monarchy arise in the first place? As we noted above, Israel lasted for several centuries after Moses without having any king. How would a society that had established itself in that manner then transition to embracing a monarchy?

The first point to understand is that the pre-monarchical period of Israel was *not* all rainbows and sunshine. Many horrific things happened during the period of the judges. As the book of Judges draws to a close, we see an incident in which the men of Israel are involved in a large scale gang rape (Judges 19:22-26). The description of the scene repeatedly echoes the language of Genesis, in which the men of Sodom attempted this same crime but were obliterated by the fire of God's wrath from heaven (Genesis 19). It is clear that towards the end of this period, Israel had become just as wicked as the nations which they were intended to displace, if not more so.

The book of Judges ends with these scathing words:

> In those days there was no king in Israel. Everyone did what was right in his own eyes.
>
> Judges 22:25

Now, it would be easy to conclude from this statement that the Bible was identifying a lack of a king as the root cause of Israel's problems. If only they would leave behind this terrible *anarchy* and install a king who would prevent this sort of behaviour, perhaps then everything would be fine? That is one explanation.

However, on reflection, I do not believe that such an explanation makes sense. Two questions make this interpretation of the text in Judges very difficult.

First, if the answer were this simple, then why would God have not set up the monarchy explicitly from Israel's beginning as a nation? Why did God allow Israel to live for centuries with no king if having a king was critical to their moral flourishing?

Second, if the reason that Israel should install a monarchy into their society is to restrain such wicked behaviour, then why is the issue of their wicked behaviour not discussed at all when the origins of the monarchy are recorded in 1 Samuel 8?

These questions push us to find an alternate explanation for the introduction of a monarchy into Israelite society. To find that explanation, we must examine the issues that led to the institution of Israel's monarchy in the first place. The monarchy actually arose due to a perceived deficiency in the system of judges:

> When Samuel became old, he made his sons judges over Israel. The name of his firstborn son was Joel, and the name of his second, Abijah; they were judges in Beersheba. Yet his sons did not walk in his ways but turned aside after gain. *They took bribes and perverted justice.*
>
> Then all the elders of Israel gathered together and came to Samuel at Ramah and said to him, "Behold, you are old and your sons do not walk in your ways. Now appoint for us *a king to judge us* like all the nations."

> 1 Samuel 8:1-5 (emphasis added)

1 Samuel 8 records that the people of Israel come to Samuel and ask for a king, explicitly so that the king might take over the role of *judging* the people. Israel already has "judges". So what is the difference between a judge and a king? We have already seen that the office of "judge" could run in families (for example, Samuel appointed his sons to be judges), so the distinction is not merely a matter of succession. Kings and judges also appear to perform the same essential functions in the society. The king adjudicates legal disputes, and the king leads the people out to battle against their enemies (1 Samuel 8:20). All the way through the book of Judges, these are precisely the activities that the judges engage in. They lead the people in battle, liberate them from the surrounding nations, and judge disputes. The critical distinction between judges and kings is this: the judges did not have the power to *tax* anyone. This distinction is made explicit with Gideon. After Gideon completes a military victory, the people try to persuade him to install himself as king:

> Then the men of Israel said to Gideon, "Rule over us, you and your son and your grandson also, for you have saved us from the hand of Midian." Gideon said to them, "I will not rule over you, and my son will not rule over you; the Lord will rule over you." And Gideon said to them, "Let me make a request of you: every one of you give me the earrings from his spoil." (For they had golden earrings, because they were Ishmaelites.) And they answered, "We will willingly give them." And they spread a cloak, and every man threw in it the earrings of his spoil.
>
> Judges 8:22-25

In this passage, Gideon refuses to "rule" over the people. This does not mean that he refuses to lead them into battle. It does not mean that he refuses to adjudicate their disputes. But he does refuse to *take their property without their consent*. He will only accept spoil from them if it is willingly given.

Why is this important? It is important because it illuminates for us what is really being said at the beginning of 1 Samuel 8. What is the event that prompts Israel to ask for a king? It is Samuel's sons, the bad judges, being tempted to take bribes. The fundamental reason why Israel asks for a king is that they are seeking to solve the problem of *judicial bribery*. So how does a monarchy solve that problem? Well, since a king has the power to tax the people, bribery becomes a non-issue. If the king can simply command the people to give him money, what benefit would he get from being offered a bribe? Whatever bribe was offered to him, he could equally demand that same amount in taxes. It must have seemed like a foolproof scheme.

But of course, Samuel sees the gigantic flaw in this plan. If Israel places a king over themselves with the power to tax, then in practice they will once again become slaves.

> So Samuel told all the words of the Lord to the people who were asking for a king from him. He said, "These will be the ways of the king who will reign over you: he will take your sons and appoint them to his chariots and to be his horsemen and to run before his chariots. And he will appoint for himself commanders of thousands and commanders of fifties, and some to plough his ground and to reap his harvest, and to make his implements of

> war and the equipment of his chariots. He will take your daughters to be perfumers and cooks and bakers. He will take the best of your fields and vineyards and olive orchards and give them to his servants. He will take the tenth of your grain and of your vineyards and give it to his officers and to his servants. He will take your male servants and female servants and the best of your young men and your donkeys, and put them to his work. *He will take the tenth of your flocks, and you shall be his slaves.* And in that day you will cry out because of your king, whom you have chosen for yourselves, but *the Lord will not answer you in that day.*"
>
> 1 Samuel 8:10-18 (emphasis added)

In spite of this warning, the people were adamant. They demanded a human king with the power to tax. They felt that this particular contract-slavery arrangement was a worthwhile price to pay to solve the judicial-bribery problem. After all, the other nations around them all had kings, and those nations seemed to be functioning well enough.

> But the people refused to obey the voice of Samuel. And they said, "No! But there shall be a king over us, that we also may be like all the nations, and that our king may judge us and go out before us and fight our battles."
>
> 1 Samuel 8:19-20

We see then that the institution of a monarchy was an attempt to prevent judicial bribery in Israel by introducing a monopoly of judicial services funded by tax slavery.

The Legal Basis for Israel's Monarchy

This raises another important question about Israel's monarchy. If the monarchy was explicitly seen, in advance, to be a form of slavery, then exactly what type of slavery was it? We saw in an earlier chapter that Scripture uses the language of "slavery" to refer to a variety of different arrangements. Some of those arrangements involve force and conquest and are rejected by Scripture as being totally immoral. Others are contractual arrangements, which are regarded as permissible though typically undesirable. So then, in which sense are we to understand the "slavery" of Israel's monarchy?

The first thing which I think we need to admit is that Israel's monarchy is not brought about by conquest. The people *voluntarily* band together and ask persistently that a king should be appointed over them (1 Samuel 8:19). Whatever else we may say, we must say that Israel's monarchy is some type of *contractual* slavery arrangement, and to that extent it is morally permissible.

But what are the terms of the contract? At no point in Scripture is the legal basis for Israel's monarchy laid out systematically. The theoretical framework for a monarchy is largely assumed knowledge. However, we can infer a lot of detail by carefully examining the text.

I will contend that the fundamental basis on which Israel's monarchy presumes to levy taxes is that the monarchy was understood as owning a property title to the *produce of the land*. The monarchy arrangement was not one made individually with each person alive in Israel at the time. It was a transfer of property title for the fruits produced by the land. I will give three core arguments for understanding the monarchy this way.

First Argument: The Human Monarchy is Derived from God's Kingship

First, the kingship of Israel's human king is explicitly understood to be a substitute for the kingship of God. When Israel asks Samuel for a king, this is understood to be a rejection of God's kingship over the people.

> But the thing displeased Samuel when they said, "Give us a king to judge us." And Samuel prayed to the LORD. And the LORD said to Samuel, "Obey the voice of the people in all that they say to you, for they have not rejected you, but *they have rejected me from being king over them.*"
>
> 1 Samuel 8:6-7 (emphasis added)

Israel is asking for a human king to judge them and to go out and fight their battles. The basis of Israelite society up until this point has been that God would do these things for them. When they sinned and were given into the hands of a neighbouring nation, they would pray to God and God would rescue them. It is God who judges their disputes by providing them with the Mosaic law and by raising up prophets, priests and judges among them. It is also God who fights for them. In the chapter immediately preceding Israel's request for a monarchy, we see God fighting *directly* against the Philistines (not through any human agent):

> As Samuel was offering up the burnt offering, the Philistines drew near to attack Israel. But the LORD thundered with a mighty sound that day against the Philistines and threw them into confusion, and they were routed before Israel.
>
> 1 Samuel 7:10

So we see that by asking for a human king, Israel is asking for a human to take over this role which had previously been held by the LORD God. When things were bad, they were supposed to come to God in prayer, trusting in Him to deliver them. But now they were asking to put their faith in one of their own.

This clear connection between the human monarchy and God's kingship is important for our argument because one aspect of God's kingship over Israel is that God *owns* all the land:

> The land shall not be sold in perpetuity, for the land is mine. For you are strangers and sojourners with me.
>
> Leviticus 25:23

On that basis, it is reasonable to conclude that the human monarchy, which is in some sense a substitute for God's kingship, would also include some kind of title to the land. This connection also explains the pre-arranged caveats of human monarchy outlined in the Mosaic law. While Israel lived with no monarchy for the first few centuries after coming into the promised land, the Mosaic law had always contained provisions for a monarchy in the event that one was ever established. These pre-existing boundaries on the monarchy give strong support to the idea that the monarchy was a *contractual* form of slavery rather than a *conquest*. Because God is the true King and Master of Israel, He reserves the right to set limitations on the powers of any human monarchy which may be established:

> "When you come to the land that the Lord your God is giving you, and you possess it and dwell in it and then say, 'I will set a

king over me, like all the nations that are around me,' you may indeed set a king over you whom the Lord your God will choose. One from among your brothers you shall set as king over you. You may not put a foreigner over you, who is not your brother. Only he must not acquire many horses for himself or cause the people to return to Egypt in order to acquire many horses, since the Lord has said to you, 'You shall never return that way again.' And he shall not acquire many wives for himself, lest his heart turn away, nor shall he acquire for himself excessive silver and gold.

"And when he sits on the throne of his kingdom, he shall write for himself in a book a copy of this law, approved by the Levitical priests. And it shall be with him, and he shall read in it all the days of his life, that he may learn to fear the Lord his God by keeping all the words of this law and these statutes, and doing them, that his heart may not be lifted up above his brothers, and that he may not turn aside from the commandment, either to the right hand or to the left, so that he may

> continue long in his kingdom, he and his children, in Israel.
>
> Deuteronomy 17:14-20

By these instructions, it is clear that God retains His ultimate rule over Israel when they appoint a king. The human king is still subject to God, still commanded to live and rule by the Mosaic law. For this reason, the claim of the human king over the land was not absolute. God had established property boundaries for the inheritance of the tribes of Israel, and those boundaries remained intact. It was not within the king's power to simply take sole ownership of the land itself. This is seen clearly by the example of king Ahab and the vineyard of Naboth:

> Now Naboth the Jezreelite had a vineyard in Jezreel, beside the palace of Ahab king of Samaria. And after this Ahab said to Naboth, "Give me your vineyard, that I may have it for a vegetable garden, because it is near my house, and I will give you a better vineyard for it; or, if it seems good to you, I will give you its value in money." But Naboth said to Ahab, "The

> Lord forbid that I should give you the inheritance of my fathers."
>
> 1 Kings 21:1-3

So when we say that the monarchy in Israel derived its ability to tax the people from a title to the land, we do *not* mean a full and absolute title. What we mean is a limited title to the *produce* of the land. This is why God warns them that the best of their crops will be taken (1 Samuel 8:14-17). It is also worth noting that there is precedent in the Mosaic law for a transfer of property title only to the produce of the land without a transfer of title to the land itself:

> "In this year of jubilee each of you shall return to his property. And if you make a sale to your neighbour or buy from your neighbour, you shall not wrong one another. You shall pay your neighbour according to the number of years after the jubilee, and he shall sell to you according to the number of years for crops. If the years are many, you shall increase the price, and if the years are few, you shall reduce the price, *for it is the number of the*

> *crops that he is selling to you.* You shall not wrong one another, but you shall fear your God, for I am the LORD your God.
>
> Leviticus 25:13-17 (emphasis added)

Second Argument: Precedent from Israel's History in Egypt

The second argument for this land-yield theory of the monarchy is that it has precedent in Israel's history in Egypt. Joseph first rose to power in Egypt by interpreting a dream that came to Pharaoh. The dream foretold seven years of great abundance, followed by seven years of famine. Joseph advised Pharaoh to diligently store up grain during the abundant years in order to get them through the years of famine.

Pharaoh put this strategy into practice. When the years of famine arrived, people came from all over Egypt (and beyond) to buy grain from Pharaoh's storehouses. First people bought grain with their money. When their money ran out, they traded their livestock for grain. When they even ran out of livestock to trade, they ultimately came to Joseph and offered to enter into a slavery contract in exchange for being provided with food. What is most interesting about this slavery contract is that it explicitly involves giving Pharaoh the title over their land. It is because Pharaoh owns their land that they function as his slaves and give him a portion of their produce each harvest.

> And when that year was ended, they came to him the following year and said to him, "We will not hide from my lord that our money is all spent. The herds of livestock are my lord's. There is nothing left in the sight of my lord but our bodies and our land. Why should we die before your eyes, both we and our land? Buy us and our land for food, and we with our land will be slaves [עבדים, ebedim] to Pharaoh. And give us seed that we may live and not die, and that the land may not be desolate."
>
> So Joseph bought all the land of Egypt for Pharaoh, for all the Egyptians sold their fields, because the famine was severe on them. The land became Pharaoh's. As for the people, he made slaves of them from one end of Egypt to the other. Only the land of the priests he did not buy, for the priests had a fixed allowance from Pharaoh and lived on the allowance that

> Pharaoh gave them; therefore they did not sell their land.
>
> Then Joseph said to the people, "Behold, I have this day bought you and your land for Pharaoh. Now here is seed for you, and you shall sow the land. And at the harvests you shall give a fifth to Pharaoh, and four fifths shall be your own, as seed for the field and as food for yourselves and your households, and as food for your little ones."
>
> Genesis 47:18-24

We see that Israel's history in Genesis contains a precedent for this idea of a king owning the land of the nation. We also see that the language of "slavery" is applied to those who work the land and give the king a portion of their produce each year.

Third Argument: Resolving the Multi-Generational Nature of the Contract

Third and finally, this land-yield theory resolves the difficulty of the slavery contract extending across multiple generations. Readers who are already familiar with the history of libertarian thought are likely aware of Lysander Spooner's works denouncing slavery in the United States. Spooner argued forcefully that, even if it were somehow possible to justify the enslavement of one person, by natural law that person's children would still be born free[60]. How then could the slavery contract of Israel's monarchy come to apply to the *descendants* of the generation that first requested the monarchy? How could people born five generations after the monarchy was instituted still be subject to the monarchy's taxes? Would not those people be born free? After all, they were not the ones who actually created the contract. But of course, this objection evaporates if the basis for the monarchy's taxes is not that the king owns the people *per se*, but that the king owns some title to the produce of the land. As even Rothbard acknowledged, if the State actually did *own* the land area over which it asserts its authority, then there would be a legitimate basis for the levying of taxes upon that land[61]. The situation is not that later generations of Israelites were born into direct slavery to the monarchy. Rather, they are born onto land for which the monarchy already holds a title to the agricultural yield.

---

60 Spooner, *The Unconstitutionality of Slavery*, Chapter XIII.
61 Rothbard, *Ethics of Liberty*, 172.

Are Modern Taxes Justified by Ancient Contracts?

Before we go on to examine the theological implications of Israel's monarchy, there is a practical question that we should consider. I have argued above that Israel's monarchy was legitimately able to levy taxes upon the nation of Israel because the king held a property title to the produce of the nation's land. The transfer of this property title to the monarchy arose through a voluntary contract with the people of that day, such that the king's taxes on Israel were a particular form of contract slavery. You will also recall that the central contention of this book is that *all* taxation is a form of slavery.

The obvious question that arises is, What about our modern taxes? What form of slavery are those? Are the taxes that we pay today a form of *conquest* slavery, and therefore inherently immoral and unjust? Or is it possible that our present tax systems are ultimately derived from voluntary contracts, and therefore potentially justifiable? Could the taxes that we pay today be justified by some historic arrangement, similar to the taxes in ancient Israel?

The answer to this question must come in two parts. First, we must examine the historical facts of the matter to see whether there is any potential that our present taxes had a contractual origin. Second, if it came to pass that there was a historic justification for our present taxes, we must consider the ethical implications that would result.

As to the matter of history, it should be plain to anyone who gives it a few minutes thought that the number of cases where a government or a monarch has held a just and genuine property title to the land that they ruled is vanishingly small. The government of your country *almost certainly* has no historical grounds for claiming that their tax system is contractual and legitimate. I will run through a few examples, just to demonstrate the point.

I myself live in Australia. The government that taxes us is the one set up by British settlers and invaders. The first fleet of British settlers and invaders came in 1788 and federated the separate states into a single nation in 1901. I have used the phrase "settlers and invaders" deliberately. Both are accurate. Some of the British who came here absolutely were invaders. The invaders marched onto land that was already being used and occupied by Australian Aboriginals and used violence to take over that land. There is no justification for that. Other British people who came were legitimate settlers. They settled on land which was not being used or occupied by anyone.

No violence was required in order for them to homestead that land and to take legitimate possession of it.

One of the central difficulties of our history is that the distinction between those who *settled* unowned land and those who *invaded* previously owned land is not drawn. All of those who came from Britain to this island during that period are lumped together. But, in any case, there was no point at which anyone, whether British or Aboriginal, entered into a contract with the British monarchy to give over title of the land which they had homesteaded. The property title to each parcel of land in Australia rightly belongs to whomever first cultivated it, whether they were Aboriginal, British or any other ethnicity (and of course, that title then passed to whomever the first owner chose to sell it or bequeath it). Therefore, all taxes levied upon residents of Australia by the British monarchy and its representatives in the Australian parliament are *illegitimate.* Those taxes constitute an act of conquest slavery.

Similar stories could be told about the USA. The parcels of land there are owned by whomever settled them first, regardless of ethnicity, and then ownership passed to whomever the first owners sold or bequeathed it. Once again, at no point in history was a contract created by which any of those landowners signed over their titles either to the British crown or to any branch of the U.S. government.

What about Britain itself? Could the monarchy there have originated with a lord who actually owned the lands of a great estate and who eventually came to own all the land of what is now called the "United Kingdom"? Well, in short, no. The modern monarchy in Britain can be traced back to William the Conqueror who took over the kingdom by force in the year 1066. Several rebellions followed, but William quashed them and doled out parcels of land to his supporters in exchange for their loyalty. The land area of Britain has been for centuries in the hands of people who do not hold a just title to it. To the extent that their title is passed down from William the Conqueror, it is an unjust title resulting from conquest and does not deserve to be respected.

Very well then. As a matter of history, it is simply a fact that our modern States have typically been installed through conquest rather than by any voluntary arrangements. The taxes they levy are arbitrary, not based on any legitimate property title, and constitute a sinful act of conquest slavery.

But suppose that this was not the case? Suppose that you, dear reader, found yourself dwelling in a nation where there *is* good reason to believe that the taxing State has a historic basis for claiming legitimate ownership of the whole land area. Or, suppose that you have read my historical claims about the three nations above and have concluded that I am simply mistaken in the details? If, for whatever reason, we came to conclude that the people who tax us really did have a *legitimate* title to the land that we live on, what would happen then?

Well, on the one hand, if it could be clearly demonstrated that a just property title to the land was indeed held by the taxing State, then yes, we would have to say that such a hypothetical government would have the right to levy taxes on the people who presumed to live there. This was the case in ancient Israel, and it would remain the case today if the legitimate property title could be demonstrated.

However, even if it were the case that the State held a legitimate property title to the land in this way, it would not mean that they were *obliged* to levy taxes on the people. Indeed, we have argued above that the world created by God works best when people operate in economic harmony. The more free the people, the more prosperous they are able to be. For that reason, it is both permissible and *deeply wise* for any ruler who currently asserts the ability to tax a whole nation to *unilaterally* repeal their taxes and allow their people to be free. There is not one ethical or Scriptural objection that could be raised against this course of action. Recall that even though Philemon had a legitimate, contractual claim to Onesimus' services as a slave, Philemon was under no obligation to exercise that claim. He could voluntarily set Onesimus free at any time, and that is exactly what Paul requested that he should do (Philemon 1:14).

This last point is critically important, because it gives us a practical answer to the problem of historic ambiguity. Suppose that, after a diligent historical enquiry, it was simply unclear to us whether or not the British monarchy had any rightful claim to the land title of Britain. Perhaps the records that we have of William's conquest are called into question or are simply too vague for us to know with certainty whether he was the aggressor or was defending a legitimate claim? It simply does not matter. Whether or not the House of Windsor currently has a legitimate claim to tax the United Kingdom, their wisest course of action would *still* be to free the people with all haste. If their title is illegitimate, then they should immediately repent of their conquest enslavement of the British people and repeal 100% of their taxes this very hour. But even if their title to the nation's land is legitimate, then wisdom would still implore them to exercise generosity, end the contract slavery of the British people, and therefore to abolish their taxes just the same.

The Gospel Implications of Israel's Monarchy

With that practical consideration out of the way, let us finish our consideration of Israel's political structure by considering what its monarchy means at a deeper level. How does our new, enriched understanding of the monarchy point us towards the gospel of Jesus Christ?

Is Monarchy Preferable to Anarchy?

The first question we must ask is, What lessons can Israel's political history teach us about the relationship between God and man? We have seen that ancient Israelite society went through two major phases before ultimately going into exile. In the first stage, they had no human king and lived in a state that therefore could reasonably be called "anarchy". It was a capitalist society which respected property rights and saw income derived from capital investment as fully legitimate. To that extent, pre-monarchical Israel could even be called an "anarcho-capitalist" society of sorts.

In the second stage, Israel had a human monarchy. There was a hereditary line of kings who exacted taxes from the people, led them into battle with foreign invaders, and ruled over them in judgement.

Of these two arrangements, which one does Scripture hold up as preferable?

On the one hand, we saw above that the testimony of Scripture about the "anarchic" period of the judges was often negative. There was plenty of sin, violence, idolatry and disobedience. But it is also true that there were sustained periods of peace. After Israel cried out to God and God raised up a deliverer, then Israel would get along quite well for a period of time. The anarchic period was a very mixed bag. What then of the monarchic period?

The monarchic period definitely had some high points. There are certainly kings of Israel who, despite some very significant shortcomings, are held up overall as examples of virtue. Among them are David, Solomon, Hezekiah and Josiah. But there are also terrible kings who arise within this royal line. Some noteworthy examples are Jeroboam, Omri and Ahab, who each led Israel into gross idolatry. The monarchy, as it turned out, was no guarantee of virtue. Israel was still subject to internal civil wars and was still a home to idolatry and violence under the monarchy, just as it had been in the days of the judges.

Furthermore, recall that God had said through Samuel that the king would tax the people until they cried out because of their oppression, but the LORD would not answer them (1 Samuel 8:18). This is precisely what happened within only a couple of generations. Solomon laid very heavy taxes on the people to fund his various building projects, including a fancy new palace that took 13 years to build (1 Kings 7:1) and a whole lot of vanity projects (Ecclesiastes 2:1-11).

When Solomon died, his son Rehoboam took the throne, and his subjects came to him, begging him to lighten the tax burden which was laid upon them by Solomon:

> ... The assembly of Israel came and said to Rehoboam, "Your father made our yoke heavy. Now therefore lighten the hard service of your father and his heavy yoke on us, and we will serve you."
>
> 1 Kings 12:3-4

Rehoboam consults with some older men of Israel, men who used to advise Solomon. Those advisors tell him to listen to the people's request and lower the taxes. They tell him that if he does, he will gain their loyalty. But then Rehoboam consults with some of his younger companions. They tell him to *raise* the taxes because that will show the Israelites who is really in charge. Rehoboam, being a terrible fool, takes the advice of his young companions:

> And the king [Rehoboam] answered the people harshly, and forsaking the counsel that the old men had given him, he spoke to them according to the counsel of the young men, saying, "My father made your yoke heavy, but I will add to your yoke. My father disciplined you with whips, but I will discipline you with scorpions."
>
> 1 Kings 12:13-14

This ultimately leads to a rebellion, which results in the splitting of the kingdom into two parts, the Northern kingdom of Israel (under Jeroboam) and the Southern kingdom of Judah (under Rehoboam).

So then, we see that the monarchy was not the great political solution for which the Israelites in 1 Samuel 8 were hoping. The monarchy did not banish wickedness from Israel. Perhaps the kings were not susceptible to "bribery", as some of the judges had been, but they were still capable of doing great injustices out of their love for wealth and power.

It is not even clear that the monarchy restrained wickedness in Israel more effectively than the judges. After all, it was under the monarchy that Israel fell into such great wickedness that they eventually triggered the Babylonian exile. When Samuel and the LORD God warned Israel that instituting a monarchy was a bad idea, perhaps we should simply take that warning at face value. The fact that Israel sinned greatly in the time of the judges does not invalidate the concept of a human society with no taxing State. Israel experienced both situations, and it is not clear that the addition of a taxing monarchy was any fundamental improvement.

What then is the overall lesson? The lesson is that the solution to the problems of human wickedness, corruption and lust for power *cannot be solved* by a sufficiently elegant political system. No amount of checks and balances, no amount of careful tinkering, can invent a political structure that will prevent people from falling into sin and oppressing one another. Anarchy does not guarantee a virtuous society, but assuredly neither does the State.

This has two practical implications. First, the overall assessment of Scripture regarding the prospect of a Stateless society is *positive*. In general, Scripture views the kings of the earth as wicked tyrants who enslave their people in conquest and who deserve God's wrath for doing so. Nothing in Scripture *compels* us to institute a government where one is absent. Many heroes of the faith lived righteously in a context with no government over them (including Abraham, Isaac, Jacob and Moses). In the one case we know of where a society has the chance to *consult God* on whether or not they should appoint a human king, God discourages it.

Second, the real solution to all of these societal problems has been clear all along. We cannot fix society by instituting a monarchy (or any other system of government). But, by the same token, we cannot fix society *merely* by dissolving the government (although dissolving government would be a positive step). What we really need is not *mere* anarchy. What we need is for *God to be our King*.

Therefore, while I am comfortable with the position described in this book being considered a form of anarcho-capitalism, given the choice, I would prefer to use the term "Divine Monarchy". The ideal societal arrangement that I would propose, at least up until the second coming of Christ, is one in which there is no taxing State governed by any human ruler. Instead, the justice system of the society should be based on market-competitive courts seeking to outdo one another in diligent application of the natural law. Courts within that system that were overtly Christian would recognise explicitly that the natural law *is* the law given to all nations by God as an ordinance of His creation. Non-Christian courts may differ on some details but would still respect the natural law to some degree simply because of common grace. Although they may attempt to reject God's rule in their lives, they would still be human beings possessing rational faculties and unable to avoid the empirical realities of life in the world that God has made.

The Divine Monarchy Fulfilled in Christ

Throughout the period of the judges and the transition to monarchy, the constant refrain is not that Israel ought to have *no* king. The refrain is that they ought to have *God* as their King. It is not for nothing that the book of Ruth begins with these words:

> In the days when the judges ruled there was a famine in the land, and a man of Bethlehem in Judah went to sojourn in the

> country of Moab, he and his wife and his two sons. The name of the man was Elimelech...
>
> Ruth 1:1-2

For readers who know some Hebrew or Arabic, the subtext in this passage will be clear. At the time when the judges ruled, the first character that we meet has a name that literally means: "God is King" ("El" = God, "Melech" = King).

When the people ask Samuel to give them a human king, God points out that this is not merely a request for a slight tweak to their political system. It is a rejection of God's direct reign as their king (1 Samuel 8:7).

What is needed in all of this is to get back to that state of affairs in which God reigns over us as our *rightful* king. Not some human king who has conquered us out of selfish ambition, but God who loves us. Not a human king, who only wishes to *take* things from us, but God, who needs nothing from human hands and instead gives us gifts. God alone is inherently *worthy* to be our King. Things are right with the world when God is the one who reigns over us, and this is precisely what is promised to us in the gospel. God will come and be with us.

> "Behold, the virgin shall conceive and bear a son, and they shall call his name Immanuel" (which means, God with us).
>
> Matthew 1:23

The ultimate plan of God to resolve this problem of human wickedness and corruption is that God the Son would become one of us. In Christ, we finally have an answer to our dilemma. Our king will not be a sinful human being. Our king will be God the Son come in human flesh, reigning as the Messiah of Israel.

The real substance of the Bible's message about human politics is *not* just Romans 13:1-7. It is not a commandment to be good little boys and girls and obediently give our earthly conquerors whatever they demand. Instead, it is a radical, prophetic decree that the days of every human king are *numbered*. The only human king who is truly worthy is Jesus Christ, and he is coming back to dethrone all pretenders, abolish all wickedness, and redeem his people.

Why do the nations rage

  and the peoples plot in vain?

The kings of the earth set themselves,

  and the rulers take counsel together,

against the Lord and against his anointed, saying,

"Let us burst their bonds apart

  and cast away their cords from us."

He who sits in the heavens laughs;

  the Lord holds them in derision.

Then he will speak to them in his wrath,

  and terrify them in his fury, saying,

"As for me, I have set my King

  on Zion, my holy hill."

I will tell of the decree:

  The Lord said to me, "You are my Son;

  today I have begotten you.

Ask of me, and I will make the nations your heritage,

  and the ends of the earth your possession.

> You shall break them with a rod of iron
>
> and dash them in pieces like a potter's vessel."
>
> Psalm 2:1-9

This is the promise of the coming Messiah, the king who is the very Son of God. He will liberate us from those who conquer and oppress us. In Luke's gospel, we see Jesus begin his earthly ministry. Having resisted Satan in the wilderness, he heads back into the synagogue in his home town of Nazareth and publicly declares his intent to fulfil the prophecies of the liberating Messiah:

> And the scroll of the prophet Isaiah was given to him. He unrolled the scroll and found the place where it was written,
>
> "The Spirit of the Lord is upon me, because he has anointed me to proclaim good news to the poor. He has sent me to proclaim liberty to the captives and recovering of sight to the blind, to set at liberty those who are oppressed, to proclaim the year of the Lord's favour."

> And he rolled up the scroll and gave it back to the attendant and sat down. And the eyes of all in the synagogue were fixed on him. And he began to say to them, "Today this Scripture has been fulfilled in your hearing."
>
> Luke 4:17-21

At long last, the true king had come. But of course, Christ's path to glory is not a simple one. He came to his own, but his own did not receive him (John 1:11). Israel had met their Messiah, but they rejected him. Finally, a man stood before them, a man of David's royal lineage, who was God in the flesh. Finally, they had the chance to undo all the errors of their national history and once again have God as their king. But they rejected him utterly. They scorned him, gave him over to be tortured and executed, and declared at the top of their lungs that they *preferred* having a wicked, violent, idol-worshipper as their king rather than this Jesus:

> They cried out, "Away with him, away with him, crucify him!" Pilate said to them, "Shall I crucify your King?" The

> chief priests answered, *"We have no king but Caesar."*
>
> John 19:15 (emphasis added)

Jesus. The king that we needed but did not deserve. The king that God sent to us, in spite of our sin, because God is gracious. This Jesus was rejected. The truth is that all of us are sinners, all of us have likewise gone astray. All of us have fallen short of the glory of God. We have worshipped and served created things rather than the Creator (Romans 1:25). If we were to condemn Israel for rejecting their Messiah, we would find ourselves to be hypocrites. Every single one of us would have done the same. Every one of us has wanted to be our own God, our own king, and to reject the God who made us.

But praise be to God, he did not leave us in that hopeless state. God steps in to rescue us. Even as Jesus is rejected and crucified, he pours out grace. He goes willingly to the cross (John 10:18), and there he takes upon himself all the sins of his people. He sheds his blood and bears the righteous wrath of a holy God that all of us deserved. Jesus died *for us*. Whatever doubt that could have remained about his worthiness to rule us, this is where it is completely demolished. Jesus Christ is no Alexander, no Caesar, no Napoleon. He is no violent conqueror. He is the Saviour who loved us unto death and rose triumphant over the grave. He is the king who rescued us from our slavery by becoming a slave himself.

> Have this mind among yourselves, which is yours in Christ Jesus, who, though he was in the form of God, did not count equality with God a thing to be grasped, but made himself nothing, taking the form of a slave [δουλου], being born in the likeness of men. And being found in human form, he humbled himself by becoming obedient to the point of death, even death on a cross. Therefore God has highly exalted him and bestowed on him the name that is above every name, so that at the name of Jesus every knee should bow, in heaven and on earth and under the earth, and every tongue confess that Jesus Christ is Lord, to the glory of God the Father.
>
> Philippians 2:5-11

Jesus comes to us as the servant king. He does not come with a royal parade, demanding that we lift him up on our shoulders. He chooses the path of humility and proves that he is worthy of our worship and our devotion. He becomes the servant of all and commands his disciples that if they will not accept him stooping down to wash their feet (the lowest, dirtiest slave job of the ancient world), then they will not have a place in his kingdom:

> He came to Simon Peter, who said to him, "Lord, do you wash my feet?" Jesus answered him, "What I am doing you do not understand now, but afterward you will understand." Peter said to him, "You shall never wash my feet." Jesus answered him, "If I do not wash you, you have no share with me."
>
> John 13:6-8

This Jesus is *worthy* to be our king. He who came not to be served but to serve, and to give his life as a ransom for many (Mark 10:45). Everything we ever hoped a political leader would do, Christ does. Every wild hope that we wrongly pinned on a human king, a president or a prime minister, Christ fulfils them all. In Christ, there is liberty for the captive and the oppressed. We wait now for this resurrected Jesus to come again in glory, when he will bring God's wrath upon every wicked ruler the Earth has produced, when his rightful rule will never be challenged again:

> Then I saw heaven opened, and behold, a white horse! The one sitting on it is called Faithful and True, and in righteousness *he judges and makes war*. His eyes are like a flame of fire, and on his head are many diadems, and he has a name written that no one knows but himself. He is clothed in a robe dipped in blood, and the name by which he is called is The Word of God. And the armies of heaven, arrayed in fine linen, white and pure, were following him on white horses. From his mouth comes a sharp sword with which to strike down the nations, and he will rule them with a rod of iron. He will tread the winepress of the fury of the wrath of God the Almighty. On his robe and on his thigh he has a name written, *King of kings and Lord of lords*.
>
> Revelation 19:11-16

Having dispatched his enemies, Christ ushers in the kingdom of peace that our hearts have been longing for, and war finally comes to an end. Israel wanted a human king to judge them in complete righteousness and to defend them from all of their enemies. That is exactly what they get when the reign of Christ is fulfilled.

> It shall come to pass in the latter days that the mountain of the house of the LORD shall be established as the highest of the mountains, and shall be lifted up above the hills; and all the nations shall flow to it, and many peoples shall come, and say:
>
> "Come, let us go up to the mountain of the LORD, to the house of the God of Jacob, that he may teach us his ways and that we may walk in his paths." For out of Zion shall go the law, and the word of the LORD from Jerusalem. *He shall judge between the nations, and shall decide disputes for many peoples*; and they shall beat their swords into ploughshares, and their spears into pruning hooks; *nation shall not lift up sword against nation, neither shall they learn war any more.*

> O house of Jacob, come, let us walk in the light of the Lord.
>
> Isaiah 2:2-5

Rothbard was fond of quoting Oppenheimer's distinction between the "economic means" and the "political means" of obtaining wealth[62]. The economic means is that of production and free exchange, where people become wealthy by helping each other to cultivate God's good creation. The political means is that of violence, where people wield the sword against one another to plunder their neighbours' wealth. What we see in this prophecy is that the political means, the methods of war and violence, are finally done away with, and the economic means flourishes all over the earth. When Christ rules, the nations will finally cease going to war. Their weapons will become unnecessary to the point where they will melt them down and turn them into tools of the field. The political means will be swallowed up by the economic means, and economic harmony will dominate Christ's kingdom.

What remains for us is a very simple question. Are we among those who will come to Christ,

---

62 Rothbard, *Ethics of Liberty*, 167.

confess our sins, confess our rebellion, and receive the mercy and forgiveness that he purchased by his blood? Or will we be among the would-be kings of the Earth, trying to rule ourselves, rejecting God, and storing up wrath for ourselves when the day of his judgement comes?

When all the dust settles, the only question of politics that will matter at all is this: have you bowed the knee to *Jesus Christ* as your king?

Appendix 1: What About Democracy?

Some readers may be surprised that it has taken up until this point in the book to mention democracy. We have discussed Reformation-era views of civil government, ancient empires ruled by Caesars, and the views of obscure church fathers. But what about our modern context? Most people reading this book are probably living in a country with some kind of democratic element. Most readers have probably had the opportunity to elect a national leader at some point in their life. Does that mean that the things we have been learning in this book are simply ancient history, not applicable to our modern, democratic societies?

At one point, I certainly believed that the introduction of democracy changed the fundamental issues. I felt that having the opportunity to vote gave us some kind of influence over what the government did, and therefore the government's actions could be seen as a reflection of the will of the society at large. However, when I began thinking more deeply about the ethics and practicalities of democracy, I gradually had to let go of those assumptions.

As I considered the way that a democracy tends to work in practice, I saw more and more cases where the democratic structure itself created perverse incentives and did harm to the society. This led me to consider the ethical foundations for democracy more carefully. Ultimately, I concluded that democracy is no more ethically justifiable than an outright dictatorship. We will consider democracy first from a practical perspective, then from a theoretical perspective.

Australian Childcare Subsidy – A Case Study in the Failure of Democracy

In my own country, Australia, the government uses our tax dollars to subsidise people's use of childcare facilities. The amount of childcare subsidy paid to a family is based on their household income and is paid on a progressive scale (i.e., the higher your household income, the lower will be the percentage of your childcare costs that are subsidised). I like to do this social experiment with people to see how realistic their suspicions of government policy are. I ask them, "How much do you think a family can earn, including both parents' incomes, before their family no longer qualifies for *any* amount of childcare subsidy?"

I have had opening guesses ranging from $50,000/year (not very cynical) up to $120,000/year (fairly cynical). In all cases, I have to say "higher" many times before a person guesses the true amount. In most cases, they give up and simply look at me in disbelief well before they hit the actual number.

In fact, a family in Australia can earn up to $351,247 per year before they will stop having their childcare costs subsidised by the taxpayer[63]. I am sure that seems absurdly high to you. How could our elected representatives conclude that a family earning over *four times* the national average wage needs to be subsidised?

The answer to this question became obvious when I looked up a list of salaries for these elected representatives in our federal government. There were four exceptional cases, those in top jobs like "Prime Minister" and "Leader of the Opposition". But for the "standard" MPs, the highest salary level was – surprise! – $348,000. Just 0.9% below of the cutoff for receiving subsidised child care.

What is the lesson here? The lesson is that giving individuals the power to make decisions for a whole group does not automatically make those

---

63 You can see the figures for yourself at https://www.education.gov.au/child-care-subsidy-combined-annual-family-income-0

individuals give up their own interests. There will always be a strong tendency for the laws of the land to be favourable to those who are given the privilege of defining the laws. If there needs to be a subsidy cutoff, is it any wonder that it will be *just above* the salary level of those who are voting on it?

I give this example to illustrate that, in practice, democracy is not nearly as "fair" as it is made out to be. People in power will always change the laws to benefit themselves. If we were to have a national referendum where we asked all of the citizens to vote on the appropriate maximum income for receiving childcare subsidy, what do you think the outcome would be? Is there any real chance that the great mass of people would vote for those earning *over four times the national average* to be given a subsidy? Clearly the votes cast by our "representatives" are not anywhere close to what *would* have been voted for by the people themselves.

Now, someone may object that isolated scandals do not invalidate the democratic system. The point of democracy is that when we uncover something like this, we can punish those representatives by voting them out at the next election. However, in practice, there are two major flaws with this strategy.

Flaw Number One: Power Corrupts

The first flaw is that it is not *who* is in power that makes the difference, it is the nature of power itself. In Australia, we have two major political parties. On the one hand, we have the tax-and-spend, left-leaning Labor Party. On the other hand, we have the fiscally conservative, right-leaning Liberal-National Coalition. Which of these two parties brought in this massively oversized childcare subsidy? Sadly, it was our so-called fiscal conservatives. It does not make much sense to express our disapproval of over-spending by electing the other major party which wants to spend even more.

What if we reject both major parties and instead try to get a minor party elected? Even if we did elect another party, one that makes bold promises to cut spending, once they were elected, they would then be subject to all of the same incentives that have corrupted their predecessors. Increasing spending tends to bring in votes, while cutting spending tends to lose votes. If politicians want to stay in power, then they have every incentive to *become* the big spenders that they used to oppose.

The sad reality is that what is good for an elected leader is *not* the same as what is good for the people they rule over.

Flaw Number Two: Weaponised Boredom

The second flaw is that having the power to create legislation also gives you the power to make that legislation very unlikely to be widely scrutinised. Before reading this book, did you know about the scandal of super-high-earning Australian politicians voting themselves a childcare subsidy? Probably not. Why did you not know? The information was freely available online. Theoretically, it is public knowledge.

The simple reason is that scanning over the technical language and sheer bulk of the tax code and other government regulations is *boring*. The only reason that I know about this example is that I have worked in the childcare industry. The more complex the legislation becomes, the *less* likely the average voter is to look into the matter. I do *not* know about similar scandals in the health sector, the education sector, etc. But I am confident that such examples do exist. The problem is that it would take many lifetimes to read and understand the relevant legislation. I would rather go to the beach.

This is weaponised boredom. If legislators make the law sufficiently frustrating to read, voters will not bother. Therefore, the more convoluted and complex they make it, the more they will be able to get away with.

Right now, do you know how much tax you have paid in the last year? You almost certainly do not. We are not just speaking about income tax. Also consider sales tax, VAT tax (what my country calls "GST"), property rates, stamp duty, vehicle registration, fuel excise, etc. You have probably never stopped to add it all up because it would be a vastly frustrating and boring activity.

Imagine how much simpler everything would be if they scrapped all of that. Instead, suppose the government gave every citizen a single bill each year for their "share" of the government's expenses. That would be so much more clear and efficient. However, if they did that, we would all be much more aware of how severely we are being fleeced, and so of course, it is never going to happen.

Lesser Magistrates: Kuyper's Justification for Democracy

I have tried to show above that democracy can lead to specific evils in practice. For that reason alone, we should have some scepticism. However, it is easy to understand that, from the perspective of people living in a world dominated by monarchies, democracy might have seemed like a huge step forward. This is certainly true for theologians and political thinkers arising after the Reformation and for Abraham Kuyper in particular.

Kuyper was committed to the idea of representative democracy as the most legitimate way to run a country. Kuyper, being a theologian as well as a politician, grounded his pro-democracy view in a doctrine arising from the time of the Reformation, the "doctrine of the lesser magistrate".

Kuyper believed that representative democracy was ultimately derived from the lesser-magistrate doctrine, and that the lesser-magistrate doctrine was itself biblical. Therefore, in Kuyper's mind, it naturally followed that representative democracy was a biblical way to order society[64].

So then, what precisely is the "doctrine of the lesser magistrate"? Put simply, the doctrine of the lesser magistrate states that lower-ranking government officials are permitted and encouraged to lead the people in resisting unjust laws given by a higher-ranking official.

So, for example, imagine that the king of a country decides that the kingdom is overpopulated and issues an order that no family shall be allowed

---

64 Kuyper, *Lectures on Calvinism*, 84.

to have more than two children. The police are ordered to go house to house, round up every child who is the third or later sibling in their family, and bring them to a camp where they will be killed. The lesser-magistrate doctrine says that the mayor of a city within that kingdom can rally the people of his city in armed resistance against the king's order.

In the Reformed tradition, the people are meant to give honour and respect to their rulers. The lesser-magistrate doctrine gives them an exit strategy in the event that their ruler becomes tyrannical. They can petition a "lesser magistrate" to lead them in resistance against the higher ruler. In this way, they maintain their principle of respecting an established authority while still being able to resist some degree of tyranny.

If the mayor refuses to lead the people in resistance, not wanting to risk his own neck, then an individual police officer may become the next lesser magistrate in line, leading the people in resistance against both the mayor and the king. At each stage, if a higher magistrate behaves wickedly, the people may rally to a lesser magistrate who is further down the chain of command.

This principle was articulated (and put into practice) by the people of a German city called Magdeburg during the Protestant Reformation (an incident already outlined earlier in this book). In

Magdeburg, the city leaders rallied the citizenry to resist the orders handed down by the king of the Holy Roman Empire, Charles V.

As far as it goes, I find the lesser-magistrate doctrine to be a very admirable idea. However, its proponents never seem to carry it to its ultimate conclusion.

Trewhella's book on the lesser-magistrate doctrine praises mid-tier rulers who are willing to "interpose" on behalf of the people that they rule (that is, to place themselves between the people and the higher ruler who is threatening them). Trewhella then goes on to give biblical examples of this interposing action. What seems to go unnoticed is that both of his key examples are conducted by people who hold *no formal office* in the government of their day. One case is the Hebrew midwives, who lie to the king of Egypt in order to protect the firstborn sons of Israel (Exodus 1:15-22). The midwives are not government officials. They are private individuals and even slaves. Yet they are lying to their king and master in order to save the lives of the Hebrew babies. The second example is the people of Israel who "interposed" for Jonathan so that Saul would not kill him on account of a rash oath that Saul had made (1 Samuel 14:45). Again, those who came to

Jonathan's defence had no official position in the hierarchy[65].

The framers of the Magdeburg Confession give the example of a wife whose husband tries to sell their daughters into prostitution. The framers say that the wife *can and should* lead the daughters in resisting the father. Again, the wife is not required to be holding any formal, political office in this scenario.

If these are all legitimate examples of exercising the lesser-magistrate doctrine, then I see no reason why the principle, consistently applied, should not lead to *every individual having freedom of their own conscience*. Yes, there may be legitimate, natural authorities over them (like the authority of parents over children), but when those authorities command them to do something wicked, they can always choose to resist. There is no minimum number of people who must be in the resistance movement for it to be legitimate. There is also no requirement that the resistance movement must be led by someone who has a formal position within the existing hierarchy. Therefore, a consistent application of the lesser-magistrate doctrine becomes indistinguishable from the exercise of individual liberty.

---

65 Trewhella, *The Doctrine of the Lesser Magistrates*, Chapter 2.

Sadly, for Kuyper, this totally undermines his basis for democracy. If a leadership hierarchy is not required in order for people to exercise their own conscience, then a parliamentary system to appoint those leaders is also not required. If we permit one lesser magistrate to resist the authority of the magistrate above them, then why not the next one down and the next one and so on? There is no logical stopping point. Once every level of magistrate in the hierarchy has been exhausted, there is no reason why a lone individual should not act as their *own* final magistrate. Suppose that the king wants to levy taxes, the mayor agrees, the local sheriff agrees, and a man's neighbours even agree. The man is left with no lesser magistrate to which he can turn. Under God, he is still not obliged to go along with the sin of taxation slavery, any more than he would be obliged to go along with any other sin committed by his rulers and neighbours.

Of course, the proponents of the lesser-magistrate doctrine rarely, if ever, take the theory to such an extreme. They typically have a pro-State reading of Romans 13, and so they feel the need to rationalise *some* kind of legitimacy for governmental authority.

Ultimately, the lesser-magistrate doctrine cannot be a justification for a democratically elected government because the lesser-magistrate doctrine logically reduces to *individual liberty* rather than reducing to *majority rule*.

Lysander Spooner's Critique of Democratic "Consent"

One common justification for democracy is the idea of a "social contract". The substance of this theory is that all the members of a society have entered into an *implicit* contract with each other, and this contract morally binds them to respect the established political structures that exist within their context.

Over the years, many people have picked up a pen to demolish this view, but perhaps none so devastatingly as Lysander Spooner. Spooner penned a work simply and provocatively titled "No Treason". In that work, Spooner begins with the claim that the government described by the Constitution of the United States of America is a government whose authority is derived from the "consent of the governed". Spooner then systematically disproves that claim. He demonstrates that there can be no logical basis for considering the Constitution to be binding upon any individual who did not personally sign it. Therefore, the alleged "consent of the governed" is only a fantasy.

Spooner begins by presenting a series of arguments to demonstrate that a majority has no inherent moral right to command the behaviour of a minority. He gives a *reductio ad absurdum*[66]. If a majority of a million people have the right to command a minority of a hundred, then why should a majority of two not rule a minority of one? If we held it to be a general principle that a majority has the right to rule a minority, then there is no reason why this principle should not extend to small groups. Suppose that two men want to take money from a third man for their own use. All they need to do is to call an election, and agree together to vote themselves in as the "government" of that three-person group. If this is unjust among three men, then it is equally unjust among three million.

Spooner goes on to point out that such an arrangement will always lead to conflict and struggle:

> The principle that the majority have a right to rule the minority, practically resolves all government into a mere contest between two bodies of men, as to which of them shall be masters, and which of them slaves; a contest, that – however

---

66 Spooner, *No Treason*, Part 1, Section 2.

> bloody – can, in the nature of things, never be finally closed, so long as man refuses to be a slave.

Spooner goes on to demonstrate, through a variety of examples, that there is no other area of life in which we would accept the premise that a man can be bound by a contract which he himself has never signed. No court would ever dream of enforcing a contract which had never been signed by the parties involved[67].

Spooner also demolishes the notion that voting implies any sort of consent by the voter. Spooner points out that the whole process of voting is generally done under *duress*. Voting is undertaken by people who find themselves forced to choose between artificially limited alternatives, rather than free to choose any course of action which nature itself has given them[68].

People generally do not vote for someone because they genuinely wish for that individual, or the party they represent, to have unlimited authority over their life. Far from indicating a person's "consent" to the government's actions, voting is typically an act of self-defence. People do

---
67 Spooner, *No Treason*, Part 6, Section 5.
68 Spooner, *No Treason*, Part 6, Section 2.

not wish to give unlimited authority to any person on the ballot, but they know that no matter what they do, the authority will be given to someone. Just because they voted for the current leader does not mean that they prefer that leader to having no leader at all. It only means that, given their artificially limited options, the current leader seemed the least bad. We see here that voting does not imply consent in the case where someone voted *for* the current leader. How much more ridiculous is it then to claim that there is consent from someone who voted *against* the current leader?

This all leads Spooner to regard taxation the same way that Augustine did over a millennium earlier[69]:

> No middle ground is possible on this subject. Either "taxation without consent is robbery," or it is not. If it is not, then any number of men, who choose, may at any time associate; call themselves a government; assume absolute authority over all weaker than themselves; plunder them at will; and kill them if they resist. If, on the other hand, taxation without

---

69 Spooner, *No Treason*, Part 2, Section 7.

> consent is robbery, it necessarily follows that every man who has not consented to be taxed, has the same natural right to defend his property against a taxgatherer, that he has to defend it against a highwayman.

The Silence of Scripture on Democracy

Given that this is meant to be a book for Bible-believing Christians, a final point must be raised against democracy. If democracy were the answer to all of our political problems, then why is it never brought up in Scripture? In all of God's special revelation, handed down to us in Scripture, He never suggested that we should appoint a leader by democratic election. In the Mosaic law, God makes provision for an anarchic society with cities of refuge, avengers of blood, and a distributed system of judges to settle disputes. God also makes provision for a future monarchy, which will remain under certain restraints within His own ultimate rule of Israel. But even while providing guidelines for multiple systems of government, God apparently saw no need to suggest a system of constitutional democracy for Israel.

If it really were the case that democracy was God's answer to the whole dilemma of governing human society, then this omission makes no sense at all. Why give His people detailed frameworks for anarchy and monarchy, all the while withholding what He knew to be a better solution?

Democracy is simply not the answer that God gave us. The answer that He gave us is to be ruled by Christ, our true and worthy king, rather than by any wicked human being, whether elected or not.

Can a Christian Vote or Hold Political Office?

These objections to democracy raise a few practical concerns. Is it permissible for a Christian to vote? Is it permissible for a Christian to join a political party and seek office? The short answer I would give is yes. If you can diminish the wicked activities of the government by voting for a better candidate than would otherwise be in office, then do it. If you can combat the plunder and aggression of the government by becoming a senator and voting against their nonsense in the legislature, then do that too. Only watch that you yourself are not corrupted by the temptations of government. Do not allow yourself to be tempted into perverting justice for personal gain. Should you ever be in a position to repeal any tax, to end any war or to repeal any law of the land which violates the natural law, then do so immediately and without apology.

Of course, you will not be perfect while in office. You will sin, you will make mistakes, and people will suffer. But Christ died for our sins and our failures, and his grace is sufficient for you.

Having said all of that, it is certainly permissible to abstain from voting. If you feel that your vote in any direction will only give greater legitimacy to the wicked actions of your rulers, then you are at liberty to abstain.

Appendix 2: Assorted Q&A

1. Cut to the chase! As a Christian, do I have to pay my taxes or not?

Let's face it, if I can't give you a clear, simple answer to this question, then there wasn't a lot of point in writing this book. So here goes.

Do you *have to* pay your taxes in order to be acting ethically as a Christian?

Short answer: No, I don't believe that you do.

Longer answer: No, it is not obligatory to pay any given tax *merely* because it is being demanded from you. Imposing taxes is a form of conquest slavery. It is a sin to impose arbitrary taxes on people. The mere fact of taxes being demanded from you by a group that calls itself "the government" does not create any moral obligation for you to pay. If it did create such a moral obligation, then we would have no explanation for the many tax revolts that occur in Scripture *with God's blessing* (for example, Ehud's resistance against the Moabites and Gideon's resistance against the Midianites).

For reasons of wisdom, you may *choose* to pay some or all of the taxes that are demanded from you. You may wish to avoid living in fear of the threats made against those who do not pay. That is totally acceptable. However, when you choose to peacefully submit to the taxes imposed on you, even though the imposition of the tax is itself an evil, you should remember to give thanks to God for any good things which the taxing State *does* do with the plunder it has taken (Romans 13:4).

Your life's testimony to the gospel may also motivate you to pay taxes in certain cases. For example, suppose that you are in a community where there is a common (false) assumption that refusal to pay a particular tax is immoral. If you flaunt your violation of this social assumption in front of a less-mature Christian, you may cause them to stumble, because they will mistakenly assume that you are legitimising immoral behaviour *in general* (Romans 14:13-23). To avoid stumbling the weaker brother or sister in their faith, you may simply choose to pay the tax. This was essentially Jesus' motivation for paying the temple tax in Matthew 17:27.

2. If we *don't* get involved in politics, how else can we apply this way of thinking in our everyday lives?

The ideas in this book may have a great variety of practical applications. There is no way to give a comprehensive answer here. However, there is a particular school of thought within libertarianism that has much to contribute and bears mentioning. That school of thought is called "agorism". The name comes from the Greek word for the "marketplace", which is αγορα ("agora"). Basically, the goal of agorism is to deliberately turn the peaceful forces of the free market against the coercion of the State.

The agorist sets out to diminish the power of the State in their own life and in the lives of others, by deliberately doing actions which are morally acceptable within the natural law but which are either outlawed or discouraged by the State. In doing so, they do not take up violence against the State, nor do they sin against anyone by violating the natural law. Instead, they deliberately *bypass* the man-made rules of the State in order to improve their own lives and the lives of their neighbours.

A simple example will demonstrate the principle. Suppose the government of country A decides to pass a law that all food sold in the country will be sold at controlled prices. They say that they are doing this to make sure that everyone can afford food. However, this policy is economically foolish. The food producers in country A quickly realise that they cannot provide food for the prices the government demands. If it costs them $1/litre to produce milk, but they are required by law to sell it for $0.90/litre, then they will make ever-increasing losses. Not wanting to be driven into bankruptcy, vast numbers of food producers will start pivoting to other lines of work. Country B also produces food and does not have these price controls, so their production continues uninterrupted. The people in country A would like to import food from country B, but the government sees that this will make their price controls ineffective. To prevent this, the government imposes large tariffs on all the food imported from country B, so that the food from country B is too costly for most people in country A to buy[70].

---

70 While this scenario might seem absurd to you, it is only a simplified summary of what is actually taking place in Venezuela at this very moment and has taken place in many other planned economies. Food and basic hygiene supplies are in dramatic shortage in Venezuela due to foolish price controls, and many Venezuelans are facing starvation.

Here the agorist sees an opportunity to help both themselves and their neighbours by practising *righteous disobedience*. The agorist travels to country B, purchases large quantities of food, and smuggles them back into country A. The agorist then sells these food parcels to hungry people in country A for a profit.

In doing this, the agorist violates no element of natural law. The people of country A have the natural right to spend their own money on whatever they desire, including food from country B. They commit no crime in buying this food, and so there is no justification for punishing them with fines (which is the effect of the tariff). The agorist is justified in getting whatever price the market will accept for the food that he has transported. He is even justified in selling the food for a higher price in country A than it would normally attract in country B. Indeed, he will need to do so since he has incurred extra costs and risks in order to smuggle the food back into country A.

By this arrangement, the sellers in country B benefit because they get more sales of their product. The buyers in country A benefit because they get the food that they need at a cheaper price than they could get otherwise. The agorist benefits because he has made a profit by engaging in non-violent, free-market transactions. His stealthy avoidance of the State authorities is nothing different to keeping thieves out of his online bank account by protecting it with a password.

The hope of the agorist is that, over time, more people will engage in this sort of righteous disobedience. The more common this practice becomes, the more people will come to see the absurdity of the State. The State claims that it has some sort of moral right to determine who people must trade with and at what prices. But people will come to see that it is the State's rules that are the source of their suffering. As the illusion of the State's authority is gradually undermined, society will grow to tolerate its wickedness less and less, causing the State to gradually wither away.

This is the substance of the agorist concept. If you would like to learn more about the philosophy of agorism, one foundational text is titled "The Agorist Primer" by Samuel E. Konklin III[71].

3. Does Acts 4 show that early Christians embraced socialism?

In Acts 4:32-37, we find a short description of an arrangement that took place in the very early church.

---

71 A PDF edition of this work is freely available at http://agorism.info

> Now the full number of those who believed were of one heart and soul, and no one said that any of the things that belonged to him was his own, but they had everything in common. And with great power the apostles were giving their testimony to the resurrection of the Lord Jesus, and great grace was upon them all. There was not a needy person among them, for as many as were owners of lands or houses sold them and brought the proceeds of what was sold and laid it at the apostles' feet, and it was distributed to each as any had need. Thus Joseph, who was also called by the apostles Barnabas (which means son of encouragement), a Levite, a native of Cyprus, sold a field that belonged to him and brought the money and laid it at the apostles' feet.
>
> Acts 4:32-37

At first glance, this passage would seem to provide strong evidence of "socialist" tendencies in the early community of believers. Indeed, the socialist motto "from each according to his ability, to each according to his need" seems to be embodied in this passage.

While the passage clearly indicates that these early Christians did in fact treat much of their property as communal, this practice must be understood in both its immediate and broader context. In the immediate context, it is clear that this practice of offering property as communal was entirely voluntary. In the verses that follow, we see a couple named Ananias and Sapphira sell a piece of land. They bring a part of the proceeds to the apostles but keep back a part for themselves. Peter calls them out for doing this, and they are struck down by God for their dishonesty. What is important to note, however, is the content of Peter's condemnation:

> But Peter said, "Ananias, why has Satan filled your heart to lie to the Holy Spirit and to keep back for yourself part of the proceeds of the land? While it remained unsold, did it not remain your own? And after it was sold, was it not at your disposal?"
>
> Acts 5:3-4

Clearly, Peter is not condemning them for keeping a part of the property for themselves. Peter openly acknowledges their right to do as they wish their own property. They were not obliged to sell it, and, after it was sold, they were not obliged to bring the money to the apostles. The dishonesty lay in them claiming to have brought the whole of the proceeds as their gift when they had really only brought a part. They were trying to have their cake and eat it too. That is, they wanted to be honoured as though they had given the whole proceeds but did not want to actually give them.

The point to note, in the immediate context, is that this practice was entirely voluntary and believers were free to participate or not. Under a socialist government, the "sharing" of property is not voluntary at all. Under socialism, property is taken from people by force. So this situation is starkly different from genuine socialism in that respect.

It is important to underscore the point that all voluntary arrangements are compatible with libertarianism. This includes a situation where a community of people voluntarily choose to put their property into a common pool to be distributed by the leaders. The libertarian does not object to this at all. If a community feels strongly that it would be more efficient or somehow spiritually helpful to share all of their property, then they are free to do that. The libertarian only objects when participation is imposed by force. As a practical matter, most communities cannot sustain a shared-property model for long. There is no economic incentive to work, and plenty of economic incentive to free ride.

Indeed, the early church does not appear to have sustained this model indefinitely. The New Testament mentions the presence of wealth disparities within the church without any indication that they are to be condemned as a violation of some shared-property mandate. Gaius is obviously richer than those travelling evangelists to whom he gives support (3 John 1:5-8). Paul counselled the women in Timothy's church at Ephesus to refrain from dressing in expensive clothing, braided hair and extravagant jewellery. This presupposes that some women in the church had the financial means required for dressing in such a manner while others did not (1 Tim 2:9).

Nevertheless, it is clear that the early church was in the habit of providing some degree of social "safety net" to its members. For example, food was being distributed daily to widows in the church (Acts 6:1). However, it is also evident that this safety net had conditions. Being poor was not enough to qualify someone for the safety net. If a person was able to work but was poor due to laziness, then they were not to be given food (2 Thessalonians 3:10). If a widow had children who could provide for her, then that responsibility should fall on the children rather than upon the broader church (1 Timothy 5:4,16). Paul counselled Timothy to refuse to enrol younger windows who were not in such great need, partly because being on the safety-net roll would teach them to be "idlers", "gossips" and "busybodies" (1 Timothy 5:13-14). That is, Scripture recognises that the social safety net carries with it a moral hazard. People are incentivised not to work when they can simply be taken care of by others. This moral hazard too easily leads them into sin.

All in all, the church safety net came with many restrictions. It was apparently at the discretion of the elders to decide whether being enrolled for the safety net would do more harm than good to the spiritual health of a person (1 Timothy 5:11). Taken together, this all sounds much more like a voluntary church charity trying to wisely allocate funds, rather than a socialist welfare state.

Did the early church embrace socialism? The short answer is "no". Within the broader context of respecting private property rights, there were pockets of the early church that voluntarily shared their wealth in a common pool. However, there was never any drive to have poorer members of the church rise up and redistribute the wealth of the richer members by force.

www.ingramcontent.com/pod-product-compliance
Lightning Source LLC
Chambersburg PA
CBHW050259010526
44107CB00055B/2088